W9-CAJ-277

2010

HR Handbook
for California Employers

Published by
California Chamber of Commerce
P.O. Box 1736
Sacramento, CA 95812-1736

ISBN 1-57997-301-9

5 4 3 2 1

The information compiled in this handbook is being provided by CalBizCentral as a service to the business community. Although every effort has been made to ensure the accuracy and completeness of this information, CalBizCentral and the contributors and reviewers of this publication cannot be responsible for any errors and omissions, nor any agency's interpretations, applications and changes of regulations described herein.

This publication is designed to provide accurate and authoritative information in a highly summarized manner with regard to the subject matter covered. It is sold with the understanding that the publisher and others associated with this publication are not engaged in rendering legal, technical or other professional service. If legal and other expert assistance is required, the services of competent professionals should be sought.

This publication is available from:

CalChamber/CalBizCentral
P.O. Box 1736
Sacramento, CA 95812-1736
(800) 331-8877
www.calbizcentral.com

Table of Contents

Chapter 3

Chapter 4

Chapter 5

Chapter 6

Chapter 7

Chapter 8

What's New for 2010?

This preface lists additions and changes for the *2010 HR Handbook for California Employers*, detailed in chapter order.

General

- Each chapter now features a Frequently Asked Questions section, immediately following the "Where do I Go for More Information" table.

Hiring Employees

- A 2009 court decision cautioned employers about provisions and disclaimers in "one-size-fits-all" employment applications. See "Receive Applications" on page 15 for more information;

- The Form I-9 is new for 2010. See "Verify the Employee's Authorization to Work" on page 26;

- Federal contractors and subcontractors are now required to use E-Verify to confirm employees' eligibility to work in the United States. See "E-Verify" on page 30 for more information.

Providing Benefits

- The 2010 National Defense Authorization Act expands the scope of FMLA for employees providing care to military members. See Table 17 in Chapter 4, page 105, for more information.

- Employers with 15 or more employees must provide leave to any employee who is a volunteer member of the California Wing of the civilian auxiliary of the U.S. Air Force (Civil Air Patrol). See Table 27 in Chapter 4, page 125, for more information.

- A court decision in 2009 affects the nature of workers' compensation awards to an employee. See Table 32 on page 134 for more information.

- Same sex couples who are legally married in another state will have the same rights, protections and benefits, and be subject to the same responsibilities, obligations and duties in California as spouses. "What Do I Need to Know About Domestic Partner Rights?" on page 149 for more information.

- Health care taxes that San Francisco-based employers must pay to the city, per the San Francisco Health Care Ordinance, increased in 2010. See "San Francisco Health Care" on page 151 for more information.

- The federal Mental Health Parity and Addiction Equity Act took effect for health plan years beginning Oct. 3, 2009. See "Mental Health and Substance Abuse" on page 153 for more information.

Paying Employees

- When a compensation package includes commission payments, employers should create a written agreement, specifying when commissions are earned, paid out and how the employee's termination impacts the commission payment. See Table 45 on page 179 for more information.

- Employees may want to change their withholding for state income tax because the state withholding on wages increased by 10 percent, effective Nov. 1, 2009. See Table 49 in Chapter 5, page 188, for more information.

- Effective Jan. 1, 2010, exempt computer professionals may be paid on a salaried basis, either monthly or annually. See "Exempt Computer Professionals" on page 180 for more information.

- Effective Jan. 1, 2010, a licensed physician or surgeon primarily engaged in performing duties that require a license is exempt from overtime if paid $69.13 or more per hour. See "Licensed Physicians and Surgeons" on page 181 for more information.

- The mileage reimbursement rate set by the IRS was 55.0 cents per mile effective January 1, 2009. See "Must I Reimburse My Employees for Their Expenses?" on page 183 for more information.

- The issue of whether employers are required to ensure employees take the unpaid 30-minute meal break or simply provide the break is in flux. See "What Happens if I Fail to Give Nonexempt Employees Meal and Rest Breaks?" on page 200 for more information.

Preventing Discrimination and Harassment

- Regulations are pending for the federal Genetic Information Nondiscrimination Act (GINA) which will govern employer benefit plans. See Table 67 on page 246 for more information.

Chapter 1

Getting Started with This Book

This simple book makes it easy to find what you need — quickly.

Structure

This book organizes the information into chapters based on topics. If you're not sure what chapter to look in to find information about a topic, please consult the Index.

Formatting

This book uses formatting conventions to help you identify important information.

Table 1. *HR Handbook* **Formatting**

Bold	Emphasizes important terms.
Italics	Identifies forms and checklists.
❗	Identifies information you should pay close attention to.
TIP	Identifies definitions of terms and helpful advice.
NEW 2010	Identifies new laws, regulations and court decisions for 2010.

Does This Employment Law Apply to Me?

Use the chart on the next page to determine if a particular employment law applies to your company, based on the number of people you employ. For further information about each law, see the Index, which refers you to material throughout this product.

Table 2. Does This Employment Law Apply to Me? (continued)

Law/Requirement	All employers	4 or more	5 or more	15 or more	16 or more	20 or more	25 or more	50 or more	75 or more
Paid Family Leave (PFL)	✓								
Plant Closing (State WARN Act)									✓
Posters and Notices	✓								
Pregnancy Disability Leave (PDL)			✓	✓	✓	✓	✓	✓	✓
Privacy	✓								
School Activities Leave							✓	✓	✓
School Appearance Leave	✓								
Sexual Harassment	✓								
Sexual Harassment 2 hour Supervisor Training								✓	
Smoking in the Workplace	✓								
State Disability Insurance (SDI)	✓								
Unemployment Insurance (UI)	✓								
Victims of Violent Crime Leave	✓								
Volunteer Civil Service Leave	✓								
Voting Leave	✓								
Wage and Hour Laws	✓								
Workers' Compensation	✓								

Online Forms

Throughout this book, you'll find references to many forms and checklists. As regulations can change throughout the year, accessing your forms online ensures that you will always have the most current version of each form. Be sure to check **www.calbizcentral.com/support** occasionally for updates to forms and descriptions of important mid-year regulatory changes.

To download the forms mentioned in this book:

1. Go to **www.calbizcentral.com/support**.

2. From the list of 2010 product titles, select **HR Handbook for California Employers**.

3. Enter your product security code in the input field and select "Continue."

> **HR Handbook for California Employers** ⬇
>
> Please enter the product code found in the back of your book in the box below and click Continue. Remember, codes are case-sensitive.
>
> [   ] [Continue]

TIP You'll find the product security code on the inside covers of the book.

4. Right-click on the link and select "Save Target As."

5. Save the compressed zip file to the location on your computer where you want to store your forms.

6. Navigate to the compressed zip file and extract the contents.

TIP To easily find the form or forms you need after downloading, open **_ViewFormsListingFirst.htm**. That page provides links to all downloaded forms and helpful descriptions of each.

About CalChamber and CalBizCentral

The California Chamber of Commerce (CalChamber) is the largest broad-based business advocate to government in California. Membership represents one-quarter of the private sector jobs in California and includes firms of all sizes and companies from every industry within the state. Leveraging our front-line knowledge of laws and regulations, we provide products and services to help businesses comply with both federal and state law. CalChamber, a not-for-profit organization with roots dating to 1890, promotes international trade and investment to stimulate California's economy and create jobs. Please visit our Web site at ***www.calchamber.com***.

CalBizCentral, presented by CalChamber, provides business and human resources managers a one-stop-shop for employment law compliance products. The comprehensive site is designed and maintained by employment law experts. For more information on CalBizCentral products, please visit ***www.calbizcentral.com***.

Contributors

Publishing Manager, Print Media: Andrea LaMattina

Managing Editor: Mike McCluskey

Editors: Angele Hill, Judy Larson and Shane Peterson

Proof Reader: Cheri Acton

Cover Design: Marcy Wacker

Index: Bayside Indexing Service

Chapter 2

Hiring Employees

If you establish a hiring procedure that covers everything from making the decision to hire someone to welcoming a new employee, you give yourself the best opportunity to avoid litigation and create a smooth, enjoyable hiring experience.

In this chapter, you'll find answers to questions about:

- Legal recruiting procedures;
- Required and recommended forms;
- Credit and background checks for applicants;
- Independent contractors; and
- Much more!

Minimum Compliance Elements

1. Hang your ***Employment Notices Poster*** (available from ***www.calbizcentral.com***), which includes mandatory postings that all employees and applicants must be able to see, in a prominent place (such as a break room).

2. Use the *Hiring Checklist* to make sure you fill out all the required paperwork for every new hire. See "Important Forms and Checklists" on page 40.

3. Look at all candidates objectively, in terms of their ability to do the job. See "Interview Candidates" on page 16.

4. Make sure you classify workers properly. See "What's the Difference Between an Exempt and a Nonexempt Employee?" on page 11.

5. Make sure you don't control your independent contractors as if they were employees. See "How Do I Make Sure That the Individual Is Truly an Independent Contractor?" on page 33.

The Basics of Hiring Employees

Many employers find hiring a new employee a complicated and daunting process. You must:

- Find the best employee for the job;
- Fulfill extensive paperwork requirements;
- Avoid violating complex discrimination laws; and
- Avoid creating/violating contracts that open you up to litigation.

To protect yourself from making a costly mistake, consider establishing a hiring policy. Before you begin the hiring process, review your policy to make sure you don't violate it.

Example: If your policy states that you open all new positions to existing employees before looking outside the company and you fail to do so, you could open yourself up to an employee complaint, and even legal action.

How Do I Hire an Employee?

To help organize the process of finding, preparing to hire an employee and complying with legal requirements, you can use the *Pre-Hire Checklist* and the *Hiring Checklist*, described in Table 8 on page 40.

The following sections provide information to help you:

- "1 — Define Job Requirements with Up-to-Date Information" on page 9.
- "2 — Recognize the Need for a New Employee and Determine the Best Type of Employee to Hire" on page 9.
- "3 — Advertise and/or Recruit for the Position" on page 12.
- "4 — Evaluate Potential Candidates" on page 14.
  - "Review Résumés" on page 14 (optional);
  - "Screen Candidates with a Phone Interview" on page 14 (optional);
  - "Receive Applications" on page 15; and
  - "Interview Candidates" on page 16.
- "5 — Conduct Background Checks" on page 18.
- "6 — Make the Hiring Decision and Offer the Position" on page 23.

- "7 — Fill Out Paperwork" on page 24.
- "8 — Welcome Your New Employees" on page 31.

1 — Define Job Requirements with Up-to-Date Information

It's vital that you start the hiring process with up-to-date information about the job requirements. If you need to fill an existing position, locate the existing job description and make sure that it's accurate. If creating a new position, write a new job description that clearly outlines the essential functions of the job.

Essential functions: fundamental job requirements of the position or the reason the job exists.

See "What Should I Know About Essential Functions?" in Chapter 7, page 253, for tips on documenting a job's essential functions. You must be sure that applicants who could perform the essential functions of the job don't get turned away based on their inability to perform a non-essential function. Beware of creating promises in a job description that you will have to keep later. See "Don't Create a Contract" on page 37.

2 — Recognize the Need for a New Employee and Determine the Best Type of Employee to Hire

The first task in the hiring process is to figure out exactly what kind of help you need and determine the resources available to meet that need.

Do you need a full-time employee? A part-time employee? Would an independent contractor or a temporary employee better suit your needs?

How Do I Know Which Type of Worker to Hire?

There are many types of worker classifications. Consider the nature of the assignment, and what level of supervision will be required before making your decision. For example, do you need a supervisor who runs a retail store during business hours? A worker who replenishes inventory when your store is closed? A worker to fill in for an employee taking medical leave?

Table 3 describes the various types of workers. To read about how workers can be classified for wages, see "What Do I Pay My Workers?" in Chapter 5, page 179.

Table 3. Types of Workers

What type	What it means
Exempt	An exempt employee is not subject to any of the laws pertaining to overtime, meal periods and rest periods. An exempt employee normally is an executive, managerial, administrative or professional employee; exempt employees can also be certain artists or outside salespeople. For more information on how to determine whether an employee is exempt or nonexempt, see "What's the Difference Between an Exempt and a Nonexempt Employee?" on page 11.
Nonexempt	A nonexempt employee is subject to all Wage Order rules and wage laws. You must pay nonexempt employees overtime for working more than eight hours in a day or more than 40 in a workweek and provide required meal and rest breaks. Paying employees a salary doesn't necessarily mean their classification changes to exempt. See Table 45 in Chapter 5, page 179.

Independent contractor	California law defines an independent contractor as "any person who renders service for a specified recompense for a specified result, under the control of his principal as to the result of his work only and not as to the means by which such result is accomplished."
	
	TIP Make sure that you classify independent contractors properly. See "How Do I Make Sure That the Individual Is Truly an Independent Contractor?" on page 33.
	
	What this means is that contractors enjoy more freedom, such as:
	• Flexible working conditions, such as the ability to set their own hours;
	• Certain tax advantages; and
	• Financial and personal rewards of self-employment.
	
	For these workers, employers don't face requirements to:
	• Provide certain statutory employment benefits, such as:
	  – Workers' compensation coverage;
	  – Unemployment benefits;
	  – Overtime payments; and
	  – Minimum wage obligations.
	• Withhold income taxes from payments for services.

Full time	A full-time employee works the number of hours that you designate as "full time."

Table 3. Types of Workers *(continued)*

What type	What it means
Part time	A part-time employee works less than the number of hours that qualify an employee as full time. You should define this in your handbook or other policy document. Part-time employees may or may not receive the same level of benefits as full-time employees.
Regular	A "regular" employee is someone who completes the introductory period and isn't employed on a casual basis. Regular employees may be either full-time or part-time employees, depending on the number of hours they work.
Introductory	An introductory employee is new to your company. You may define the introductory period in terms of calendar days or working days. Be sure to reserve the right to extend such periods in appropriate cases.
Temporary	Temporary employees are hired for specific assignments of limited duration. They may work full time or part time, but the length of their employment is usually specified. You should reserve the right to extend the duration of temporary employment without implying such employees' rights to benefits during the extension. Benefits established by law, such as State Disability Insurance and Unemployment Insurance, generally apply to temporary employees who otherwise qualify.
Casual (on call, per diem, irregular)	Casual workers perform intermittent service on an as-needed basis. For example, a retail establishment might have an employee who floats among departments as needed, or a preschool might bring in an additional teacher for a week to make sure state teacher/child ratios are met during attendance peaks, but the teacher isn't on staff all the time.

What's the Difference Between an Exempt and a Nonexempt Employee?

For details about exempt and nonexempt workers, see Table 3 on page 10.

When deciding to hire an employee, you need to determine whether the position merits exempt or nonexempt status. The difference between exempt and nonexempt is that though nonexempt employees are subject to the laws pertaining to overtime, meal periods and rest periods, exempt employees aren't.

 Don't pay nonexempt employees a salary. This doesn't make them exempt, and requires you to track and document all hours they work. See "What Do I Pay My Workers?" in Chapter 5, page 179, for more information.

In other words, nonexempt employees:

- Earn overtime pay, (see"What Is Overtime and How Does It Affect Me?" in Chapter 5, page 183);

- Receive payment of at least minimum wage (see "What Is the Minimum Wage?" in Chapter 5, page 181); and

- Must take meal and rest periods (see "What Meal and Rest Break Requirements Must I Comply With?" in Chapter 5, page 174).

Whether you can classify an employee as exempt depends mostly on the employee's duties and responsibilities. Exempt employees typically hold managerial-level positions and assume responsibility for getting their job duties done regardless of the time it takes them. Exempt employees don't keep time records for purposes of recording overtime. Exempt status is also determined by a minimum salary level of at least two times the minimum wage; see "What Is the Minimum Salary?" in Chapter 5, page 180. Employment laws create five main types of exempt positions:

- Administrative;

- Computer professional;

- Executive/managerial;

- Professional; and

- Outside salesperson.

Use the Exempt Analysis Worksheets (described in Table 8 on page 40) to help you decide how to classify your employee. You can find these in your online formspack, described in detail in "Online Forms" on page 4.

3 — Advertise and/or Recruit for the Position

You can use a variety of methods to let potential candidates know about the position:

- Advertise in magazines, newspapers or trade publications;

- Post job announcements on the Internet;

- Recruit in person at trade shows and job fairs; and

- Send a job request to a staffing agency, California's Employment Development Department or schools.

Whatever method you choose, make sure the language you use doesn't:

- Imply a secure contract, overriding employment at-will — although California is an at-will state, courts ruled that various factors, including employment advertisements and applications, can create an implied contract. For more information, see "Don't Create a Contract" on page 37. At-will is a legal concept, under by California law, assuring both employer and employee that either party can terminate the relationship at any time, for any reason, or for no reason.

Avoid advertisements with language that seems to guarantee future employment, such as:

- "Secure position";

- "Looking for candidates willing to make a long-term commitment to the company"; and

- "Looking for someone who can grow with the company."

Make sure that recruiters know they don't have the authority to promise job security to applicants.

Example: "Don't worry, we'll find a place for you" creates an oral contract that is just as binding as a written one. For more information, see "Don't Create a Contract" on page 37.

• Violate any state and federal discrimination laws — state and federal law prohibits limiting or excluding someone from employment because they have, or you think they have, certain characteristics. See "What Is Discrimination?" in Chapter 7, page 244, for more details. Make sure to avoid words and phrases that single out characteristics that could belong to a protected class.

Avoid even the appearance of the intent to discriminate by advertising in general interest venues or in a wide range of special interest ones, rather than in publications geared to one protected class.

The only time you can use prohibited language is when it identifies a bona fide occupational qualification (BFOQ). For example, an advertising agency looking for a model to advertise men's suits may specify "male model" in a job announcement. Being male is a BFOQ for this job.

A 2003 California law raises doubts about the validity of gender-related BFOQs. AB 196 added "gender" to the definition of sex discrimination under the California Fair Employment and Housing Act (FEHA), and in particular, provides protection for transgender employees who come to work dressed according to their "gender identity," so long as they meet reasonable appearance standards. Being male may no longer be a BFOQ for modeling men's clothing if a female who maintains a male gender identity and dresses appropriately as a male seeks employment to model men's suits or other clothing.

4 — Evaluate Potential Candidates

A thorough examination of the potential candidates gives you the best chance of finding an employee who matches well with your company. This person should have the necessary skills to do the job, but you should also find out about his/her work style, personality and employment-related interests to make sure this employment relationship will be a good fit for both of you. Though not required by law, each of the following activities can help you find a high quality employee:

- "Review Résumés" on page 14;

- "Screen Candidates with a Phone Interview" on page 14;

- "Receive Applications" on page 15; and

- "Interview Candidates" on page 16.

Review Résumés

Sometimes an applicant will submit a résumé providing helpful information about his/her education, skills, past work experience and accomplishments. A résumé is the candidate's marketing tool, and does not contain all of the information you should gather about a potential candidate. But it can give you a way to preview the person before beginning the application process.

You are not required to keep unsolicited résumés. You can send them back to the applicant along with a note explaining that no openings currently exist for the position sought, or keep the unsolicited résumés in a separate folder as a pool of potential employees.

Screen Candidates with a Phone Interview

A phone interview presents another, more informal way to preview a potential employee. This gives you a chance to talk over points of the résumé or application and clarify anything you want to know more about.

As in all conversations, be careful not to create an implied contract or to open yourself up to a discrimination charge. You might consider developing a script for the person conducting the phone interview. You can use the *Guide for Pre-Employment Inquiries*, described in Table 8 on page 40, to make sure your script doesn't contain any illegal questions. You can also see the *Employment Interview Checklist* described in Table 8 on page 40, for a series of questions you can ask. You can find these forms in your online formspack, described in detail in "Online Forms" on page 4. For tips on steering clear of implied contracts, see "Don't Create a Contract" on page 37.

Receive Applications

Applications can provide you with a broad range of standardized information that can help you evaluate applicants more equally. An application may request information such as:

- Applicant's availability;

- Experience and skills, including related military experience;

- Licensing and/or certification;

- Employment history;

- Specialized knowledge or training, such as proficiency in a language other than English; and

- Certification that all information provided is true and accurate.

To reduce the possibility of liability for discrimination, compare your own application with the provided sample *Employment Application – Short Form*, and review your application using the *Guide for Pre-Employment Inquiries*, both described in Table 8 on page 40, (especially if you use applications created out of state). Also, read "Interview Candidates" on page 16 for more information and tips on correct note-taking techniques.

 Interstate employers should use caution with provisions and disclaimers for applications used in multiple states. Job applicants might not notice certain provisions in "one-size-fits-all" applications. In some situations, this could create potential liability for employers.[1]

---

1. *Starbucks v. Superior Court of Orange County* 168 Cal. App. 4th 1436 (2008)

You should include the following "damage-control" provisions in the application and require the applicant to separately initial each provision.

Table 4. Application Provisions

What	Why
An authorization to check all references listed by the applicant	Since you may be liable for "negligent hiring" if you fail to check an applicant's references, this provision will help protect you from a claim that the applicant's privacy was invaded. It's also easier to gain information from former employers if they know that their former employee authorized disclosure to you. This release can't protect you against claims of intentional misconduct or employment discrimination (such as asking about protected information like the employee's medical history).
A statement that all answers given by the applicant are true, and any omissions or false information are grounds for rejection of the application or for termination	The courts allow employers to use an applicant's placement of false information on a job application as evidence in their defense of wrongful termination lawsuits, even when the employer did not discover the information was false until after the employee was terminated.
A statement that any future employment will be on an at-will basis	This helps applicants understand that employment is at-will. State that for any contrary representations to be binding, they must be in writing.

Interview Candidates

Interviewing candidates is your opportunity to learn more about your applicants and to determine which applicant is best for you, based on:

- Skills;
- Suitability for the position;
- Work style;
- Personality; and
- Employment-related interests.

 You will probably only select a small fraction of the candidates for interviews and/or background checks.

Be careful of questions that can put you at risk for a discrimination lawsuit and statements that can establish contracts or violate your policies. Read "Don't Create a Contract" on page 37 and the *Employment Interview Checklist*, described in Table 8 on page 40, for more information.

In general, don't ask questions about:

- Marital status or children;

- Age;

- Disabilities; and

- Hobbies and outside activities that might indicate race, religion, age, etc.

The *Guide for Pre-Employment Inquiries*, described in Table 8 on page 40, can guide you in asking appropriate questions. Also see "What Can I Do to Defend Myself Against a Claim?" in Chapter 7, page 274, for exceptions to these guidelines.

 Managers and supervisors who conduct interviews should beware of exaggerating the employment opportunity. California courts continue to award damages to employees promised increased compensation, promotions or job security during the employment process, and the promises went unfulfilled. Damages can reach millions of dollars if the court finds that an employer induced an applicant to leave secure employment by knowingly making false promises regarding the terms of future employment.

Consider a number of tips when conducting your interviews.

Table 5. Tips for Conducting Interviews

When?	Providing a deadline for applicants to respond to job openings can make it easier to evaluate all of your applicants and offer interviews all at once. Others prefer to leave a position open until filled.
Where?	Invite candidates to visit your office for the interview. This is their chance to learn more about your company and work environment, and to meet potential co-workers. Additionally, it's a professional way to receive applicants and allows you to select a quiet place for talking with the candidate without distractions.
How long?	Interviews generally last between 30 and 60 minutes, depending on the job requirements and the candidate's experience. Tell the candidate at the beginning how long the interview will last, and allow time to answer any questions the candidate may want to ask.

Table 5. Tips for Conducting Interviews *(continued)*

What?	Using "Don't Create a Contract" on page 37 and the *Fmployment Interview Checklist*, described in Table 8 on page 40, create a script of questions to ask each applicant. Make sure other interviewing managers understand the guidelines for interviewing.
Notes?	You may take notes during the interview, but you must exercise caution in how you phrase your written comments because the notes could be used in a legal claim. See "Don't Create a Contract" on page 37 for more details.

5 — Conduct Background Checks

Before selecting a new employee, perform some research on your applicants. Researching your applicant's background can provide you with valuable information, and can make costly litigation far less likely. See "Negligent Hiring" on page 23 for details.

 Researching an applicant's background can create an invasion of the applicant's privacy if improperly performed.

Remember that you are looking for information that will help you evaluate a candidate's job-related abilities. Also remember that records of a credit check, medical exam, etc., must be kept separate from the employee's regular personnel file — keep these records confidential.

You might examine each candidate's:

- Need for a work permit;

- Criminal background;

- Credit history and/or investigative consumer report;

- Drug/alcohol screening results;

- Physical health;

- References; and

- Educational background.

For financial reasons, you may wish to do some of this research post-offer, only on the lead candidate and make your offer contingent upon satisfactory results.

Table 6. Background Checks

What	Why
Proof of legal working age or work permit	Hiring someone less than 18 years old will probably require a work permit. See "What If the Applicant Is a Minor?" on page 34.
Criminal background check	You can choose not to hire someone based on past felony convictions if you can show a legitimate business purpose. Don't automatically deny employment to any applicant with a record of criminal conviction. The decision not to hire someone on this basis should be job related.

The law requires the Department of Justice to send conviction and pending arrest information to the employer and the applicant if he/she is applying for a license, employment or volunteer position with supervisory or disciplinary power over vulnerable persons under his/her care. This includes the care of minors, the elderly or the mentally impaired. The request for records must include the applicant's fingerprints.

If you hire an applicant convicted of any of the crimes listed below, you must notify the parents of any minor who will be supervised or disciplined by the employee or volunteer. You must provide the notice at least 10 days prior to the day that the employee or volunteer begins his/her new duties or tasks.

The violations that must be reported include:

- Assault with intent to commit mayhem, rape, sodomy or oral copulation;
- Unlawful sexual intercourse with a minor;
- Rape;
- Bodily harm to a child;
- Cruel or inhuman corporal punishment to a child; and
- Corporal injury to another.

The Department of Justice accepts only electronically submitted fingerprints.

If your organization employs or uses volunteers who care for minors, the elderly or the mentally impaired, consult with your legal counsel about criminal history checks. |

Table 6. Background Checks *(continued)*

What	Why
Credit check	If the job description demands that the employee will handle large amounts of money or be responsible for your company's finances, you may want to obtain a consumer credit report. The process requires many mandatory forms, which you can find in your online formspack, described in detail in"Online Forms" on page 4. The process is as follows: **1.** Written disclosure — tell the applicant, in writing, that you intend to obtain a consumer report. You can use the *Notice of Intent to Obtain Consumer Report*, described in Table 8 on page 40. **2.** Written Authorization — obtain the applicant's authorizing signature. You can use the *Authorization to Obtain Consumer Credit Report*, described in Table 8 on page 40. **3.** Certification to Consumer Reporting Agency — provide the agency with written certification that you made the disclosure and obtained authorization and that the information will not be used in violation of any federal or state law. You can use the *Certification to Consumer Credit Reporting Agency*, described in Table 8 on page 40. If the information on the consumer credit report leads you to take adverse action against the applicant, you must give the applicant written notice of the following: • Name, address and toll-free telephone number of the agency that provided the report; • A statement that the agency didn't make the adverse decision and can't explain why the decision was made; • A statement of the applicant's right to obtain a free copy of his/her files from the reporting agency (if requested within 60 days); • A statement of the applicant's right to dispute directly with the consumer reporting agency the accuracy of any information provided by the agency; • A statement to the applicant that the decision to take adverse action was based in whole or part upon the information obtained in the consumer credit report; and • A copy of the *Summary of Your Rights Under the Fair Credit Reporting Act*, described in Table 8 on page 40. You can use the *Pre-Adverse Action Disclosure* and the *Adverse Action Notice*, described in Table 8 on page 40.

Table 6. Background Checks *(continued)*

What	Why
Investigative consumer report	Helps you discover information about an applicant's character, general reputation, personal characteristics and mode of living, obtained through personal interviews. If you intend to obtain such a report, you are required to provide: **1.** Written disclosure — tell the applicant, in writing, that an investigative consumer report may be obtained. The disclosure must describe the applicant's right to request additional disclosures of the nature and scope of the investigation, and must include a summary of consumer rights. **2.** Certification to the consumer reporting agency — provide the agency with written certification that you made proper disclosure to the applicant. **3.** Additional requested disclosure — if the applicant requests it, you must fully disclose the nature and scope of the requested investigation. The Fair Credit Reporting Act (FCRA) prohibits consumer reporting agencies from providing consumer reports that contain medical information for employment purposes or in conjunction with credit or insurance transactions, without the specific prior consent of the applicant. It's prudent to limit the scope of these investigations to specifically job-related information, since investigative reports that aren't job-related may violate federal and state civil rights laws if they create an unequal impact on minority applicants. See "What Is Discrimination?" in Chapter 7, page 244 for details. **TIP** Always prepare a detailed job description, identifying the essential job functions and specific job duties, before advertising or interviewing candidates.

Table 6. Background Checks *(continued)*

What	Why
Drug testing	In general, the law doesn't require drug testing. Certain transportation employees must pass drug tests, and certain companies with state or federal contracts must maintain drug-free workplace programs. See "Where Do I Go for More Information?" on page 51 for helpful resources. If you wish to require drug testing for applicants, you should follow these guidelines: • Be consistent. Decide whether drug testing is required for all positions or just those with potential safety concerns; • Determine at what stage of the hiring process that you will test for drugs and what levels of what substances will be considered "passing" levels; • Obtain the applicant's signed authorization; and • Use an independent testing facility. Be aware that the law limits drug testing on employees. If you want to perform any drug testing, it needs to happen in the application phase after a job offer is made. If you make your offer contingent on a medical evaluation or a drug test, be sure to note this in the employment offer letter. The offer should be contingent on passing the exam. If an applicant refuses to take a drug test, you can refuse to hire the applicant.
Medical evaluation	The position may require job-related physical fitness, such as being able to lift a certain amount of weight. You may test for necessary qualifications only, and only after you have made an offer of employment. You may not test for an individual's HIV status. If your offer is contingent on the candidate passing a medical evaluation or drug test, be sure to note this in the employment offer letter.
Reference check	Though you are not required to check your future employee's references, doing so will make your hiring decision easier. See "Negligent Hiring" on page 23. When contacting your applicant's listed references, you should stick to questions that directly relate to job performance to avoid liability for invasion of privacy. You may need written permission from the applicant to obtain salary information.
Education check	This is not required, but verifying an applicant's transcript and a university's accreditation can save headaches later.

Negligent Hiring

The law does not specifically obligate you to check an applicant's references and background. However, a court could hold you liable for negligent hiring if you don't perform an investigation and the employee commits an offense that you could have predicted if you made a reasonable effort to research that person. A reasonable effort, even if former employers don't cooperate, can protect you from negligent hiring claims.

 It's considered negligent to hire someone whose documented past presents an unreasonable risk of harm to others; specifically, to co-workers and customers.

Example: If an employee with a record of violent behavior assaults someone in your office, the assaulted person may bring a suit of negligent hiring against you, alleging that you should have known about the employee's violent past and not hired the person.

6 — Make the Hiring Decision and Offer the Position

Once you've done the work of reviewing résumés and applications and interviewing candidates, it's time to make your hiring decision. Make all hiring decisions carefully. To prevent claims of unfair hiring practices:

- Be sure you have valid reasons for making the hiring decision, based on the person's:

  - Qualifications;

  - Experience;

  - Skills;

  - Knowledge; and

  - Education.

- Document the reasons why one person was selected over other candidates; and

- Review documents from hiring supervisors to ensure decisions were based on valid reasons, and that no applicant was rejected for a discriminatory reason.

How Do I Offer the Position to the Successful Applicant?

You can send an employment offer letter to the applicant you've chosen that clarifies the terms of employment, such as:

- Start date;

- At-will employment status;

- Exempt or nonexempt status (see "What's the Difference Between an Exempt and a Nonexempt Employee?" on page 11);

- Wage or salary — if the employee is exempt, phrase the pay rate in terms of dollars weekly, biweekly or monthly; if the employee is nonexempt, phrase the pay rate in terms of dollars per hour; and

- Whether the offer depends on the applicant passing a medical exam, drug test or reference or background check.

 If you send an offer letter, be sure that the salary for an exempt employee meets the minimum salary requirements for an employee to be exempt. See "What Is the Minimum Salary?" in Chapter 5, page 180.

You don't have to write a letter, but many employees won't want to leave their current jobs until they have something in writing confirming the new job.

 Be careful that you don't create a contract in your letter, overriding employment at-will. For more information, read "Don't Create a Contract" on page 37. To see a sample letter that contains no contractual language, read the *Employment Offer Letter*, described in Table 8 on page 40.

How Do I Handle Unsuccessful Applicants?

Although not required, you might consider sending a letter to all applicants not hired after the successful applicant accepted the position, letting them know that they are no longer under consideration for the position. This is a courtesy to the applicants that pursued employment with your company. You can send a standard letter to all unsuccessful applicants. To see a sample letter, read the *Letter to Applicants Not Hired*, described in Table 8 on page 40.

7 — Fill Out Paperwork

The paperwork involved with hiring a new employee is extensive. Use a *Hiring Checklist* to help you keep track of which forms/notifications you have provided and processed. This checklist is described in Table 8 on page 40.

Use the following forms throughout the hiring process:

- Applications (see "Receive Applications" on page 15);

- Forms for checking background (see "5 — Conduct Background Checks" on page 18);

- Forms for special types of workers, such as:

    - Minors. See "What If the Applicant Is a Minor?" on page 34; and

    - Independent contractors. See "How Do I Make Sure That the Individual Is Truly an Independent Contractor?" on page 33.

TIP You can find these forms in your online formspack, described in detail in "Online Forms" on page 4.

Fill Out or Provide These Forms on the Employee's First Day of Work

- Information about benefits and employee rights, such as:

    - Workers' Compensation (see "What Do I Need to Know About Workers' Compensation?" on page 133);

    - State Disability Insurance (see "What Do I Need to Know About SDI?" in Chapter 4, page 128);

    - COBRA and Cal-COBRA rights notifications;

    - *Paid Family Leave* (see "What Do I Need to Know About Paid Family Leave?" in Chapter 4, page 129);

    - *HIPAA Questionnaire*; and

    - Sexual harassment forms.

- Safety information, such as:

    - *Emergency Information* form; and

    - *Individual Employee Training Documentation – Initial Safety Training* (see Table 65 in Chapter 6, page 234).

- Government forms, such as:

    - *W-4 Form (federal) - Employee's Withholding Allowance Certificate*;

    - *Form DE-4 (state) - Employee's Withholding Allowance Certificate;* and

    - *Report of New Employee(s) (Form DE 34).*

- Personnel policy forms, such as:
  - *Confidentiality Agreement*; and
  - *Property Return Agreement.*

TIP You can find these forms in your online formspack, described in detail in "Online Forms" on page 4. CalBizCentral's Required Notices Kit includes pamphlets on Unemployment Insurance, State Disability Insurance, Paid Family Leave, Sexual Harassment and Workers' Compensation.

Verify the Employee's Authorization to Work

All new workers must fill out their portion of the Form I-9 and provide the documents listed on the back of the Form I-9 (described in Table 8 on page 40) within three business days of beginning work.

NEW 2010 On Aug. 7, 2009, U.S. Citizenship and Immigration Services issued a new Form I-9. Employers should use the most current version of Form I-9, which bears a revision date of 08/07/09 and an expiration date of 8/31/12.

The departments of State and Homeland Security now issue "passport cards," considered a "List A" document that may be presented by newly hired employees during the employment eligibility verification process to show work authorized status. Employees use "List A" documents to prove both identity and work authorization when completing the Form I-9.

The "passport card" is more limited in its uses for international travel (for example, it can't be used for international air travel), but it's a valid passport that attests to the bearer's U.S. citizenship and identity. The card may be used for the Form I-9 process, and can also be accepted by employers participating in the E-Verify program. For more information on E-Verify, see "E-Verify" on page 30.

 You may not require more or different identity and work authorization documents than specified by the USCIS on the Form I-9, nor can you specify which documents an employee must provide. If the employee can't produce the documentation at the time of hire, you may still hire the employee. However, the employee must give you:

- A receipt demonstrating that he/she applied for the required documents within three days after he/she begins work; and

- The actual documents, within 90 days after he/she begins work.

If the employee works for you for less than three business days, Section 2 of the Form I-9 must be completed at the time employment begins. For a non-citizen, make sure you re-verify expiring work authorization documents before the expiration date noted in Section 1 of the Form I-9. For more information about hiring non-U.S. citizens, see "What If the Applicant Is Not a U.S. Citizen?" on page 36.

> The receipt rule only covers documents that indicate the employee was eligible to work in the United States on or before the date employment with you started. Receipts for an initial application for the right to work in the U.S. aren't acceptable.

Electronic I-9 Retention

Employers and employees may complete and sign the Form I-9 electronically. The rule also permits employers to electronically scan and store the Form I-9, as long as the employer meets certain performance standards set forth in the rule for the electronic filing system. The rule provides a reasonable set of standards for creating a trustworthy system for Form I-9 completion and storage. The technology-neutral standards allow businesses the flexibility to keep records in a manner consistent with other business processes. The standards also provide DHS investigators with a framework for inspecting the records and assessing their trustworthiness.

The rule sets standards for electronic retention of the Form I-9. The rule doesn't limit employers to using one system for the storage of the Form I-9 electronically, nor does it identify one method for acceptable electronic signatures. If you complete the Form I-9 electronically using an electronic signature, your system for capturing electronic signatures must allow signatories to acknowledge that they read the attestation and attach the electronic signature to an electronically completed the Form I-9.

In addition, the system must:

- Affix the electronic signature at the time of the transaction

- Create and preserve a record verifying the identity of the person producing the signature; and

- Provide a printed confirmation of the transaction, at the time of the transaction, to the person providing the signature.

If the employer uses an electronic signature to complete the Form I-9, but the electronic signature capturing system doesn't comply with these standards, the DHS will determine that the Form I-9 has not been properly completed. This will subject the employer to fines and penalties.

Whether the Form I-9 gets filled out manually or electronically, an employer representative must still physically examine required identification and work eligibility documentation.

Verify That Social Security Numbers and Names Match

The Social Security Administration (SSA) offers two methods of verifying Social Security numbers (SSNs) of employees. The first method, the Telephone Number Employer Verification (TNEV), is an automated telephone service that employers may use to verify up to 10 employee names and SSNs at one time, without speaking to an agent. This service can only be used for wage reporting purposes.

The second method, the Social Security Number Verification Service (SSNVS), allows registered users (employers and certain third-party submitters) to verify employees' names and SSNs against SSA records.

With SSNVS, you may:

- Verify up to 10 names and SSNs online and receive immediate results. You may use the SSN Verification Web page an unlimited number of times per session.

- Upload electronic files of up to 250,000 names and SSNs and usually receive results the next government business day.

Registration and use of the TNEV and SSNVS is free, and employers can register through SSA's Business Services Online Web site at **www.socialsecurity.gov/bso/bsowelcome.htm**.

What If the Documents I'm Shown Aren't Valid?

You aren't liable for accepting documents that appear reasonably authentic, unless you know or have reason to know that the documents are false. In fact, you may not refuse to honor documents that appear valid on their face.

For Form I-9 purposes, new employees may use one item from List A, or one item from List B and one item from List C of the Form I-9. For example, the individual who uses a California driver's license to establish identity must also present a valid document that establishes his/her right to work in the United States.

On the Form I-9, five documents no longer appear on "List A" of the "List of Acceptable Documents":

- Certificate of U.S. Citizenship (Form N-560 or N-561);

- Certificate of Naturalization (Form N-550 or N-570);

- Alien Registration Receipt Card (I-151);

- Unexpired Reentry Permit (Form I-327); and

- Unexpired Refugee Travel Document (Form I-571)

The following documents do appear on "List A" of the "List of Acceptable Documents," and all documents must be unexpired:

- Employment Authorization Document (Form I-766) that contains a photograph;

- U.S Passport or U.S. Passport Card;

- Permanent Resident Card or Alien Registration Receipt Card (Form I-551);

- Foreign passport that contains a temporary Form I-551 stamp or a temporary Form I-551 printed notation on a machine-readable immigrant visa;

- In the case of a nonimmigrant alien authorized to work for a specific employer incident to status, a foreign passport with Form I-94 or Form I-94A bearing the same name as the passport and containing an endorsement of the alien's non-immigrant status, as long as the period of endorsement has not yet expired and the proposed employment is not in conflict with any restrictions or limitations identified on the form; and

- Passport from the Federated States of Micronesia (FSM) or the Republic of the Marshall Islands (RMI) with Form I-94 or Form I-94A indicating nonimmigrant admission under the Compact of Free Association Between the United States and the FSM or RMI.

Instructions for Section 1 of the Form I-9 now indicate that the employee is not obliged to provide his or her SSN in Section 1 of the I-9 unless he or she is employed by an employer who participates in the E-Verify program. For more information on this program, see "E-Verify" on page 30.

Employers may now sign and retain Forms I-9 electronically. See "Electronic I-9 Retention" above. Don't file the Form I-9 with U.S. Immigrations and Customs Enforcement (ICE) or USCIS. You must keep the Form I-9 for either:

- Three years after the date of hire; or

- One year after employment is terminated, whichever is later.

- The form must also be available for inspection by authorized U.S. government officials (e.g., ICE, Department of Labor).

The Spanish version of Form I-9 may be filled out by employers and employees in Puerto Rico ONLY. Spanish-speaking employers and employees in the 50 states and other U.S. territories may print this for their reference, but may only complete the form in English to meet employment eligibility verification requirements. Any documents used for Form I-9 purposes that must be "unexpired" will require you to reconfirm the employee's ability to work in the United States once the document expires. You should note when the document is to expire and several months prior to the expiration date, and remind your employee that he/she will need to provide new Form I-9 documentation. The employee doesn't have to provide the same document again, and may provide any document from List A or C that establishes the employee's right to work in the United States.

E-Verify

E-Verify is an Internet-based system operated by the Department of Homeland Security (DHS) and the Social Security Administration that allows employers to electronically verify the employment eligibility of newly hired employees. Some important points regarding E-Verify include:

- California employers' participation in E-Verify is voluntary.

- E-Verify must be used for new hires only. It can't be used to verify the employment eligibility of current employees.

- E-Verify must be used for all new hires regardless of national origin or citizenship status. It may not be used selectively.

- E-Verify must be used only after hire and after completion of the Form I-9. Employers may not pre-screen applicants through E-Verify

- The program is currently free to employers.

Employers who use the E-Verify system to determine employment eligibility must display the notices supplied by the DHS in a prominent place clearly visible to prospective employees. The notices, "You Should Know Your Rights and Responsibilities Under E-Verify" and "OSC Employee Rights Poster," can be found on the DHS Web site. The formspack associated with the *HR Handbook for California Employers* also contains the forms, in English and Spanish versions.

As of Sept. 8, 2009, federal contractors and subcontractors must now use E-Verify to confirm their employees' eligibility to work in the United States. You must enroll in E-Verify if and when you're awarded a federal contract or subcontract that requires participation in E-Verify as a term of the contract.

To find out more or to sign up for E-Verify, visit ***www.dhs.gov/e-verify***.

8 — Welcome Your New Employees

Your new employee's first day of work is the ideal point in the employment relationship to make sure that your new employee:

- Understands your policies and work rules;

- Is informed of his/her legal rights and obligations; and

- Receives the necessary training to do the job safely and efficiently.

All training and orientation should be documented. Proper records can help protect you from lawsuits. Use the *Employee Orientation* checklist, described in Table 8 on page 40, and keep it in the employee's personnel file.

 You might be tempted to designate the first few weeks or months of work as a "probationary" period, but this could be understood as a promise that, when the probationary period is over, the employee will have permanent status. Calling this time an "introductory period" is acceptable and won't compromise the idea of at-will employment.

Employee Orientation

Verify that the employee:

- Fills out and returns the required forms (see Table 8 on page 40);

- Tours the building/facilities and learns the exits' location;

- Meets managers and other employees;

- Understands information on company processes and resources;

- Receives an employee handbook (see "How Do I Create an Employee Handbook?" in Chapter 3, page 62) and returns a signed *Confirmation of Receipt* (see Table 13 in Chapter 3, page 92);

- Receives a copy of all required pamphlets, including:

  - *Sexual Harassment*;

  - *Workers' Compensation Rights and Benefits*;

  - *Paid Family Leave*; and

  - *State Disability Insurance.*

- Receives a copy of the company's IIPP (see "Injury and Illness Prevention Program" in Chapter 6, page 213); and

- Gets a chance to ask questions about anything he/she doesn't completely understand.

TIP You can find these forms in your online formspack, described in detail in "Online Forms" on page 4.

Employee Training

You must provide all of your employees with the necessary knowledge and training to complete their tasks safely. If employees get hurt because you did not take the time to make sure that they understood how to operate a machine properly, you will be liable. See "How Should I Cover Safety Training?" in Chapter 6, page 224.

If you employ 50 or more people, you must provide at least two hours of sexual harassment training to all supervisory employees every two years. All new supervisory employees must receive training within six months of assuming supervisory positions, either as a new hire or through a promotion. For more information, see "Provide Training" in Chapter 7, page 259.

What if I Use Independent Contractors?

Engaging an independent contractor can offer significant advantages over hiring an employee. In an independent contractor relationship, business owners don't have to:

- Provide certain benefits, such as workers' compensation and unemployment insurance;

- Meet overtime and minimum wage obligations; and

- Withhold income taxes from payments.

Be careful! It isn't enough that the two parties agree to an independent contractor relationship. You can classify an individual as an independent contractor only if the individual meets the requirements.

If you misclassify an employee as an independent contractor, you might have to:

- Pay huge fines imposed by the IRS and the EDD;

- Pay workers' compensation from the date of hire, plus possible penalties; and

- Pay retroactive employee benefits, such as health insurance, vacation time and retirement plan contributions.

How Do I Make Sure That the Individual Is Truly an Independent Contractor?

Various state and federal agencies use their own tests to determine whether an individual meets the criteria to be classified as an independent contractor. These tests cover concepts that have been used in California for several years.

 Be careful in making your decision. Each case is unique, and the penalties for making a mistake can be costly. We recommend you consult your legal counsel to help you determine an individual's status.

Independent Contractor Test

The California Common Law and the "Balancing" tests measure a worker's right to control when, how and where work is performed. Factors include:

- The employer:
  - Has the right to terminate the contract; and
  - Pays by job, not by time.
- Both parties believe they are creating an independent contractor relationship;
- The worker:
  - Engages in a distinct occupational business;
  - Possesses significant skills or education required for the particular occupation;
  - Supplies the instruments and tools for performing the work;
  - Performs services over a short or specified period of time;
  - Has opportunity for profit or loss, depending upon his/her own managerial skills; and
  - Employs additional help at his/her own expense.
- The work:
  - Usually occurs under the employer's general direction, by a specialist, without supervision; and
  - Is not part of the employer's regular business.

You can also use the *Employment Determination Guide (Form DE 38)* to help you determine if the worker is an independent contractor. This form is described in Table 8 on page 40.

What Special Forms Do I Need for Independent Contractors?

Each independent contractor you hire needs to sign a contract, approved by your legal counsel, that includes the scope of work and the terms of the agreement.

You must also report independent contractors to the EDD's New Employee Registry within 20 days of the start-of-work date. Use the *Report of Independent Contractor(s) (Form DE 542)*, described in Table 8 on page 40, and in your online formspack, described in detail in "Online Forms" on page 4.

What If the Applicant Is a Minor?

TIP A **minor** is any person under the age of 18 required to attend school, or any person under the age of six.

When you employ a minor, you must comply with child labor laws designed to help young people acquire work experience and income while safeguarding their scholastic advancement and physical well-being. You can use the *Checklist for Employing Minors* as a guide, described in Table 8 on page 40.

To employ a minor, you must have a work permit on file year-round, even when school is not in session. You must have the permit on file the day the minor begins work. You can get the permit from the minor's local school district office, even if the student attends a charter school.

TIP A **work permit** sets limits on the maximum number of days and hours of work as well as the spread of hours allowed for that minor. It may also contain limitations on other aspects of the minor's work.

This rule applies to any minor, even:

- High-school dropouts;

- Emancipated minors (minors who declare independence from their parents for IRS purposes), although they can apply for a work permit without their parent's permission;

- Minors who are not state residents, such as children who live out of state with one parent during the school year and visit the other parent in California during the summer; and

- Children who work for their parents.

What Circumstances Don't Require a Work Permit?

Direct all questions regarding the need for work permits to the minor's school district (or the school district in which the minor would go to school, if he/she does not currently attend).

You don't need a work permit for minors who:

- Graduated from high school, though in certain hazardous occupations even these minors need a work permit unless they completed a certificate program for that industry;

- Work irregularly at odd jobs, such as yard work and babysitting in private homes;

- Participate in any horseback riding exhibition, contest or event;

- Are self-employed;

- Are at least 14 years of age and deliver newspapers to consumers; and

- Work for a parent or guardian in connection with property he/she owns, operates or controls for:

  - Agriculture;

  - Horticulture;

  - Viticulture; and

  - Domestic labor.

How Do I Obtain a Work Permit?

1. Complete a *Statement of Intent to Employ Minor and Request for Work Permit (Form B1-1)*, described in Table 8 on page 40. The minor's supervisor and parent/guardian must both sign the form.

2. File Form B1-1 with the minor's school district.

3. The minor's school district completes and issues a *Permit to Employ and Work (Form B1-4)*, described in Table 8 on page 40.

You must keep the work permit on file the entire length of employment. For more information on handling these forms, see Table 8 on page 40.

What If the Applicant Is Not a U.S. Citizen?

You may not knowingly hire, contract for labor, recruit, retain or refer for a fee for employment an individual unauthorized to work in the United States. If you do, you could face progressive fines from $375 up to $16,000 per unauthorized worker. Repeat offenders can face up to six months in jail.

How Do I Protect Myself?

You must verify that every person you hire is either:

- A U.S. citizen; or

- Authorized to work in the United States.

See "Verify the Employee's Authorization to Work" on page 26 for instructions on the verification process.

If you later discover that the employee is an unauthorized worker, you may not continue to employ him/her. However, you will still need to pay the worker for all hours worked.

What Other Things Should I Be Careful of When Employing Non-U.S. Citizens?

You may not:

- Adopt an English-only policy; or

- Discriminate against any employee who has valid documents of eligibility on the basis of:

  - National origin;

  - Citizenship status; or

  - Future expiration date of verifying documents.

An **English-only policy** prohibits the use of other languages in the workplace. It's illegal in California unless certain conditions are met, including business necessity and employee notice.

The Hitches, Glitches and Pitfalls of Hiring Employees

Understanding the potential for lawsuits will help you avoid them. The most important thing you can do is watch your language to avoid:

- Creating a contract that may lead to a wrongful termination lawsuit at the end of the employment relationship; and

- Making an employment decision or acting in any way that may lead to a claim of discrimination.

See "How Can I Avoid a Discrimination/Harassment Claim?" in Chapter 7, page 256, for guidelines on non-discriminatory employment decisions.

Don't Create a Contract

California is an at-will employment state. In brief, this means that as long as you don't break a law or violate a specified public policy, you can hire or terminate an employee whenever you want, and workers can accept or leave employment whenever they want.

In every employment relationship, an implied covenant exists requiring you to exercise good faith and fair dealing in the employment relationship. An employment contract can create explicit limitations on when, and under what circumstances, you can terminate the employment relationship.

Essentially, **good faith and fair dealing** means that you should make decisions on a fair basis, and treat in like manner employees who are similarly situated.

To emphasize the at-will nature of employment, you can use an employment agreement that outlines the terms and conditions of employment and restates the definition of at-will employment. However, if you create employment that is not at-will, you create a contract that overrides the presumption of at-will employment because the contract usually creates a promise that you will only terminate an employee for just cause. Remember, contracts can be written, oral or implied

Just cause means a fair and honest cause or reason, acted on in good faith by the employer.

Table 7. Types of Contracts

What kind?	What about it?
Written contracts are the most obvious. An employee with a written and signed contract has the right to have that contract honored.	Written contracts can work to your benefit if your contract clearly states how and why employment may be terminated. You should also consider adding these provisions to the contract: • Specify the duration of the contract and the time period required for notice for termination of the contract; • State that the contract can be renewed at the option of the company; and • State that the written document constitutes the entire agreement, that no representations or promises other than those documented can be relied upon, and that the contract can be modified only in writing signed by a corporate officer. Written contracts do carry disadvantages; they are less flexible, and any inadvertent omissions or ambiguities in the contract will be interpreted in the employee's favor, not yours.
Oral contracts, based on conversations between employer and employee, aren't as obvious, but just as binding as signed, written contracts.	Watch what you say to an employee in every phase of the employment relationship. Promises such as, "As long as you do a good job, you will have a job here," create oral contracts. See "Don't Create a Contract" on page 37 for details.
Implied contracts are based upon the length of employment and indicators of job security that an employee receives.	The courts determine whether an implied contract exists on a case-by-case basis. The best defense against an implied contract claim is a signed, at-will employment agreement. You should also maintain an explicit at-will employment policy in your employee handbook. See Table 11 in Chapter 3, page 64.

Be Aware of the Laws That Apply

Though employment in California is considered at-will, federal and state laws require that you treat all qualified candidates equally. You can't make hiring decisions based (in whole or in part) on an applicant's race, gender, nationality, sexuality, marital status, religion, disabilities, medical condition, age, union activity, past bankruptcy or status as an authorized immigrant or a veteran. California's laws create more strict protections for applicants than do federal laws. The definition of disability is broader, and more classes are included as protected.

If an aggrieved person files a discrimination lawsuit against you, you will bear the burden of proving that you acted on legitimate reasons for not hiring that individual. This might be tougher than it sounds. Any documents or notes on documents will be used either to defend you against accusations of discrimination, or to prove those accusations. Only constant vigilance and consistent behavior will protect you.

See "How Can I Avoid a Discrimination/Harassment Claim?" in Chapter 7, page 256, for more details.

What Forms and Checklists Do I Use to Hire Employees?

The following tables describe required and recommended forms associated with the hiring process.

TIP You can find these forms in your online formspack, described in detail in "Online Forms" on page 4.

Table 8. Important Forms and Checklists

Notification/ Form	What do I use it for?	When do I use it?	Who fills it out?	Where does it go?
Adverse Action Notice	To take adverse action (such as not hiring an applicant or terminating an employee) based on a credit report you have obtained.	This form is required when you know you are taking adverse action based on information in the credit report (see "5 — Conduct Background Checks" on page 18).	You do.	Give it to the employee. Keep a copy in a private file away from personnel file. Restrict access to the form to a "need to know" basis.
Authorization to Obtain Consumer Credit Report	To obtain a credit report of any type.	This form is required before you obtain the report (see "5 — Conduct Background Checks" on page 18).	You and the employee or applicant fill out respective sections of the form.	Keep in personnel file. Restrict access to the form to a "need to know" basis.
Checklist for Employing Minors	Tracking legal issues to consider when hiring a minor.	During the recruiting and hiring processes.	You do.	Keep the checklist in the minor's personnel file.
Confidentiality Agreement	Obtaining employee acknowledgement that there is information necessary for his/ her job that he/ she may not disclose.	At the time of hire or change in duties of an employee.	You prepare the agreement and have it reviewed by an attorney. Employee signs the agreement.	The original agreement goes in the employee's personnel record. Give the employee a copy.

Table 8. Important Forms and Checklists *(continued)*

Notification/ Form	What do I use it for?	When do I use it?	Who fills it out?	Where does it go?
Form DE-4 - Employee's Withholding Allowance Certificate	All employees. This is the California tax withholding form if employees want different federal and state tax withholding.	Before employee's first pay date.	The employee.	Keep the form in the employee's personnel record. If you send the original to payroll, keep a copy of the form.
Emergency Information	Recording important medical information and contacts in case of an emergency.	At the time of hire. Keep the form updated throughout employment.	The employee.	Keep emergency information readily accessible. You may keep the forms in your personnel records, but you might want to use a separate binder for quicker access.
Emergency Information - Spanish	Recording important medical information and contacts in case of an emergency for employees whose primary language is Spanish.	At the time of hire. Keep the form updated throughout employment.	The employee.	Keep emergency information readily accessible. You may keep the form in your personnel records, but you might want to use a separate binder for quicker access.
Employee Orientation	Tracking completed orientation tasks.	In the first weeks of employment.	The managers.	Keep in the employee's personnel file.

Table 8. Important Forms and Checklists *(continued)*

Notification/ Form	What do I use it for?	When do I use it?	Who fills it out?	Where does it go?
Employment Application – Short Form	Gathering key work history information from an applicant, obtaining authorization to check references and background, and certification that all information is truthful.	During the recruiting process.	The applicant.	Keep in the employee's personnel file, if the applicant is hired. If you don't hire the applicant, keep the paperwork for two years.
Employment Determination Guide (Form DE 38)	Determining employee versus independent contractor status.	During the hiring process.	The employer.	Keep in the applicant's file, or if the applicant is hired, in the personnel file.
Employment Interview Checklist	Listing which questions to ask applicants during an interview.	During the applicant's interview.	The interviewer.	Keep in the employee's personnel file, if hired. If you don't hire the applicant, keep the paperwork for two years.
Employment Offer Letter	Informing an applicant that he or she has been selected for employment.	When the employment decision has been made.	The employer.	Mail to the applicant. Keep a copy in the employee's personnel file.
Exempt Analysis Worksheet – Administrative Exemption	Determining whether an employee's duties meet the requirements for exempt status.	During the hiring process.	The employer.	Keep in the employee's personnel file.

Table 8. Important Forms and Checklists *(continued)*

Notification/ Form	What do I use it for?	When do I use it?	Who fills it out?	Where does it go?
Exempt Analysis Worksheet – Computer Professional Exemption	Determining whether an employee's duties meet the requirements for exempt status.	During the hiring process.	The employer.	Keep in the employee's personnel file.
Exempt Analysis Worksheet – Executive/Managerial Exemption	Determining whether an employee's duties meet the requirements for exempt status.	During the hiring process.	The employer.	Keep in the employee's personnel file.
Exempt Analysis Worksheet – Professional Exemption	Determining whether an employee's duties meet the requirements for exempt status.	During the hiring process.	The employer.	Keep in the employee's personnel file.
Exempt Analysis Worksheet – Salesperson Exemption	Determining whether an employee's duties meet the requirements for exempt status.	During the hiring process.	The employer.	Keep in the employee's personnel file.
Guide for Pre-Employment Inquiries	Outlining what you can and can't ask during the recruiting process.	During the recruiting process.	N/A	Use as a reference.
Hiring Checklist	Tracking completion of recommended and required hiring procedures and forms.	During the recruiting and hiring process.	The manager or other person in charge of hiring employees.	Keep in the employee's personnel file.

Table 8. Important Forms and Checklists *(continued)*

Notification/ Form	What do I use it for?	When do I use it?	Who fills it out?	Where does it go?
Letter to Applicants Not Hired	Informing an applicant that he or she wasn't selected for employment.	When the employment decision has been made.	The employer.	Mail to the applicant. You should keep a list of the applicants to whom the letter is mailed.
Pre-Hire Checklist	Organizing the process of finding and preparing to hire an employee.	During the recruiting process.	The employer.	Keep the checklist in the employee's personnel file, if the applicant is hired.
Property Return Agreement	Obtaining employee acknowledgement that he/she received property from you (tools, uniforms, etc.) and agrees to return the property.	When your property is issued to the employee.	The employee signs the form.	Keep the original agreement in your personnel records.
Certification to Consumer Credit Reporting Agency	To obtain a credit report of any type.	This form is required before you obtain the report (see "5 — Conduct Background Checks" on page 18).	The employer.	Send form to the agency creating the report. Keep in personnel file. Restrict access to the form to a "need to know" basis.

Table 8. Important Forms and Checklists *(continued)*

Notification/ Form	What do I use it for?	When do I use it?	Who fills it out?	Where does it go?
Direct Deposit Authorization - English	To get employees' permission to deposit paychecks directly into their bank account instead of receiving a paper check.	As part of the hiring process or whenever an employee requests direct deposit.	The employee.	Keep in personnel and/or payroll file (if separate).
Direct Deposit Authorization - Spanish	To get permission from employees whose primary language is Spanish to deposit paychecks directly into their bank account instead of receiving a paper check.	As part of the hiring process or whenever an employee requests direct deposit.	The employee.	Keep in personnel and/or payroll file (if separate).
HIPAA Questionnaire	To respond to a *Certificate of Group Health Plan Coverage* (a HIPAA Certificate) from a new group health plan participant.	On the day the employee enrolls for the benefit.	Prior employer or plan administrator fills out Question 6. Current employer or plan administrator fills out the rest of the form.	Send the *HIPAA Questionnaire* to the prior employer or plan administrator. Keep a copy of the questionnaire in your personnel records.

Table 8. Important Forms and Checklists *(continued)*

Notification/ Form	What do I use It for?	When do I use it?	Who fills it out?	Where does it go?
Form I-9 NEW ~2010 Note: Employers should use the current version of the Form I-9, which bears a revision date of 08/07/09 and an expiration date of 08/31/12.	To verify the employment eligibility of **all** employees.	Section 1: at the time of hire. Section 2: within three business days after the employee's first day of work. Section 3: on or before the expiration date in Section 1.	Section 1: The employee fills out. Section 2: The employer fills out. Section 3: The employer fills out if necessary for updating or reverifying.	Keep the forms for all employees in a common file rather than separate personnel records.
General Notice of COBRA Continuation Coverage Rights (California Employees)	To inform California employees of their rights to continuation of health care coverage. Applies only to employers with 20 or more employees, and only to employees in California.	This form is required on the day the employee enrolls for the benefit.	N/A	Include this notice in the group health plan's Summary Plan Description. Send a copy of the notice to the spouse of a married employee, preferably by registered mail. Keep a record of the mailing and/or distribution at hire of this notice to both employee and spouse on the *Hiring Checklist*.

Table 8. Important Forms and Checklists *(continued)*

Notification/ Form	What do I use it for?	When do I use it?	Who fills it out?	Where does it go?
General Notice of COBRA Continuation Coverage Rights (Outside California)	To inform employees outside California of their rights to continuation of health care coverage. Applies only to employers with 20 or more employees, and only to employees outside California.	This form is required on the day the employee enrolls for the benefit.	N/A	Include this notice in the group health plan's Summary Plan Description. Send a copy of the notice to the spouse of a married employee, preferably by registered mail. Keep a record of the mailing and/or distribution at hire of this notice to both employee and spouse on the *Hiring Checklist*.
Notice of Intent to Obtain Consumer Report	To obtain a credit report of any type.	This form is required before you obtain the report (see "5 — Conduct Background Checks" on page 18).	The employer.	Keep in personnel file. Restrict access to the form to a "need to know" basis.
Paid Family Leave pamphlet (available in ***2010 Required Notices Kit at www.calbiz central.com***)	To provide notice to employees of their rights to paid family leave benefits.	This pamphlet must be given it to all new employees and any employees taking leave for a covered reason.	N/A	Give the pamphlet to employees and make sure they understand its contents.

Table 8. Important Forms and Checklists *(continued)*

Notification/ Form	What do I use it for?	When do I use it?	Who fills it out?	Where does it go?
Permit to Employ and Work (Form B1-4)	To obtain permission to employ a minor.	This is required before the minor begins working [and after the *Statement of Intent to Employ Minor and Request for Work Permit (Form B1-1)* has been approved]. See the form's description following in this table.	The minor's school district fills out and issues the permit.	Keep form (permit) on file as long as the minor is employed. Keep it in your personnel records or in a common binder for all minor employees.
Pre-Adverse Action Disclosure	To notify an employee or potential employee of the possibility of adverse action.	This form is required when you know you're taking adverse action based on information in the credit report (see "5 — Conduct Background Checks" on page 18).	The employer.	Give to employee. Keep a copy in a private file away from personnel file. Restrict access to the form to a "need to know" basis.
Recruiting Checklist	Use this checklist to guide you through the recruiting process for new and existing positions.	When you need to advertise and recruit for a new position.	The employer.	In your files.

Table 8. Important Forms and Checklists *(continued)*

Notification/ Form	What do I use it for?	When do I use it?	Who fills it out?	Where does it go?
Independent Contractor(s) Report (Form DE 542)	All new independent contractors. **TIP** The District Attorney uses the information in this form to locate parents who owe child support funds.	This form must be completed and submitted as soon as possible after signing the contract.	The employer.	Mail or fax the form to: Employment Development Department P.O. Box 997350 MIC 99 Sacramento, CA 95899-7350 Fax: 916-255-3211
New Employee(s) Report (Form DE 34)	All new employees. Permits registered domestic partners to file joint state income tax and have their earnings treated as community property on par with married couples. **TIP** The District Attorney uses the information in this form to locate parents who owe child support funds.	This form must be completed and submitted within 20 days of hire.	The employer.	Mail or fax the form to: Employment Development Department P.O. Box 997016, MIC 23 West Sacramento, CA 95799-7016 Fax: 916-255-0951

Table 8. Important Forms and Checklists (*continued*)

Notification/ Form	What do I use it for?	When do I use it?	Who fills it out?	Where does it go?
Sexual Harassment pamphlet (available in **2010 Required Notices Kit at www.calbiz central.com**)	This form describes the problem and the penalties of sexual harassment.	You must provide this form whenever you hire a new employee. It's recommended that this form is given to independent contractors.	N/A	Give a copy to your workers and make sure they understand its contents.
Statement of Intent to Employ Minor and Request for Work Permit (Form B1-1)	To obtain permission to employ a minor. **TIP** Be sure to finish the permit process with the *Permit to Employ and Work (Form B1-4)*, supplied by the minor's school district.	Before the minor begins working.	Each completes the appropriate part: • Minor; • Employer; • Parent; and • School district.	File it with the minor's school district. Keep a copy in your personnel records.
Summary of Your Rights Under the Fair Credit Reporting Act	To obtain a credit report of any type.	This form is required when you give the employee a copy of the credit report.	N/A	Give it to applicant.

Table 8. Important Forms and Checklists *(continued)*

Notification/ Form	What do I use it for?	When do I use it?	Who fills it out?	Where does it go?
W-4 Form – Employee's Withholding Allowance Certificate	All employees.	Before employee's first pay date.	The employee.	Keep the form in the employee's personnel record. If you send the original to payroll, keep a copy of the form.
Workers' Compensation Rights and Benefits pamphlet	To provide notice to employees of their right to workers' compensation benefits should they sustain an on-the-job injury.	This must be given to all new employees at hire and again to any employee injured at work.	The employee fills out the *Personal Physician or Personal Chiropractor Predesignation Form*, then gives it to his/her physician to sign, accepting the predesignation; the rest is informational.	Put the predesignation form in the employee's regular personnel file and send a copy to your contact at your insurer or claims administrator. The employee keeps the rest of the brochure for reference.

Where Do I Go for More Information?

CalBizCentral and federal and state government agencies offer a variety of resources to help you hire employees in compliance with the law.

Table 9. Additional Resources

For information on	Check out these resources
General	From CalBizCentral: • The **2010 California Labor Law Digest**, the most comprehensive, California-specific resource to help employers comply with complex federal and state labor laws and regulations; • **www.calbizcentral.com**; and • **www.hrcalifornia.com**.

Table 9. Additional Resources *(continued)*

For information on	Check out these resources
Equal opportunity	The Equal Employment Opportunity Commission (EEOC) offers prepared guidelines for the types of disability-related pre-employment questions that you may and may not ask of a job applicant under the ADA. The guidelines also address the effect of the ADA on medical examinations given to applicants and employees. Enforcement Guidelines at ***www.eeoc.gov/policy/guidance.html*** You can request publications at no cost to you, including posters, fact sheets, manuals, pamphlets and enforcement guidelines. For a list of EEOC publications, or to order publications, write, call or fax: U.S. Equal Employment Opportunity Commission Publications Distribution Center P.O. Box 12549 Cincinnati, Ohio 45212-0549 Toll-free: (800) 669-3362 TTY: (800) 800-3302 FAX: (513) 489-8692 California's Department of Fair Employment and Housing (DFEH) also offers informational material on discrimination in employment. Its reach is generally much broader in California than that of the EEOC. Department of Fair Employment and Housing, Sacramento District Office 2000 O Street, Suite 120 Sacramento, CA 95814-5212 Telephone: (9160 445-5523 Toll-free: (8000 884-1684 *Disability Under the Fair Employment & Housing Act: What you should know about the law (DFEH-208 DH)* at ***www.dfeh.ca.gov/DFEH/Publications/PublicationDocs/DFEH-208DH.pdf***
Consumer reporting agencies	Federal Trade Commission Consumer Response Center 600 Pennsylvania Ave, NW Room H-130 Washington, D.C. 20580 (2020 382-4357 ***www.ftc.gov*** *Using Consumer Reports: What Employers Need to Know* at ***www.ftc.gov/bcp/edu/pubs/business/credit/bus08.shtm***

Table 9. Additional Resources *(continued)*

For information on	Check out these resources
Immigration	The USCIS established a 24-hour toll-free hotline to provide information regarding the IRCA. Call (800) 255-8155 or (800) 362-2735 (hearing impaired). ***www.uscis.gov/portal/site/uscis*** Handbook for Employers at ***www.uscis.gov/files/nativedocuments/m-274.pdf***.
Workers' compensation	California Workers' Compensation Institute 1111 Broadway, Suite 2350 Oakland, CA 94607 Telephone: (510) 251-9470 FAX: (510) 251-9485 ***www.cwci.org*** California Division of Workers' Compensation ***www.dir.ca.gov/dwc/dwc_home_page.htm***
Fingerprinting information	California Department of Justice ***http://caag.state.ca.us/fingerprints/index.htm***

TIP CalBizCentral also provides many ongoing and comprehensive educational opportunities for small business owners, HR beginners and experienced HR professionals alike. These include online sexual harassment training, DVDs and special HR seminars. For more information, please visit our Web site at ***www.calbizcentral.com***.

Hiring Frequently Asked Questions

What is the minimum salary for an exempt employee? Exempt employees must earn a minimum salary which is the equivalent of two times the state minimum wage for full-time employment, currently $2,773.33. Much higher exempt hourly rates apply to exempt computer professionals and doctors; these rates are subject to annual revision.

If I put an employee on salary, does that mean the employee is exempt from overtime? Placing an employee on salary doesn't mean that employee is exempt from wage and hour laws, including keeping track of hours worked and paying overtime. A nonexempt employee placed on a "salary" earns overtime the same as hourly wage earners.

To be considered exempt under California law, the employee must primarily perform duties that meet the law's exemption requirements and earn a salary equivalent to no less than two times the minimum wage for full-time employment.

Where can I find copies of what an employee's acceptable identification documents should look like? The new U.S. Citizenship and Immigration Services Handbook for Employers (Rev. 07/31/09) now includes color pictures of acceptable documents. The guide also contains useful information about Form I-9 requirements and commonly asked questions and answers. This document may be downloaded directly at *www.uscis.gov/files/nativedocuments/m-274.pdf*.

How long must I keep each Form I-9 on file? The completed Form I-9 must be retained for at least three years from the date of hire or one year from the date of termination, whichever is longer.

May employers legally make copies of the documents an employee presents with the Form I-9? Although it's not illegal to copy the documents, the form doesn't require the copies be retained. All that's required is that the employer certifies that it saw the original documents and that they appeared genuine.

What can happen to me if I classify someone as an independent contractor, and she/he is really an employee? The consequences for an employer misclassifying an employee as an independent contractor can be significant tax, wage and benefits liabilities, and massive fines that may be imposed by the Internal Revenue Service and by California's Employment Development Department.

What is the difference between an independent contractor and an employee? A person who provides services to another for payment can be either an employee or an independent contractor.

The relationship between an independent contractor and a principal differs significantly from an employer/employee relationship. The difference is largely in the degree of control over the person performing the services and the multitude of obligations an employer has to an employee which are not part of the independent contractor relationship. Some of the factors that determine independent contractor status include:

- Whether the principal had the right to discharge at-will without cause;

- Whether the person performing services is engaged in a distinct occupational business;

- Whether the work is usually done under the direction of the principal or by a specialist without supervision;

- Whether the principal or the worker supplied the instruments, tools and place of work for the person performing the work; and

- Whether the work is part of the regular business of the principal.

May employees view and copy their personnel files? Every employee has the right to inspect the personnel records that the employer maintains. The employer must make the personnel records available to the employee at reasonable intervals and at reasonable times.

An employee doesn't have an absolute right to a copy of his or her entire personnel records, but an employee does have a right to a copy of any document he/she signed relating to obtaining or holding employment, subject to a reasonable fee for each copy. This right extends to current and past employees.

What types of information about employees do I need to keep private from other employees? California's constitutional right to privacy protects employee personnel files from improper disclosure to third parties. As a general rule, financial records should be kept confidential, and records of investigations, such as those related to sexual harassment, should be kept confidential.

Employers must establish appropriate procedures to ensure all employee medical records and information will remain confidential and will be protected from unauthorized use and disclosure. It's recommended that another personnel file be maintained containing the more confidential information.

Access to an employer's computer files containing sensitive information must be closely guarded, and an employer may be held liable for negligently failing to protect its system from unauthorized access.

Other laws protect the privacy of employees taking time off for drug or alcohol abuse treatment, for assistance with an illiteracy problem or to cope with domestic violence.

Chapter 3

Developing Policies

Every company creates policies, particular ways of doing things and rules about what employees can and can't do at work. However, informal and inconsistent policies can potentially create big problems later. Developing carefully considered polices and communicating them clearly to your workers leads to effective workforce management and helps avoid lawsuits.

An employee handbook serves as the best tool for communicating company policy. If you don't currently maintain a handbook, look at the sample *Employee Handbook* in your online formspack. You can quickly fill in the blanks and create a handbook for your employees that contains the minimum recommended language.

If you already maintain a handbook, the information in this chapter will help you make it a strong legal document that will protect your interests and your employees'.

To understand the importance of creating and communicating your company's policies, or if you don't know what the law requires you to tell your employees, this chapter will give you answers to questions about:

- Basic employment policies and practices;

- Creating an employee handbook;

- Keeping employee records; and

- Much more.

Minimum Compliance Elements

1. Hang your *Employment Notices Poster* (available from *www.calbizcentral.com*), which includes mandatory postings that all employees and applicants must be able to see, in a prominent place (such as a break room).

2. Adapt the sample *Employee Handbook* to fit your company's needs and, after review by your own legal counsel, follow the policies consistently for every employee (see Table 13 on page 92).

3. Give each employee a copy of your handbook.

4. Get a signed *Confirmation of Receipt* from each employee, indicating that he or she read the handbook (see Table 13 on page 92).

The Basics of Developing Policies

This chapter will help you get the most out of your personnel policies. The law requires only a few written policies, but writing down all of your policies and distributing them to your employees in the form of a handbook is a good practice.

What Information *Must* I Provide to Employees?

State and federal laws require you to:

- Post information in public areas in a language your employees can understand. The *Employment Notices Poster* (part of the *Required Notices Kit*, available at *www.calbizcentral.com*) includes all the basic required information:

  - Wages — the minimum wage, pay dates and where to pick up paychecks;

  - Safety — hazardous material information, emergency contact information and notices of any violations or inspections for violations; and

  - Discrimination — Equal Employment Opportunity (EEO) statements, unlawful harassment notices and your company's sexual harassment policy.

  You can order additional posters in English or Spanish from CalBizCentral at *www.calbizcentral.com*.

- Give new employees certain notices and brochures. These include:

  - *Workers' Compensation Rights and Benefits* pamphlet;

- *Paid Family Leave* pamphlet; and

- *Sexual Harassment* pamphlet.

- Notify employees of their legal rights and entitlements, such as:

  - *General Notice of COBRA Continuation Coverage Rights (California Employees)* or *General Notice of COBRA Continuation Coverage Rights (Outside California);*

  - *State Disability Insurance Provisions* pamphlet; and

  - *For Your Benefit, California's Program for the Unemployed* pamphlet.

For a comprehensive list of these notices, see the "Forms and Checklists" tables in Chapter 2, "Hiring Employees"; Chapter 7, "Preventing Discrimination and Harassment"; and Chapter 8, "Ending the Employment Relationship."

What Information *Should* I Provide to Employees?

If your company follows a certain policy or offers a benefit governed by legal requirements, you may need to communicate these requirements to avoid misunderstandings and potential lawsuits.

> *Example:* Paid vacation is not a legal mandate. But if you provide it, you must follow legal requirements that govern how vacation is offered, and you should clearly communicate your vacation policy to any employee affected by it.

Why Should I Establish and Write Down Company Policies?

You may not realize the need for formal and comprehensive policies and procedures until you encounter an unanticipated problem. Don't wait until you find yourself in a lawsuit.

Properly conceived, written and communicated policies can help you:

- Comply with complex federal and state regulations;

- Ensure fair and consistent treatment of employees;

- Avoid misunderstandings that could potentially lead to lawsuits;

- Orient new employees;

- Educate supervisors and managers; and

- Establish legal protections.

Many small- and medium-sized companies find effective workforce management challenging. If your company doesn't employ an experienced personnel administrator, you can especially benefit from written policies.

Should I Be Aware of any Special Circumstances?

Written policies are legal documents, and you should write them with precision. Some circumstances merit special treatment in written policies.

Table 10. Special Circumstances

Changing laws	Employment laws change over time; your policies should, too. Review and revise your policies accordingly.
Specialized industries	The policies recommended in this chapter cover the most commonly encountered subjects. Your company may need to develop additional policies based on its unique characteristics, such as including rules about child/teacher ratios for a preschool or waste handling guidelines for a medical office. Check with your trade association about available resources.
Government contractors	Government contractors must comply with a multitude of federal and state laws and regulations, such as strict drug-free workplace rules and affirmative action obligations. Government contractors should consult legal counsel for assistance in drafting appropriate policies and procedures.
Local ordinances	Cities and counties sometimes legislate in traditional employment practice areas, such as domestic partner benefits and "living wage" ordinances. Consult legal counsel to determine whether additional local mandates impact your employment policies.
Unionized workers	Unionized employers may have a duty to negotiate before implementing written policies. Unionized employers, regardless of whether the specific policies cover unionized employees, should consult an experienced labor relations attorney.

How Can I Communicate Company Policies?

You can use a variety of methods to communicate company policies to managers, supervisors and employees:

- Along with the notices and posters required by law, you can post your company policies in a place where employees can easily access them;

- Conduct training sessions with written materials. You can go over the policy point by point, answering questions as they come up;

- Send written communication on policies to all employees in at least one of the following methods:

  - In an e-mail;

  - Mailing them to the employee's home address;

  - Including them in paychecks;

  - Hand delivering; and

  - Putting them in employee mail boxes.

- Draft and distribute an employee handbook. An employee handbook, sometimes called an employee manual, combines your policies in one document and provides employees with an overview of your:

  - Personnel policies;

  - Work rules;

  - Standards of performance; and

  - Benefits.

  You can also explain operational functions, such as:

  - Dealing with customers;

  - Production methods; and

  - Health, safety and housekeeping practices.

- As part of your overall training program for supervisors and managers, consider creating a special manual for them that explains in greater detail personnel procedures that the average employee doesn't need to know.

How Do I Create an Employee Handbook?

To prepare an effective handbook, you need to understand your current policies (both written and oral), past practices and anticipated future needs. Remember that, as a legal document, your handbook must adapt to the ever-changing needs of your company and the laws that govern employment practices. You can find a sample of the *Employee Handbook* form in your online formspack, described in detail in "Online Forms" on page 4.

1 — Assess Your Current Policies

Written or not, your company does follow policies and practices. Current policies provide a foundation for your handbook. To find your current policies:

- Gather all existing written policies;

- Survey managers and supervisors to determine unwritten policies and practices;

- Review payroll and business practices and personnel record maintenance procedures;

- Obtain copies of benefit plans; and

- Review any recent litigation documents (for example, wrongful termination claims, discrimination lawsuits, Cal/OSHA citations, etc.).

2 — Determine Your Need for New Policies

Looking at what you have, you may identify issues for which you don't have clear policies. To help make sure you've got everything, interview employees to consider long-range goals and identify operational needs that you haven't addressed.

3 — Begin the Drafting Process

Though you might find the thought of writing an important document intimidating, the sample *Employee Handbook* contains language for the most common handbook policies that you can use as-is, or use as a model for your own handbook.

The important thing to remember is that the ideal handbook contains policies that are:

- Carefully and clearly worded — make sure you don't accidentally override at-will employment or give up your right to make updates to policies;

- Accurate reflections of your policy — don't make promises you don't intend to keep, because these policies could be used against you in any legal action by an employee;

- Consistent with applicable legal requirements — your policies can't violate state or federal law; and

- Understood by the audience — if no one understands your policy, they can't follow it.

 Detailed guidelines for supervisors concerning the treatment, management and discipline of employees belong in a supervisor's manual given to managers and supervisors, rather than to regular employees.

4 — Review Your Document

It may take several drafts to get your handbook just right. Because your managers will implement these polices, ask them to review the initial draft and incorporate their recommendations into the document.

Before you distribute your handbook to employees, ask legal counsel to review it. Your handbook provides structure for employees and guidance for managers, but it's primarily a legal document. Make sure that you don't violate the law or put yourself in a vulnerable position with the language you use.

5 — Distribute Your Handbook

Carefully and thoughtfully orchestrate distribution of your handbook to underscore its importance. Orientation presents the perfect opportunity to give a new hire the handbook. For existing employees, either meet with them or prepare a cover letter to accompany the handbook when you distribute it. Encourage employees to ask questions, and explain any provisions about which they express uncertainty or skepticism.

Each employee should sign a *Confirmation of Receipt* of an employee handbook. Keep the signed form in the employee's personnel file.

6 — Monitor Your Handbook's Effectiveness

You must verify that the terms in the handbook are uniformly applied throughout the company and that employees, supervisors and managers follow them.

7 — Revise Your Handbook Periodically

Ask managers, supervisors and legal counsel to review your handbook periodically. Determine if you need to delete or revise certain provisions or create additional provisions due to a change in the law or business need.

Issue any changes in writing, and make sure you state that this version supersedes all previous versions. Keep a copy of all changes and new policies in a central file so you can track and reference them easily.

 If you make substantial changes, employees should sign new confirmation of receipt forms. You can also send updates via e-mail with return receipt required so you can later show that the employee received notice of the policies.

What Policies Must I Include in My Handbook?

The following table contains policies required by California and federal law or to provide you with legal protection. If you maintain an employee handbook, you must put these policies in writing and make them available to your employees:

Table 11. Mandatory Policies for a Handbook

Policy	What it should say	Why should I have it?
At-Will Employment Status	Clearly state that: • Employment is at-will; and • You or the employee can terminate the employment relationship at any time, with or without cause.	A written at-will employment policy is critical in defending wrongful discharge claims because it can refute an employee's claim that he/she could be fired only if you had just cause.

Table 11. Mandatory Policies for a Handbook *(continued)*

Policy	What it should say	Why should I have it?
Right to Revise	Clearly state that: • You have the right to change the policies and procedures contained in the handbook; and • The handbook embodies the entire agreement between you and the employee, and that no other oral or written agreements exist. Describe the procedure for changing policies.	Though not required by law, this policy makes your other policies (and your handbook as a whole) solid legal documents. This gives you the flexibility you need to cope with unforeseen changing circumstances and protects you against an employee claim that he/she is not governed by the handbook policies, but has a prior or different agreement.
Confirmation of Receipt	Clearly state that the employee: • Received; • Read; and • Is aware of the policies and procedures as described in your company's handbook. Include at-will language to reinforce at-will employment status. ❗ A Confirmation of Receipt form that does not include such language may leave you more vulnerable to a lawsuit for wrongful discharge.	Retain signed forms in each employee's personnel file as a written record of the employee receiving the handbook.

Table 11. Mandatory Policies for a Handbook *(continued)*

Policy	What it should say	Why should I have it?
Introductory Statement	This brief introduction should: • Welcome new employees; • Describe the working conditions for different sets of employees; • Specifically state that the new handbook supersedes any previously issued handbooks, policies or benefit statements that are inconsistent with policies in the new handbook; and • Explain the handbook's purpose. You may also wish to provide a brief overview of company history and/or philosophy. ❗ Avoid using terms such as "permanent" or "long-term" employment" or suggesting the prospect of "a promising career with the company." Such promises or statements contradict the concept of at-will employment.	This statement makes it difficult for employees to claim that the terms of their employment were defined in other documents previously issued.

Table 11. Mandatory Policies for a Handbook *(continued)*

Policy	What it should say	Why should I have it?
Equal Employment Opportunity **TIP Equal employment opportunity** ensures that all applicants and employees receive equal treatment without regard to race, sex, etc.	Clearly state your commitment to equal employment opportunities for all persons. Describe the procedure for filing complaints relating to perceived discrimination. If you work under government contracts, you must include an affirmative action provision that states your commitment to equal opportunity and the steps you take to encourage opportunities for women and minorities. Draft your policy carefully so that it expresses a promise to comply with the law but doesn't inadvertently create additional equal employment rights. Registered domestic partners and same sex married couples enjoy the same protection from discrimination on the basis of marital status as heterosexual couples.	State and federal law requires you to communicate to your employees your commitment to equal opportunities for everyone. For more information on EEO, see Chapter 7, "Preventing Discrimination and Harassment."

Table 11. Mandatory Policies for a Handbook *(continued)*

Policy	What it should say	Why should I have it?
Unlawful Harassment **TIP** **Harassment** is any behavior toward a person that a reasonable person would find unwelcome or hostile.	Clearly describe the kinds of conduct that constitute harassment of a protected class. Clearly state that: • Such conduct violates your rules and state and federal law; and • You will take forceful and appropriate measures to investigate any claims, stop any harassment and take effective remedial action, if necessary. Tell employees: • They have the right to complain about harassment; • They can resist such harassment without fear of retaliation; • What procedure to follow when making harassment complaints; and • That you will promptly, fully and objectively investigate complaints of harassment. Legislation prohibiting sexual harassment includes "gender" in the definition of sex. You must allow employees to appear or dress consistently with their gender identity. Registered domestic partners enjoy the same rights as spouses. This includes the right to be free from harassment on the basis of registered domestic partner status. Same sex, married couples also enjoy the same protections.	California law requires you to provide information to employees about harassment and your company's complaint process. You may be liable for sexual harassment by non-employees if you, your agents or supervisors knew or should have known of the harassment and you failed to take immediate and appropriate corrective action. For more information, see "How Should I Handle a Discrimination/Harassment Complaint?" in Chapter 7, page 265.

What Policies Are Recommended for a Handbook?

Table 12 contains important policy topics and provisions that should be defined for all employees, though not technically required by law. The sample *Employee Handbook*, in your online formspack, contains sample language for the most important policies.

Table 12. Recommended Policies for a Handbook

Policy	What it should say	Why should I have it?
Hiring		
Arbitration **TIP** **Arbitration** is a non-court procedure for resolving disputes using one or more neutral third parties to evaluate the issues and make a decision.	State which circumstances arbitration will cover.	To avoid lengthy and costly litigation. This is a very dynamic area of law. Be sure to talk to legal counsel if you wish to use arbitration agreements.
Employee Classification	Clearly and unambiguously define employee classifications both in your handbook and for each individual you hire. Take care not to promise anything other than at-will employment. Establish no more classes than reasonably necessary. The most common employee classes: • Full time; • Part time; • Regular; • Introductory; • Temporary; • Exempt; • Nonexempt; • Commissioned; and • Casual. For descriptions of these classes, see Table 3 in Chapter 2, page 10.	Employee classifications affect eligibility for benefits, duration of employment, compensation and expectations regarding employment.

Table 12. Recommended Policies for a Handbook (*continued*)

Policy	What it should say	Why should I have it?
Job Duties	Clearly state that you: • May occasionally require employees to work on special assignments in addition to normal job duties; and • As an at-will employer, reserve the right to change job responsibilities, transfer job positions or assign additional job duties at any time.	This policy preserves your flexibility in assigning job duties that differ from job descriptions at any time during employment.
Leaves of Absence		

Leaves of Absence
 	
TIP **Leaves of absence** are temporary absences from work without loss of employment status. Some specific types:
 	
• Pregnancy disability leave;
 	
• Family medical leave;
 	
• Disability leave;
 	
• Sick leave; and
 	
• Personal leave.
	Tell employees:
	
	• Eligibility requirements;
	
	• Conditions for using the leave;
	
	• Procedures for:
	  – Requesting leave;
	  – Extending leave; and
	  – Returning to work.
	
	• Whether and under what conditions the leaves are paid;
	
	• What period of time the leave covers;
	
	• Whether medical certification is required, the timelines associated with submitting it and consequences for not providing it; and
	
	• Effects of the leave on benefit accrual.
		Stating the terms of these benefits will prevent misunderstandings and help you comply with legal requirements.
		
		You can choose to provide a generic policy that only discusses basic concepts, or you can provide separate policies that detail specific types of leaves.
		
		For more information, see Chapter 4, "Providing Benefits."

Table 12. Recommended Policies for a Handbook *(continued)*

Policy	What it should say	Why should I have it?
Vacation	Tell employees: • Eligibility requirements; • Accrual rate; • Conditions for using accrued vacation; • Payment for unused accrued vacation; • Carryover and caps on accrual of vacation; • The effect of holidays or sickness during vacation; and • Vacation accrual during leaves of absence. Most employees at companies of all sizes are eligible for Paid Family Leave (PFL). You may require that an employee use up to two weeks of paid vacation before receiving PFL benefits.	The law doesn't require you to provide any vacation benefits. If you do, you must comply with laws that regulate vacation policies, requiring you to treat accrued vacation as wages due an employee upon termination. Stating the terms of this benefit will prevent misunderstandings by employees. For more information, see "What Do I Need to Know About Vacation?" in Chapter 4, page 141.
Paid Time Off (PTO) **TIP** Some employers use PTO to consolidate different types of time off into time off without condition. You can consolidate vacation and sick pay while continuing to provide paid holidays, or use some other combination.	Tell employees: • Eligibility requirements; • Accrual rate; • Conditions for using accrued PTO; • Payment for unused accrued PTO; • Carryover and caps on accrual of PTO; and • PTO accrual during leaves of absence.	If you provide this benefit, you must comply with laws that regulate vacation policies, requiring you to treat accrued PTO as wages due an employee upon termination. Stating the terms of this benefit will prevent misunderstandings. For more information, see "What Do I Need to Know About PTO?" in Chapter 4, page 147.

Table 12. Recommended Policies for a Handbook *(continued)*

Policy	What it should say	Why should I have it?
Leave for Protected Activities TIP Like other leaves of absence, employees can take these temporary absences from work without loss of employment status. Some protected types of leave: • Jury duty/witness leave; • Domestic violence leave; • Military leave; • Volunteer civil service leave; • School activities leave; and • Time off for voting.	Tell employees: • The conditions for using the leave; • Procedures for using the leave; and • That you will not discriminate against an employee who must take a protected leave.	State and federal law prevents you from discriminating or discharging employees who must take off time from work for protected activities. This policy provides consistency in the treatment of your employees, and informs your employees of their rights. For more information, see Chapter 4, "Providing Benefits."

Table 12. Recommended Policies for a Handbook *(continued)*

Policy	What it should say	Why should I have it?
Benefits		
Insurance Benefits	Provide general descriptions and refer employees to their insurance plan booklets for further information. ❗ You aren't required to provide this benefit, but if you do, don't put complete information in your handbook. Just distribute the plan description booklets provided by the insurance company. Insurance carriers must provide registered domestic partners benefits in the same manner as those provided for spouses. For more information, see "What Do I Need to Know About Health Care?" in Chapter 4, page 151.	This policy provides consistency in the treatment of your employees and informs them of their rights.
Retirement Plans	Provide no more than general statements that: • Recognize the existence of such plans; • Outline available benefits; and • Identify which employees are eligible. ❗ You don't have to fully describe these benefits in your handbook, but you must distribute summary plan descriptions (SPDs) to participants and beneficiaries of all ERISA plans.	This policy provides consistency in the treatment of your employees and informs them of their rights. For more information, see "What Do I Need to Know About Retirement or Pension Plans?" in Chapter 4, page 154.

Table 12. Recommended Policies for a Handbook *(continued)*

Policy	What it should say	Why should I have it?
Workers' Compensation	Most employers face requirements to provide workers' compensation. Tell your employees: • Where they will receive emergency medical care; • How to report injuries and accidents on the job; and • Their rights to care, compensation and rehabilitation.	This policy informs your employees of their rights, provides basic information about the benefit and notifies employees about the penalties for workers' compensation fraud. For more information, see "What Do I Need to Know About Workers' Compensation?" on page 133.
Holidays	Tell employees: • Which holidays you recognize; • Who can take paid holidays; • Any conditions that qualify for holiday pay; • The holiday pay rate; and • What happens if a holiday falls on a weekend, on an employee's normal days off and during vacations or other leaves of absence.	The law doesn't require you to provide paid time off for holidays or premium pay for work performed on holidays. If you do, stating the terms of this benefit will prevent misunderstandings.
External Employee Education	If you reimburse employees for voluntary training programs, your policy should describe what the employee needs to do to: • Get approval for the training; and • Receive reimbursement.	Stating the terms of this benefit will prevent misunderstandings.

Table 12. Recommended Policies for a Handbook *(continued)*

Policy	What it should say	Why should I have it?
Management		
Personnel Records	Tell employees: • That personnel records are confidential; • Who to contact to access their records; and • Any restrictions on access, such as times of the day or who must be present. ❗ Be sure that employees understand their obligation to update their names and addresses whenever changes occur.	To inform employees of their rights and prevent misunderstandings. ❗ Many laws govern personnel records retention. For more information, see *Records Retention Requirements*, described in Table 13 on page 92, and in your online formspack, described in detail in "Online Forms" on page 4.
Performance Evaluations	Tell employees: • If, when and how often performance evaluations occur; • What criteria you use to evaluate performance; • Who gives the evaluations; and • What happens to the evaluations (placed in file, signed copies, etc.). ❗ If you follow a policy of regular evaluations, communicate the timing to employees so they don't develop unrealistic expectations. If you can't stick to the schedule, don't create a policy. Be clear if you associate pay increases with evaluations.	This policy advises employees of performance expectations. Don't tie pay increases to evaluations. Focus evaluations on performance.

Table 12. Recommended Policies for a Handbook *(continued)*

Policy	What it should say	Why should I have it?
Employment of Relatives	Clearly state that you will review decisions regarding potential employment of relatives individually. Describe: • The types of circumstances and relationships prohibited; and • Any circumstances that might qualify as exceptions to the policy. ❶ You can't prohibit the employment of relatives. You can, for reasons of security, morale or conflict of interest, prohibit one relative from reporting to another. A blanket prohibition against the employment of relatives can expose you to liability for marital status and national origin discrimination so make sure to phrase your policy carefully. See "What Is Discrimination?" in Chapter 7, page 244 for more details. Registered domestic partners and same sex married couples enjoy the same rights and protections as opposite-sex spouses.	Employing relatives of current employees can often lead to morale problems, such as favoritism or conflicts of interest, particularly when one family member supervises another.
Employee Property	State that you reserve the right to inspect employee's personal property under certain circumstances. If you have reasonable suspicion that the employee stole your property, then you may search their personal property. Define the employee's property that is subject to inspection, such as packages, purses and backpacks.	You must notify employees of this right in advance of an inspection.

Table 12. Recommended Policies for a Handbook *(continued)*

Policy	What it should say	Why should I have it?
Telecommuting	Define: • How you evaluate eligibility for telecommuting; • The equipment required and who must provide it; • How to keep information and/or shared data secure; and • Policies that will change as a result of telecommuting. ❗ You aren't required by law to provide equipment for tele-commuters if the telecom-muting is done for the employee's convenience.	If you permit telecommuting, this policy will clarify basic conditions for it.
Company Property		
Employer Property	List the company-owned facilities and property available for employees' use. State that the property: • Belongs to the company; and • Is subject to inspection by the company at any time. Tell employees what they can and can't use your property for. Employees have a right to privacy over information held on third-party servers — as opposed to company owned and controlled servers. An employer received information from a third-party vendor that employees had transmitted through company-owned equipment. A California court said the vendor should not have released that information to the employer. Plan your policies accordingly.	This policy helps avoid a claim that you committed an invasion of privacy by searching the property.

Table 12. Recommended Policies for a Handbook *(continued)*

Policy	What it should say	Why should I have it?
Off-Duty Use of Facilities	State specifically that employees may not: • Remain on company premises while not on duty; and • Use company property for their personal use while not on duty.	This policy can protect you from workers' compensation liability if your supervisors consistently enforce it.
Personal Use of Company Electronic Equipment	State whether you allow employees to use company-provided cell phones, BlackBerries, iPhones, etc., for personal use. If you permit employees to use company equipment for personal use, describe any restrictions on such use.	This policy can protect you from having to pay additional charges for an employee's personal use of company electronic equipment.
Prohibiting Use of Company Cell Phone While Driving	State that you prohibit the use of cell phones while driving on company business and/or in a company vehicle. California law prohibits talking on a cell phone while driving unless using a hands-free device, and it's unlawful to send text messages, instant messages or e-mail while driving.	This policy protects the safety of your employees and other drivers, and follows the law prohibiting use of cell phones without a hands-free device in the most conservative manner. It also helps you avoid liability if your employee kills or injures someone while driving and using a cell phone for company business.
Prohibiting Camera Phones in the Workplace	State that you prohibit the use of camera phones: • Anywhere in the workplace; • In specified areas; or • In "secure" areas.	This policy prevents employees from using a camera phone in an area where other employees have an expectation of privacy, or in a sensitive or secure area.

Table 12. Recommended Policies for a Handbook *(continued)*

Policy	What it should say	Why should I have it?
Electronic and Social Media Policy	List the electronic media that your company uses. State that: • This media belongs to the company; • The media communications and files are subject to inspection by the company at any time; • Employees must use this media for company business; and • Employees may not use this media in any manner that conflicts with your discrimination/harassment policies.	This policy prevents employees from misusing your electronic media, and helps avoid a claim that you committed an invasion of privacy by searching the files.
Bulletin Boards	If you make bulletin boards available to employees, tell your employees: • The approval process, if any, for hanging materials; and • Any limitations on postings (size, content, etc.).	This policy helps you maintain control over the types of material posted in the workplace.
Solicitation and Distribution of Literature	Tell employees when and where they may solicit and distribute literature. ❗ You can ban nonemployees from soliciting/distributing literature on company property at any time. You can also ban employees from distributing literature in working areas at any time. You can't prohibit employees from soliciting/distributing literature in nonworking areas of company property during nonworking hours.	This policy will help you prohibit solicitation and distribution of literature which can cause distractions in the workplace.

Table 12. Recommended Policies for a Handbook *(continued)*

Policy	What it should say	Why should I have it?
Housekeeping	State your expectations about the cleanliness of employee workstations and common areas.	This policy promotes safe working conditions and efficiency in the workplace.
Parking	State: • Whether you provide parking; • Whether you take responsibility for damage that occurs in the parking lot; and • If you reserve any spots for clients, guests or visitors.	This policy will help prevent misunderstandings.
Smoking	Tell employees what areas you designate for smoking.	No federal law prohibits smoking in private workplaces. California law substantially limits smoking in enclosed places of employment in California. Many city laws contain regulations that restrict smoking even further.
Employee Conduct		
Prohibited Conduct	• List your rules of conduct; • Define the rules as "conduct that will not be tolerated"; and • State that the examples of conduct cited are illustrative and not all-inclusive.	Creating a prohibited conduct policy preserves your right to take action for violations of company rules.
Off-Duty Conduct	Explain what types of off-duty conduct you prohibit and what you allow. ❶ You may not discriminate against an employee for lawful activities outside work. For more information, see Table 67 in Chapter 7, page 246.	This type of policy protects your legitimate business interests.

Table 12. Recommended Policies for a Handbook *(continued)*

Policy	What it should say	Why should I have it?

Drug and Alcohol Abuse	Clearly state your company's:
	
	• Concerns about the use of drugs and alcohol in the workplace;
	
	• Prohibition against their use;
	
	• Specific rules and regulations concerning drugs and alcohol, including the consequences of failure to comply with the company's drug and alcohol policy;
	
	• Exceptions to these rules; for example, if your company:
	
	  – Permits parties on company property or allows sales staff to entertain clients during working hours; or
	
	  – Has employees taking prescription medication that may affect their ability to safely perform their jobs; and
	
	• Commitment to reasonably accommodate any employee who wishes to participate in an alcohol or drug rehabilitation program.
		This policy lets your employees know the consequences of not abiding by your workplace policy.
		
		This policy is required if you work under government contracts.
		
		California law requires a company with 25 or more employees to reasonably accommodate any employee who wishes to participate in an alcohol or drug rehabilitation program, as long as the accommodation does not impose an undue hardship on the employer.
		
		❗ Because of the complexity of this issue, consult legal counsel before implementing any alcohol- and drug-abuse policies and testing or screening programs.

Punctuality and Attendance	Tell employees: • Who to report to in the event of absence or tardiness; • What constitutes excessive tardiness or absenteeism; and • The consequences of excessive tardiness or absenteeism. Clearly state if excessive tardiness or absenteeism can result in termination.	This policy lets employees know what is expected of them when they are going to be late or absent, and what consequences they face if they fail to call in or report to work.

Table 12. Recommended Policies for a Handbook *(continued)*

Policy	What it should say	Why should I have it?
Conducting Personal Business	State how you expect employees to use their time while on the job, for example, whether you want them to: • Devote all of their time to performing their job assignments; and • Refrain from conducting personal business or business for another company while on duty.	This type of policy protects your legitimate business interests.
Dress Code and Other Personal Standards ❶ Dress codes are one place where men and women can be treated differently and expected to wear different types of clothing.	Explain your general or specific clothing and appearance standards: • General — properly groomed and wearing appropriate apparel; and • Specific — certain types of clothing or uniforms, even separate standards for different classes of employee. If you observe a "casual dress" day, describe: • The standard of casual dress; and • Which days you designate as casual dress days. You must allow an employee to appear or dress consistently with his/her gender identity. Make sure that your dress codes can accommodate an employee's religious creed that affects his/her style of dress.	Following this policy will help avoid inconsistencies.

Table 12. Recommended Policies for a Handbook *(continued)*

Policy	What it should say	Why should I have it?
Customer Relations	Describe: • How employees should interact with customers; and • The procedures for handling problems or extraordinary events.	This policy stresses the importance of customer satisfaction.
Business Conduct and Ethics	Outline what constitutes unethical behavior or the appearance of unethical behavior.	Gifts, entertainment or money from an external organization or business may influence your employee's business decisions. This policy seeks to prevent businesses from using gifts to interfere with and/or influence employees.
Confidentiality 🛈 Under state law, you may not prohibit employees from disclosing the amount of their wages or other information about their working conditions. This prohibition against disclosure does not include proprietary or trade secret information. Consult with legal counsel before implementing such a policy.	Tell employees: • The type of information that they must not disclose; • Your reasons for prohibiting disclosure; • Any circumstances under which they may divulge such information; • Whether they must obtain permission before disclosing confidential information, and from whom they should ask permission; and • What disciplinary action will result if they use confidential information in violation of the policy.	To protect confidential company information. You can draft a stand-alone agreement that the employee signs at time of hire. For more information, see "7 — Fill Out Paperwork" in Chapter 2, page 24. **TIP** To enhance enforceability, carefully tailor your confidentiality statement to describe the actual information and work process you want protected.

Table 12. Recommended Policies for a Handbook *(continued)*

Policy	What it should say	Why should I have it?

Conflicts of Interest
 	
TIP A **conflict of interest** is a conflict between the private interests and the official responsibilities of a person in a position of trust.
	Tell employees:
	
	• What types of activities you prohibit, such as:
	   – Directly competing with the employer; and
	   – Using company time or resources for anything other than company business.
	
	• What corrective action can result if an employee participates in an activity that creates a conflict of interest.
	
	Clearly state that the rule addresses job related concerns or problems with employee morale.
		This type of policy protects your legitimate business interests.

Wages		
Payment of Wages	Specify: • Paydays; • Pay periods; • Location where paychecks are available; and • Time paychecks are available. Indicate when paychecks will be available for scheduled paydays that fall on a Saturday, Sunday or company holiday. If you offer automatic payroll deposit, notify employees of this service. ❶ You may not make automatic payroll deposit mandatory.	To inform employees of their rights and prevent misunderstandings. For more information, see Chapter 5, "Paying Employees."

Table 12. Recommended Policies for a Handbook *(continued)*

Policy	What it should say	Why should I have it?
Pay Differentials Many employers offer premium wages to workers who work undesirable shifts.	Tell employees: • Which employees and which shifts you make eligible for pay differentials; • The amounts of the differentials; and • The circumstances under which differentials may be granted.	This policy will prevent misunderstandings by explaining your choice whether to pay premium rates.
Advances	State that you don't advance wages or lend money.	Opinion letters from the state Labor Commissioner's office indicate that it's impossible to require and enforce the repayment of a "loan" through payroll deductions. If you want to advance money to employees, consult with legal counsel before doing so.
Miscellaneous Time	This can be: • Makeup time; • Travel time; • Time for mandatory meetings and training; and • Call-in time. Briefly define the type of time and circumstances that it applies to. Tell employees: • The criteria/procedure to qualify for the time; and • Pay rates, if applicable.	This policy provides the conditions for makeup time, if available, and helps prevent misunderstandings about how these types of time will be paid. For more information on how to pay employees for time spent not working, see "How Do I Handle Time Spent Traveling, on Rest Breaks or Between Shifts?" in Chapter 5, page 176.

Table 12. Recommended Policies for a Handbook *(continued)*

Policy	What it should say	Why should I have it?
Overtime (for nonexempt employees only) **TIP** **Overtime** means any hours worked beyond eight hours per day or 40 hours per week. For employees with an alternative workweek, see "What Scheduling Options can I Choose From?" in Chapter 5, page 172.	State that: • You comply with all state and federal overtime requirements; • Time off with pay for any reason will not accrue toward overtime calculation; and • Nonexempt employees must get overtime authorized in advance. You must define a "workday" and "workweek" for use in computing overtime.	This policy will help prevent misunderstandings regarding overtime hours and payments. For more information, see the "Work Schedules" policy in this table, and "How Do I Set Up Work Schedules?" in Chapter 5, page 170.
Work Schedules	Tell employees: • Normal office and/or production work hours; • Whether you permit employees to exchange work schedules; and • The process for requesting an exchange of work schedules. For the purposes of overtime calculation, define the: • 24-hour period that makes a workday; and • 7-day period that makes a workweek. **!** If you create different workdays, workweeks or work shifts for different employees, describe those as well.	This policy will help prevent misunderstandings regarding work hours. For more information, see "How Do I Set Up Work Schedules?" in Chapter 5, page 170.

Table 12. Recommended Policies for a Handbook *(continued)*

Policy	What it should say	Why should I have it?
Timekeeping Requirements	Clearly define timekeeping practices, including the need to keep accurate records worked by nonexempt employees. Warn employees of the consequences for: • Falsification, destruction, modification or removal of time records; • Late or early recording of time; and • Recording another employee's time records. Specify the: • Classes of employees who must record their time; • Date and time the timesheet is due; and • Appropriate methods of recording.	To inform employees of their rights, prevent misunderstandings and notify them about the penalties for fraud.
Expense Accounts	Tell employees the schedule and deadlines for submitting business expense reports for reimbursement.	You must reimburse employees for reasonable business expenses they incur while performing their work, even if they miss the deadline for submitting expense reports.

Table 12. Recommended Policies for a Handbook *(continued)*

Policy	What it should say	Why should I have it?
Health and Safety		
Health and Safety	• Express your company's commitment to healthy and safe conditions for all employees; and • Refer employees to your Injury and Illness Prevention Program (IIPP) guide for specific details.	Maintaining an IIPP is required by law. If you employ 10 or more staff, your IIPP must be in writing. Your IIPP should be a stand-alone document. A simple reference to this document in your handbook alerts employees that the IIPP exists and must be followed. For more information, see "Injury and Illness Prevention Program" in Chapter 6, page 213.
Ergonomics **TIP** **Ergonomics** is the scientific study of the relationship between people and their work environments.	• Establish your policy on workplace ergonomics; and • Notify employees of your company's commitment to the prevention of repetitive motion injuries (RMIs).	The law doesn't require you to maintain an ergonomics policy, but the Cal/OSHA ergonomics standard for minimizing workplace RMIs does require your company to maintain an ergonomics program if certain conditions are met. For more information, see "Repetitive Motion Injuries (Ergonomics)" in Chapter 6, page 219.
Security and Workplace Violence	• Discuss potential security threats, such as theft or violence; • Discuss the presence of strangers on company premises; • Describe procedures for reporting any suspicious activity to the company; and • Encourage employees to report such activity.	This policy permits your company to express concern for employee welfare and safety, and supports your IIPP. Depending on the risk factors in a particular workplace, the law may require you to address workplace violence in your IIPP. For more information, see "Injury and Illness Prevention Program" in Chapter 6, page 213.

Table 12. Recommended Policies for a Handbook *(continued)*

Policy	What it should say	Why should I have it?
Recreational Activities and Programs	If your company sponsors voluntary recreational activities (for example, a softball team) you should create a policy that protects you from liability for injuries that happen at such activities. State that: • Employees face no obligation to participate; and • You are not responsible for injuries that happen.	This policy will help you avoid workers' compensation claims that arise out of non-work activities.
Employees Required to Drive	Tell employees who must drive their own vehicles on company business: • That you require each driver to show proof of license and insurance; and • The rate at which you reimburse their mileage. California considers the IRS reimbursement rate as the most reasonable rate.	This policy lets employees know what to expect when they drive their own vehicle for company business or a company vehicle.

Table 12. Recommended Policies for a Handbook *(continued)*

Policy	What it should say	Why should I have it?
Termination		
Termination	• State that employment with the company is at-will and can be terminated at any time, with or without advance notice and with or without cause; • Exclude any statements suggesting that cause is required for termination; • Define conduct that constitutes a voluntary resignation; and • Require terminated employees to return all company property. You can't unilaterally deduct payments for unreturned company property from an employee's final paycheck.	Following an established termination procedure can help you avoid costly mistakes when you end the employment relationship. For more information, see Chapter 8, "Ending the Employment Relationship."
Progressive Discipline 🛈 Avoid listing "cardinal offenses" that could lead to termination. California courts ruled that this could limit the effectiveness at-will employment status.	If you want to establish a progressive discipline system, clearly state that: • Employment with the company is at-will and can be terminated at any time, with or without advance notice and with or without cause; • You use a disciplinary process, but don't describe the stages and consequences in detail; • Employees face immediate termination under certain circumstances and at your company's sole discretion; and • Any listing of infractions that may result in discipline is not all-inclusive and is meant only to illustrate examples.	This policy: • Demonstrates your company's fairness and good-faith efforts to assist employees; and • Notifies employees of your expectations and the consequences of failing to meet them.

Table 12. Recommended Policies for a Handbook (*continued*)

Policy	What it should say	Why should I have it?
Employee References	Tell employees: • Where to direct requests for references; • Who can release references; and • The information provided in a reference.	This policy can reduce your risk of liability for defamation. For more information, see "How Should I Handle Employee References?" in Chapter 8, page 295.

The Hitches, Glitches and Pitfalls of Developing Policies

Written policies serve a variety of important purposes, but can also cause problems if you don't exercise caution.

What Do I Need to Watch Out for When I Create Policies/Handbooks?

- Don't create policies that violate federal or state laws. To read about some of the laws you should be aware of, see "Glossary of Terms, Laws and Agencies" on page 305.

- Don't override the employment-at-will relationship by promising fairness or equity in termination decisions or setting forth discipline or termination procedures that conflict with employment-at-will.

  Include precisely written at-will language (see page 37) in your handbook, making sure that the language is consistent with other policies and statements in employment applications (see "3 — Advertise and/or Recruit for the Position" in Chapter 2, page 12), employment contracts (see "6 — Make the Hiring Decision and Offer the Position" in Chapter 2, page 23), and other materials.

- Don't open yourself to claims that a secondary or pre-existing agreement defines an employee's terms and conditions of employment. See "Right to Revise" in Table 11 on page 64.

  Include a statement in the introduction of your current handbook that specifically states that the new handbook supersedes any previously issued handbooks or policy or benefit statements inconsistent with policies described by the new edition of the handbook.

Include an integration clause that states that the current handbook embodies the entire agreement between employer and employee and that no other oral or written agreements exist.

- Don't forget to allow room for change.

Include a right to revise provision that states you have the right to change the policies and provisions contained in the handbook. See Table 11 on page 64.

What Do I Need to Watch Out for When I Update Policies/Handbooks?

If you do change or terminate a policy:

- Communicate the change to all employees, and obtain written acknowledgement that employees have read and understood the changes; and

- Do not interfere with employees' vested benefits, such as accrued but unused vacation or PTO.

What Forms and Checklists Do I Use to Develop Policies?

The following table describes forms associated with policy development.

TIP You can find these forms in your online formspack, described in detail in "Online Forms" on page 4.

Table 13. Forms and Checklists

Form Name	What do I use it for?	When do I use it?	Who fills it out?	Where does it go?
Confirmation of Receipt	To document that the employee received and understands your company policies.	When hiring a new employee, or when you make significant changes to your handbook.	The employee signs it.	Keep in each employee's personnel file.

Table 13. Forms and Checklists *(continued)*

Form Name	What do I use it for?	When do I use it?	Who fills it out?	Where does it go?
Employee Handbook	Use as a guide when drafting and reviewing your own policies. You don't have to use the sample as a guide, but the sample language presents clear and correct policy statements.	Not required by law. If you publish one, all employees should get a copy. Be sure to provide a copy to every new hire. You can distribute the handbook via your company intranet.	You create the handbook. You should ask legal counsel to review it.	Employees keep the completed handbook in their possession. You should keep a copy of the sample to use as reference when making updates.
Guest and Visitor Policy	Notifying employees regarding your policy on bringing guests or visitors to work.	Not required by law, but should be part of your employee handbook or distributed to employees upon hire.	N/A	Employees keep their own copies. You should keep a copy as part of your employee handbook or personnel policies file.
Guest and Visitor Request Form - English	Give to employees who wish to bring a guest or visitor to work.	When employees request to bring a guest or visitor to work.	Employees fill it out and you sign it.	In the employee's personnel file and in your files. You should also provide a copy of this form to your receptionist or security team.
Guest and Visitor Request Form - Spanish	Give to employees whose primary language is Spanish who wish to bring a guest or visitor to work.	When employees request to bring a guest or visitor to work.	Employees fill it out and you sign it.	In the employee's personnel file and in your files. You should also provide a copy of this form to your receptionist or security team.

Table 13. Forms and Checklists *(continued)*

Form Name	What do I use it for?	When do I use it?	Who fills it out?	Where does it go?
Records Retention Requirements	To check how long to keep personnel records.	For reference.	N/A	N/A
Telecommuting Agreement	Use this form to describe your company's expectations of employees who telecommute.	After you approve a tele-commuting rela-tionship.	The employer.	In the employee's personnel file and in your files.
Telecommuting Policy	Use this sample to communicate your company's policy regarding telecommuting and how tele-commuting plans will be reviewed and imple-mented.	Not required by law, but should be part of your employee hand-book or distrib-uted to employees upon hire.	N/A	Employees keep their own copies. You should keep a copy as part of your employee handbook or personnel poli-cies file.
Telecommuting Request	Provide this form to employees who request to telecommute. This form will help you under-stand why they wish to telecom-mute and whether such accommodation is appropriate.	When an employee requests a tele-commuting arrangement.	The employee.	In the employee's personnel file and your files.

Table 13. Forms and Checklists *(continued)*

Form Name	What do I use it for?	When do I use it?	Who fills it out?	Where does it go?
Telecommuting Request Checklist	This checklist should be completed to evaluate whether telecommuting is appropriate for the individual and the job the employee performs.	After receiving a request for telecommuting plan	The employer.	In the employee's personnel file and your files.
Telecommuting Safety Checklist	Use this form in conjunction with your company's safety checklist for your workplace to ensure that the telecommuter's workspace is safe.	After approving a telecommuting plan.	The employer.	In your files.
Workplace Violence Policy	To communicate your company's policy against workplace violence.	Not required by law, but should be part of your employee handbook or distributed to employees upon hire.	N/A	Employees keep their own copies. You should keep a copy as part of your employee handbook or personnel policies file.

Where Do I Go for More Information?

CalBizCentral and federal and state government agencies offer a variety of resources to help you develop written employee policies.

Table 14. Additional Resources

For information on	Check out these resources
General	From CalBizCentral: • *2010 California Labor Law Digest*; • *2010 California Labor Law Administration*; • *2010 Employee Handbook Software*; • *www.calbizcentral.com*; and • *www.hrcalifornia.com*.
Equal Employment Opportunity	Complete regulations with Office of Federal Contract Compliance Programs summaries at *www.dol.gov/esa/ofccp/index.htm*
Workplace Violence and Security	Cal/OSHA's Guidelines for Workplace Security at *www.dir.ca.gov/DOSH/dosh_publications/worksecurity.html*
Drugs and Alcohol	Rules for drug and alcohol testing at *www.dot.gov*
Legal Counsel	American Bar Association at *www.abanet.org* or The California Bar Association at *www.calbar.ca.gov*

TIP CalBizCentral also offers many ongoing and comprehensive educational opportunities for small business owners, HR beginners and experienced HR professionals alike. These include online sexual harassment training, DVDs and special HR seminars. For more information, please visit our Web site at *www.calbizcentral.com*.

Developing Policies Frequently Asked Questions

Does the law require me to create an employee handbook? The law doesn't require an employer to maintain an employee handbook. However, if an employer chooses to maintain a handbook, certain policies may be required by law.

An employer with 50 or more employees must offer a family leave policy if the employee handbook describes other kinds of personal or disability leaves available to employees.

An employer with five or more employees must offer a pregnancy disability leave policy in its handbook if the handbook describes other kinds of temporary disability leaves or transfers available to employees.

What is arbitration? Arbitration, an alternative to litigation, is the final and binding settlement of employment-related disputes between parties by a method voluntarily agreed to by the parties themselves, including selection of the person to serve as arbitrator.

May I read my employees' e-mail and/or listen to their voice mail? In general, employers may access employees' voice mail and e-mail messages. The key is to establish and communicate a policy that eliminates any reasonable expectation that employees' e-mail and voice mail will be private.

Listening to confidential communications is prohibited if either party to the conversation has a reasonable expectation that it will be private. The law prohibits recording confidential conversations without the consent of all parties.

What if an employee refuses to sign for a new employee handbook or for a change in policy? A new handbook or policy applies to an employee regardless of whether the employee signs for it. Simply ensure that the employee receives the new handbook or policy, tell the employee that the handbook or policy applies to him or her and ask another manager to sign an acknowledgement of these facts.

You can't force an employee to sign an acknowledgement form, and you don't need to do so. The policies will apply to the employee so long as he/she continues to work for you.

May I change my employees' paydays? Yes. No law prohibits an employer from changing regular paydays. But whenever you make a change, it's advisable to give employees 30 days' notice of the change in paydays.

Am I required to offer paid holidays to my employees? No. Private sector employers aren't required to provide time off or premium pay for holidays. No state or federal holiday requirements exist for private sector employers, and holiday pay policies are a matter of contract between the employer and employee.

Though the law doesn't require that employers offer paid holidays, many employers offer this benefit as part of their benefits package.

Chapter 4

Providing Benefits

Employee benefits present one of the most complicated areas of employment law. Benefits include anything that's part of an employee's compensation package that isn't a wage or salary. Federal and California laws mandate some benefits, such as unemployment insurance. You can choose to offer others, such as health care or paid vacation. But if you offer these optional benefits, you must comply with certain legal guidelines that expand your employees' rights to use them.

This chapter describes the different benefits you can — or *must* — provide, and guides you through the processes of providing them.

In this chapter, you can find answers to questions about:

- Vacation, holidays and sick leave;
- Unemployment insurance;
- Workers' compensation;
- Pregnancy and family and medical leave; and
- Much more.

Minimum Compliance Elements

1. Hang your **Employment Notices Poster** (available from **www.calbizcentral.com**), which includes mandatory postings that all employees and applicants must be able to see, in a prominent place (such as a break room).

2. Give employees information on their workers' compensation, paid family leave and disability insurance benefits (all located in the **Required Notices Kit**, available at **www.calbizcentral.com**).

3. Pay particular attention to the overlapping requirements of pregnancy disability leave, family and medical leave and workers' compensation; see:

   - "What Do I Need to Know About PDL?" on page 101;

   - "What Do I Need to Know About Family and Medical Leaves?" on page 105;

   - "How Do Different Types of Leave Interact?" on page 113;

   - "What Do I Need to Know About SDI?" on page 128;

   - "What Do I Need to Know About Paid Family Leave?" on page 129; and

   - "What Do I Need to Know About Workers' Compensation?" on page 133.

The Basics of Providing Benefits

You must provide some benefits to your employees, and you can offer many more at your discretion.

Federal and California laws require that you provide certain benefits to your employees. Not every employer is required to provide all of these benefits — some are only required for companies over a certain size. See "Does This Employment Law Apply to Me?" in Chapter 1, page 1.

You may choose to offer other benefits. But if you do offer them, California law regulates how you apply them and the way you provide them.

Table 15. Benefits

Required benefits	Optional benefits
Benefits	
• Pregnancy disability leave (PDL), page 101; • Family and medical leave, page 105; • Disability leave, page 112; • Domestic violence leave, page 116; • School activities leave, page 120; • Jury/witness duty leave, page 121; • Military service leave, page 122; • Victims of violent crime leave, page 118; • Volunteer civil service leave, page 124; • Volunteer Civil Air Patrol Leave, page 125; and • Voting leave, page 125.	• Vacation, page 141; • Holidays, page 143; • Floating holidays and personal days, page 144; • Sick leave, page 145; • Paid time off, (PTO) page 147; • Compensatory time off, (CTO) page 147; • Bereavement leave, page 147; and • Personal leaves of absence, page 148.
Insurance/Type of Payment	
• State Disability Insurance (SDI), page 128; • Paid Family Leave (PFL), page 129; • Workers' Compensation, page 132; and • Unemployment Insurance (UI), page 131;	• Health care, page 151; • Voluntary disability insurance, page 153; • Bonuses, page 154; and • Retirement and pension plans, page 154.

What Do I Need to Know About PDL?

Pregnancy disability leave (PDL) is covered by a California law created to protect pregnant employees against discrimination and to allow for time off from work for pregnancy, childbirth and related medical conditions. Employees may not take PDL for baby bonding. See "What Do I Need to Know About Family and Medical Leaves?" on page 105 for information on baby bonding leave.

Table 16. Pregnancy Disability Leave

Question	Answer
Do I have to provide this benefit?	You must provide PDL if you: • Employ five or more full- or part-time staff; or • Are the State of California, its counties or any other political or civil subdivisions of the state and cities. If you refuse to provide PDL to an eligible employee or discriminate against an employee exercising her right to PDL, you can be penalized. See "What do I Need to Know About the Penalties for Discrimination/Harassment?" in Chapter 7, page 273.
Is this time off paid?	Only if you also pay for other temporary disability leaves. Consult your legal counsel. You can require employees to use accrued sick pay during PDL, before using unpaid PDL. The employee may choose to use accrued vacation (see page 141) or PTO (see page 147) during PDL, before using unpaid PDL. If the employee becomes disabled, she may be eligible for SDI benefits. See "What Do I Need to Know About SDI?" on page 128 for more information.
Who's eligible?	All pregnant employees, regardless of length of service.
How does this start?	When the employee's health care provider determines that she is disabled by pregnancy, childbirth or related medical conditions. This time off also covers severe morning sickness and prenatal care, including doctor's visits. **Disabled by pregnancy** means that, according to a medical professional, an employee is unable to work, perform one of her essential duties, suffers from severe morning sickness or needs prenatal care. The employee must provide you with verbal or written notice of the need for PDL, when it will start and approximately how long it will last. If possible, she must provide 30 days' notice whenever the PDL is foreseeable.

Table 16. Pregnancy Disability Leave *(continued)*

Question	Answer
How long does it last?	PDL covers the actual period of disability, up to four months, even if your policy for other temporary disability leaves allows less. In addition, if your policy provides for a longer period of leave, you must allow the employee the extra time off. The law requires that the employee can use the leave intermittently, in increments as small as one hour. The four months' leave is actually the number of days the employee would work in a four-month period. **Example:** If the employee works full time, she is entitled to up to 704 hours of leave. If she works 40 hours per week, the formula goes as follows: (22 work days per month x 4 months x 8 hours = 704 hours). If the employee works part time, she is entitled to part of the 704 hours of leave. If she works 20 hours per week, the formula goes as follows: (22 workdays per month x 4 months x 4 hours = 352 hours).
What's the process like?	1. Your employee notifies you that her health care provider determined she is disabled by her pregnancy, childbirth or related medical condition. 2. Respond to the request as soon as possible, but no later than 10 calendar days after the request. Give the employee a copy of *FMLA/PDL - Approval*, described in Table 39 on page 156. If you must comply with the Family and Medical Leave Act (see page 105), and the employee is eligible for FMLA running concurrently with PDL, give the employee a copy of *Employee Letter - PDL Only* or *FMLA/PDL - Approval*, described in Table 39 on page 156. 3. You can require a medical certification for the leave if you also require certifications for other disability leaves. See the *Certification of Physician or Practitioner for PDL or PDL/FMLA*, described in Table 39 on page 156. You can also require a medical release to allow the employee to return to work if you require releases for other disability leaves. See the *Certification of Physician or Practitioner for Employee Return to Work*, described in Table 39 on page 156. 4. When the PDL ends, you must reinstate the employee to the same position.

Table 16. Pregnancy Disability Leave *(continued)*

Question	Answer
What if the employ-ment relationship ends?	If the employee decides to leave the company (voluntary quit), PDL ends. If you need to fire an employee on PDL, consult legal counsel. If you need to lay off an employee on PDL, remember that the employee retains the same rights and seniority that she would have earned if she had been at work. See "Layoff" in Chapter 8, page 288 for more information.
What other benefits are related/can be affected?	**Family Leaves** See "How Do Different Types of Leave Interact?" on page 113. **Health Benefits** Employees taking PDL are entitled to the following health benefits: • The same access to participation in health and benefits plans as with any other unpaid disability leave. If you provide health insurance during other disability leaves, you must do so for PDL; and • COBRA coverage, if triggered by PDL. Contact your insurance provider for information. **Employee Benefits** PDL covers the following employee benefits: • Seniority — employees continue to accrue seniority as with your paid and unpaid leave policies; • Holidays — regular holidays when your business is closed count as PDL days; • Company closures — if your business closes for an extended vacation, such as summer vacation, or for other reasons, such as for maintenance, inventory or remodeling, this time does not count toward PDL days; and • Sick leave, vacation and PTO — if the employee is on company-paid leave, these benefits continue to accrue; if on unpaid leave, they only accrue if your other disability policies allow.

What Do I Need to Know About Family and Medical Leaves?

Family and medical leaves cover time off for:

- Bonding with a newborn or adopted child;

- Caring for a family member with a serious health condition;

- Caring for the employee's own serious health condition;

- Caring for a military servicemember with a serious injury or illness; and

- A qualifying exigency relating to a family member's military service. For more information see the *FMLA - Family Member Leave for a Qualifying Exigency* form.

Table 17. Family and Medical Leave

Question	Response
Do I have to provide this benefit?	You must provide family and medical leave if you: • Employ 50 or more staff; or • Are a public agency. If you fail to comply with these laws, you face civil lawsuits which could result in: • Compensatory and punitive damages; • Reinstatement; and • Back pay, court costs and attorneys' fees.

Table 17. Family and Medical Leave *(continued)*

Question	Response
Is this time off paid?	Family and medical leaves are generally unpaid, although you can, as a matter of policy, require or allow employees to substitute accrued sick pay, vacation or PTO for unpaid leave.
	❗ Although FMLA and CFRA are unpaid, the employee may be eligible for Paid Family Leave (PFL). See "What Do I Need to Know About Paid Family Leave?" on page 129 for more information.
	❗ If the employee is pregnant, she may also be covered by PDL. See "What Do I Need to Know About PDL?" on page 101 for information about paying employees on PDL.
	❗ If the employee becomes disabled, he/she may be eligible for SDI benefits. See "What Do I Need to Know About SDI?" on page 128 for more information.
	❗ If the employee is on FMLA and receives any disability benefits (state disability insurance, workers' compensation insurance or other disability benefit payments), you may not require the use of paid sick leave, vacation or other accrued paid time off benefits.
Who's eligible?	Employees eligible for family and medical leave are those who worked: • For a covered employer for at least 12 months (this time does not have to be consecutive); • At least 1,250 hours in the past 12 months; and • At a worksite with at least 50 or more company employees within a 75 mile radius.
	❗ In California, if you do not inform the employee at the time of request of his/her ineligibility for family and medical leave, the employee is presumed eligible for these benefits.
	❗ If the leave is FMLA only, the 12 months of service does not include any employment prior to a break in service of seven years or more.

Table 17. Family and Medical Leave *(continued)*

Question	Response
Who's eligible?	NEW 2010 The 2010 National Defense Authorization Act expands the scope of FMLA for employees providing care to military members to cover a member of the Armed Forces (including a member of the National Guard or Reserves) undergoing medical treatment, recuperation or therapy, and veterans undergoing medical treatment, recuperation or therapy for a serious illness or injury and who was a member of the Armed Forces at any time during the five years preceding the date the medical treatment began. This also includes a serious illness or injury incurred in the line of duty or that existed before military service and was aggravated by the military service.
	For regular Armed Forces members, "covered active duty" means duty during the deployment with the Armed Forces to a foreign country. Reservists are covered when on duty during deployment with the Armed Forces to a foreign country under a call to active duty.
	"Qualifying exigency" leave is no longer limited to a military member on active duty or on call to active duty in support of a contingency operation.
	It's likely that implementing regulations will be issued by the U.S. Department of Labor in the future.
How does this start?	Once the employee informs you that he/she needs leave, you must provide up to 12 weeks of family or medical leave, or 26 weeks to care for an injured servicemember.
	Generally, you can require that employees give you 30 days' notice when requesting family or medical leave (for example, the expected birth of a child or a planned medical treatment). If the condition is not planned or foreseeable, employees must provide the notice as soon as practical. Employees must state the reason for the leave request.
	In situations where FMLA leave runs concurrently with CFRA leave, you must respond to the employee's request, at least verbally, within two business days. If the leave is FMLA only, you must respond within five business days. See *Family Medical Leave - Approval/Conditional Approval*, described in Table 39 on page 156.
	If the employee is eligible for both PDL and FMLA concurrently, see the *FMLA/PDL - Approval Letter* and the *Family Medical Leave - Approval/Conditional Approval*, described in Table 39 on page 156.

Table 17. Family and Medical Leave *(continued)*

Question	Response
How long does it last?	FMLA and CFRA both provide for up to 12 weeks of leave, but they run concurrently unless the leave involves PDL (see page 101). If the employee is eligible for FMLA/CFRA leave, the employee can take a maximum of 12 weeks of leave. Registered domestic partners enjoy the same rights under the law as a spouse. An eligible employee who needs time off to care for his/her registered domestic partner would be entitled to a maximum of 12 weeks of leave under CFRA. For more information on domestic partner rights, see "Domestic Partners and CFRA" on page 110. The employee may take the leave all at once, or in shorter increments of hours, days or weeks. ***Example:*** If the employee works full time, (five days a week times 12 weeks, which equals 60 days; or 40 hours a week times 12 weeks, which equals 480 hours) he/she is entitled to up to 60 days or 480 hours of leave. If the employee works part time, then he/she is entitled to part of the 480 hours or 60 days of leave. The individual who works 20 hours a week would be eligible for 30 days, or 240 hours, of leave. For more information on how these different leaves interact, see "How Do Different Types of Leave Interact?" on page 113. If the leave is for a "qualifying exigency" relating to an employee's spouse, parent, son or daughter serving in the military, the employee will be eligible for 12 weeks of leave in a 12 month period beginning on the first day of leave, regardless of how the 12 month period is defined for other types of FMLA leave. These 12 weeks may be in addition to 12 weeks the same employee is eligible for under CFRA. Regulations defining "qualifying exigency" took effect January 16, 2009. These are described in the *FMLA - Family Member Leave for a Qualifying Exigency* form, available in your online formspack. If the leave is to care for a close family member injured during military service, the leave is a maximum of 26 weeks in a 12-month period. The 12-month period begins on the first day of leave for this purpose, regardless of how the 12-month period is defined for other types of FMLA leave.

Table 17. Family and Medical Leave *(continued)*

Question	Response
What's the process like?	**1.** Inquire if the employee is seeking FMLA/CFRA leave, because the employee doesn't have to ask specifically for family and medical leave. You are responsible for designating the leave as family or medical leave. If you don't designate leave as FMLA/CFRA, you may retroactively designate leave as FMLA/CFRA leave with appropriate notice to the employee if your failure to timely designate leave doesn't cause harm or injury to the employee. You and the employee may mutually agree that leave be retroactively designated as FMLA leave. **2.** You must notify employees of the method you use to calculate the 12-month period in which the 12 weeks of entitlement occurs. The method that allows you the most control uses a "rolling" 12-month period measured backward from the date the employee first uses any leave. Remember that for qualifying exigency leave or leave to care for a servicemember, the 12 month period begins the day the leave starts. **3.** You can require medical certification within 15 calendar days of your request. If you wish, you may require a second and third opinion of the employee's illness, but you must pay for it. See the *Medical Certification – FMLA/CFRA* form, described in Table 39 on page 156. **4.** You must reinstate the employee to his/her position either by an agreed-upon date, or within two days of the employee's notification of readiness to return. You can require a medical release to allow the employee to return to work if you also require releases for other disability leaves. See the *Certification of Physician or Practitioner for Employee Return to Work*, described in Table 39 on page 156.
What if the employment relationship ends?	If the employee decides to leave the company (voluntary quit), family and medical leave ends. If you need to fire an employee on family and medical leave, consult legal counsel. If you need to lay off an employee on family and medical leave, remember that the employee enjoys the same rights and seniority that he/she would have earned if he/she been at work. See "Layoff" in Chapter 8, page 288 for more information.

Table 17. Family and Medical Leave *(continued)*

Question	Response
What other benefits are related/can be affected?	Several other benefits can be affected by an employee taking family and medical leaves: **Health benefits** Employees taking family and medical leaves are entitled to the following health benefits: • Continued group health plan coverage at the same level and under the same conditions as when the employee was working (including dental, eye, mental health and dependent coverage); and • Continuation of benefits as provided by any disability leave and/or COBRA. **Other benefits** Family leave laws cover the following employee benefits: • Seniority — employees continue to accrue seniority as with your paid and unpaid leave policies; • Holidays — regular holidays when your business is closed count as family leave days; • Company closures — if your business closes for an extended vacation, such as summer vacation, or for other reasons, such as for maintenance, inventory or remodeling, this time does not count toward family leave days; and • Sick leave, vacation and PTO — if the employee is on company paid leave, these benefits continue to accrue; if on unpaid leave, they only accrue if your other disability policies allow.

Domestic Partners and CFRA

The federal Family and Medical Leave Act (FMLA) doesn't provide domestic partners with leave. In California, registered domestic partners enjoy the same legal rights as a spouse, and an eligible employee would be entitled to up to 12 weeks of CFRA-only leave to care for his/her domestic partner. This doesn't affect the employee's FMLA entitlement.

Potential for Discrimination

In one circumstance, a recent California law appears to provide registered domestic partners with more leave than single or married employees.

If, before taking any FMLA leave, a registered domestic partner takes CFRA leave (up to 12 weeks) to care for his/her domestic partner, he/she would still have 12 weeks of FMLA leave available during that 12-month period. The employee could then use FMLA leave to care for his/her own serious health condition or that of a parent or child.

In contrast, a married employee who takes leave to care for a spouse is entitled to the same 12 weeks of CFRA leave, but it runs concurrently with FMLA leave because a spouse is covered under FMLA. If that married employee later needs leave to care for his/her own serious health condition or that of a parent or child, he/she is not entitled to any more leave in the same 12-month period. This creates the potential for a claim of discrimination on the basis of marital status — because the individual is married, he/she is denied a benefit available to a registered domestic partner.

Your company could voluntarily remedy this by providing additional leave to the married employee whose first absence is to care for a spouse, and who then needs additional time to care for his/her own serious health condition or that of a parent or child.

The legislation's effect on FMLA rights for married couples creates an unsettled area of the law. Consult legal counsel before granting or denying FMLA leave or an additional leave of absence to any employee.

For more information about domestic partner rights, see "What Do I Need to Know About Domestic Partner Rights?" on page 149.

What Do I Need to Know About Disability Leave?

Any leave for a non-work-related disability beyond what is mandated by law is a matter between employer and employee. Your policy should specify exactly what leave is available and what benefits, if any, will continue to accrue during such leave. See "Leaves of Absence" in Table 11 in Chapter 3, page 64.

Table 18. Disability Leave

Question	Answer
Do I have to provide this benefit?	Certain leaves for disability are mandated by law. See: • "What Do I Need to Know About PDL?" on page 101; • "What Do I Need to Know About Family and Medical Leaves?" on page 105; • "What Do I Need to Know About SDI?" on page 128; and • "What Do I Need to Know About Workers' Compensation?" on page 133. A leave of absence for an employee with a non-work-related disability could constitute a required "reasonable accommodation." See "What Is Reasonable Accommodation?" in Chapter 7, page 252, for details. Other than these legally-mandated leaves, the law doesn't require you to provide leave or hold a job for an individual with a non-work-related disability. Check to see if you're covered under the FMLA, CFRA, FEHA or the ADA. See "Glossary of Terms, Laws and Agencies" on page 305 and "Does This Employment Law Apply to Me?" in Chapter 1, page 1 for details about these laws. If those laws don't cover you and your situation, you can freely set and follow your own policy.
Is this time off paid?	You decide.
Who's eligible?	You decide. You may want to offer this type of leave to employees not eligible for legally mandated leave, or who used up other types of leave. If you grant this type of disability leave to one employee, be prepared to grant it to other employees in similar situations.
How does this start?	Your employee becomes disabled. He/she will notify you in some way.
How long does it last?	The leave can last any length of time that you decide.

Table 18. Disability Leave *(continued)*

Question	Answer
What's the process like?	You should document whatever length of leave you are willing to grant the employee.
What if the employment relationship ends?	If the employee decides to leave the company (voluntary quit), disability leave ends. If you need to fire an employee on disability leave, consult legal counsel. If you need to lay off an employee on disability leave, remember that the employee enjoys the same rights and seniority that he/she would have earned if he/she had been at work. See "Layoff" in Chapter 8, page 288, for more information.
What other benefits are related/can be affected?	If you decide to grant a disability leave, you can still require that your employee use up any accrued but unused vacation. The employee may be eligible for SDI benefits. See "What Do I Need to Know About SDI?" on page 128 for more details.

How Do Different Types of Leave Interact?

California and federal laws mandate several different types of leave, some of which overlap. If you're confused, you're not alone; it's a very complex area of the law. Table 19 on page 114 provides an overview of the ways PDL, FMLA/CFRA, workers' compensation and disability leaves interact. Also see the *PDL Timeline.* You can find this form in your online formspack, described in detail in "Online Forms" on page 4. If you need help understanding the exact impact on your company, consult legal counsel.

For these leaves to run concurrently, you must provide notice to the employee taking the leave as soon as possible before he/she takes the leave.

TIP **Concurrently** means that as a week of Leave Type A is used up, so is a week of Leave Type B.

Table 19. How Different Types of Leave Interact

This leave	Runs concurrently with	Under these conditions
PDL (see page 101)	FMLA	Always, if you notify the employee.
	CFRA	Never.
	Workers' Compensation	Never.
	Disability	If your disability policy says so (it should).
FMLA (see page 105)	CFRA	For all leaves except: • Leave due to pregnancy disability or • Leave to care for a registered domestic partner; see "Domestic Partners and CFRA" on page 110. • Leave due to a qualifying exigency related to a family member's service in the military or to care for a service-member, see "What Do I Need to Know About Family and Medical Leaves?" on page 105.
	Workers' Compensation	If there is a work-related injury or illness, the employee can't work, and you notify the employee.
	Disability	If your disability policy says so (it should) and you notify the employee.
	PDL	If the employee takes leave due to pregnancy disability and you notify the employee.

Table 19. How Different Types of Leave Interact *(continued)*

This leave	Runs concurrently with	Under these conditions
CFRA (see page 105)	FMLA	For all leaves except due to pregnancy disability or to care for a registered domestic partner; see "Domestic Partners and CFRA" on page 110.
	Workers' Compensation	If there is a work-related injury or illness, the employee can't work, and you notify the employee.
	Disability	If your disability policy says so (it should) and you notify the employee.
	PDL	Never.
Workers' Compensation (see page 133)	FMLA/CFRA	Always, if there is a work-related injury or illness, the employee can't work, and you notify the employee.
	Disability	If your disability policy says so (it should) and you notify the employee.
	PDL	Never.
Disability (see page 112)	FMLA/CFRA	If you are covered, your disability policy says so (it should), and you notify the employee.
	Workers' Compensation	If your disability policy says so (it should) and you notify the employee.
	PDL	If your disability policy says so (it should) and you notify the employee.

What Do I Need to Know About Domestic Violence Leave?

An employee who victimized by domestic violence may request time off from work to ensure his/her health, safety or welfare, or that of his/her child.

Table 20. Domestic Violence Leave

Question	Response
Do I have to provide this benefit?	All employers must grant leave for employees to obtain a restraining order or other court assistance.
	If you employ 25 or more people, you must also grant leave for employees to:
	• Seek medical attention for injuries, including counseling;
	• Obtain services from a domestic violence shelter or rape crisis center; and
	• Take action to protect him/herself from future domestic violence, including relocation and safety planning.
Is this time off paid?	For exempt employees, it depends on the duration of the absence and whether he/she has available sick leave, vacation or PTO. You must pay exempt employees for any day in which they perform any work.
	For nonexempt employees, you decide.
Who's eligible?	Any employee victimized by domestic violence.
How does this start?	When your employee becomes a victim of domestic violence. He/she will notify you in some way.
How long does it last?	An employee can take anywhere from a few hours (to obtain a restraining order) to 12 weeks (for recovering physically/mentally). You can determine whether the leave runs concurrently with leave granted by FMLA/CFRA. See "What Do I Need to Know About Family and Medical Leaves?" on page 105.

Table 20. Domestic Violence Leave *(continued)*

Question	Response
What's the process like?	1. Your employee gives you reasonable advance notice, unless it isn't feasible for him/her to do so. If he/she can't give notice prior to an absence within a reasonable time, he/she must provide one of the following: • A police report regarding the domestic violence; • A court order protecting or separating the employee from the abuser; • Evidence that he/she appeared in court; and • Documentation from a medical professional, domestic violence advocate, health advocate, health care provider or counselor that the employee underwent treatment for injuries resulting from domestic violence. 2. Keep all requests for time off as a result of domestic violence confidential. 3. Make the necessary adjustments to the work schedule and paycheck of the affected employee. If the request is for ongoing leave (counseling appointments once a week or several court appointments) this may mean planning for long-term adjustments.
What if the employment relationship ends?	If the employee decides to leave the company (voluntary quit), then domestic violence leave ends. If you need to fire an employee on domestic violence leave, consult legal counsel. If you need to lay off an employee on domestic violence leave, remember that the employee enjoys the same rights and seniority that he/she would have earned if he/she had been at work. See "Layoff" in Chapter 8, page 288, for more information.
What other benefits are related/can be affected?	Rather than taking unpaid time, an employee may use available vacation, personal leave or PTO.

What Do I Need to Know About Leave for Victims of Violent Crimes?

An employee victimized by a violent crime, or whose immediate family member is a victim, may take time off to attend judicial proceedings related to that crime.

Table 21. Victims of Violent Crime Leave

Question	Response
Do I have to provide this benefit?	All employers must grant leave for eligible employees to attend judicial proceedings.
Is this time off paid?	For exempt employees, it depends on the duration of the absence and whether he/she has available sick leave, vacation or PTO. You must pay exempt employees for any day in which they perform any work. Exempt and nonexempt employees may choose to take accrued paid vacation, personal leave, sick leave or unpaid time off.
Who's eligible?	Any employee victimized by a violent crime; an immediate family member of a victim; a registered domestic partner of a victim; or the child of a registered domestic partner of a victim. Immediate family members include: • Spouse • Registered domestic partner • Child • Stepchild • Brother • Stepbrother • Sister • Stepsister • Mother • Stepmother • Father • Stepfather
How does this start?	Your employee notifies you in some way that he/she or someone else listed above is the victim of a violent crime.
How long does it last?	There are no restrictions on the length of time. However, the time off from work must be used to attend judicial proceedings related to the violent crime.

Table 21. Victims of Violent Crime Leave *(continued)*

Question	Response
What's the process like?	Your employee gives you reasonable advance notice, unless it isn't feasible for him/her to do so. As documentation for the absence, the employee must provide you with a copy of the notice of each scheduled proceeding that is provided to the victim by the agency responsible for providing notice. If advance notice is not feasible, you shouldn't take any action against the employee if, within a reasonable time after the absence, he/she provides you with documentation of the judicial proceeding from: • The court or government agency setting the hearing; • The district attorney or prosecuting attorney's office; or • The victim/witness office advocating on behalf of the victim.
What if the employment relationship ends?	If the employee decides to leave the company (voluntary quit), the violent crime leave ends. If you need to fire an employee on violent crime leave, consult legal counsel. If you need to lay off an employee on violent crime leave, remember that the employee enjoys the same rights and seniority that he/she would have earned if he/she had been at work. See "Layoff" in Chapter 8, page 288, for more information.
What other benefits are related/can be affected?	An employee may elect to use accrued paid vacation, personal leave, sick leave or unpaid time off.

What Do I Need to Know About Time Off for School Activities?

Parents or guardians of a child in school may occasionally need to participate in school activities, such as parent/teacher conferences, field trips or meetings.

Table 22. Time Off for School Activities

Questions	Response
Do I have to provide this benefit?	Yes, all employers must comply. You must grant time off: • To any employee who must appear at a school in connection with his/her child who was suspended; and • For other school activities if you employ 25 or more people at the same location.
Is this time off paid?	For exempt employees, it depends on the duration of the absence. You must pay exempt employees their full week's salary for any week in which they perform any work. See "Deductions for Exempt Employees" on page 191. For nonexempt employees, you decide.
Who's eligible?	Any employee who is the parent or legal guardian of a child in grades K–12, or attending a licensed day-care facility.
How does this start?	N/A
How long does it last?	You must provide up to 40 hours off per calendar year for school activities. You can limit the use of this time off to no more than eight hours in any one calendar month.
What's the process like?	1. Your employee will notify you that he/she wants to take time off to participate in a school activity. You might want to create a form for requesting time off. 2. You either approve the requested time or ask the employee to reschedule. 3. You may require documentation from the school as proof that the employee participated in the activity on a specific date and at a specific time.
What if the employment relationship ends?	Nothing. This is not an accrued benefit.
What other benefits are related/can be affected?	If the employee is on company paid leave, then sick pay, vacation and PTO continue to accrue. If on unpaid leave, they only accrue if your other policies require.

What Do I Need to Know About Time Off for Jury/Witness Duty?

According to state law, a person called to serve jury duty or participate as a witness in a trial must do so, unless the court releases him/her from service.

Table 23. Time Off for Jury/Witness Duty

Question	Response
Do I have to provide this benefit?	Yes, all employers must comply. You may not terminate or discriminate against any employee who takes time off to serve as a juror or a witness, provided he/she gives reasonable notice.
Is this time off paid?	This depends on the employee's status as exempt or nonexempt. • Nonexempt — you don't have to pay wages while he/she serves on jury duty or as a witness; or • Exempt — if an employee performs any work in a workweek, you must pay him/her for the full week. You don't need to pay him/her for a workweek when he/she performs *no* work.
Who's eligible?	Any employee called to serve.
How does this start?	Your employee gets a summons for jury duty or a subpoena to appear in court as a witness.
How long does it last?	It depends on how long the court proceeding lasts, or how long his/her responsibilities as a witness last.
What's the process like?	1. Your employee gives you notice. 2. Make the necessary changes to the work schedule and paycheck of the affected employee.
What if the employment relationship ends?	Nothing. This is not an accrued benefit.
What other benefits are related/can be affected?	Rather than taking unpaid leave, a nonexempt employee may use any available vacation or PTO. If the employee takes company paid leave, then sick pay, vacation and PTO continue to accrue. If on unpaid leave, they only accrue if your other policies require.

What Do I Need to Know About Military Service Leave?

When your employees serve in the military, you must protect their jobs. Several available government resources explain the details of this benefit.

Table 24. Military Service Leave

Question	Response
Do I have to provide this benefit?	Yes, all employers must comply. When your employees serve in the military during their employment, you must either hold their jobs or re-employ them in similar positions when they return.
	The Veterans Benefits Improvement Act, enacted by Congress in December 2004, requires all employers to provide a notice of rights under the Uniformed Services Employment and Reemployment Rights Act (USERRA) to all persons entitled to rights and benefits under USERRA.
	The most efficient way to comply is to post the notice in a prominent place where employees customarily check for such information.
	TIP The notice is part of CalBizCentral's all-in-one *Employment Notices Poster*. You can order this product, in English or Spanish, from CalBizCentral at *www.calbizcentral.com*.
Is this time off paid?	• Nonexempt — no.
	• Exempt — if an employee performs any work in a workweek, you must pay him/her for the full week. You don't need to pay him/her for a workweek when he/she performs no work.
Who's eligible?	Virtually anyone absent from work due to "service in the uniformed services" is protected. "Service" includes active duty, active duty for training, initial active duty for training, inactive duty training, full-time National Guard duty and examinations to determine fitness for duty. "Uniformed services" include:
	• The Army, Navy, Air Force, Marine Corps and Coast Guard (and the Reserves for each of those branches);
	• The Army National Guard, Air National Guard and commissioned corps of the Public Health Service;
	• National Disaster Medical System; and
	• Any other category of persons designated by the president in time of war or emergency.
How does this start?	Have your employee notify you as soon as he/she learns of the need for military leave.

Table 24. Military Service Leave *(continued)*

Question	Response
How long does it last?	Military service leave may take almost any length, with a maximum of a cumulative five years.
What's the process like?	1. Your employee will notify you before he/she leaves. 2. When the service is over, he/she will provide notice of intent to return. 3. Under most circumstances, you must reinstate the employee. For exceptions, see the Uniformed Services Employment and Reemployment Rights Act (USERRA) Web site at **www.dol.gov/elaws/userra.htm**.
What if the employment relationship ends?	If the employee decides to leave the company (voluntary quit), military leave ends. If you need to fire an employee on military leave, consult legal counsel. If you need to lay off an employee on military leave, remember that the employee enjoys the same rights and seniority that he/she would have earned if he/she had been at work. See "Layoff" in Chapter 8, page 288.
What other benefits are related/can be affected?	The employee is entitled to all rights and benefits as if he/she had remained continuously employed. The employee can also choose COBRA-like health care coverage.

What Do I Need to Know About Military Spouse Leave?

In October 2007, Gov. Arnold Schwarzenegger signed emergency legislation creating a new leave of absence for spouses of military personnel.

Table 25. Military Spouse Leave

Question	Response
Do I have to provide this benefit?	All California employers with 25 or more employees must comply.
Is this time off paid?	• Nonexempt — no. • Exempt — if an employee performs any work in a workweek, you must pay him/her for the full week. You don't need to pay him/her for a workweek when he/she performs no work. For more information, see "Deductions for Exempt Employees" on page 191.

Table 25. Military Spouse Leave *(continued)*

Question	Response
Who's eligible?	Employees who work an average of 20 hours or more per week with a spouse in the United States Armed Forces, National Guard or Army Reserve who was deployed during a period of military conflict.
How does this start?	The employee must provide the employer with notice within two business days of receiving official notice that their spouse will be on leave from deployment.
How long does it last?	The leave lasts for up to 10 days.
What if the employment relationship ends?	Employers subject to this law can't retaliate against an employee who requests or takes this leave.
What other benefits are related/can be affected?	You can allow employees to use sick, vacation or PTO during this leave, but you can't require them to.

What Do I Need to Know About Time Off for Volunteer Civil Service?

You may employ people who also provide volunteer emergency services. They may be called away during work hours to help in an emergency or go through training.

Table 26. Time Off for Volunteer Civil Service Duty

Question	Response
Do I have to provide this benefit?	Yes. All employers must provide the time off for emergency service. Employers with 50 or more employees must also provide up to 14 days off per year for training.
Is this time off paid?	For exempt employees, it depends on the duration of the absence. You must pay exempt employees their full week's salary for any week in which they perform any work. For more information, see "Deductions for Exempt Employees" on page 191. For nonexempt employees, you decide.
Who's eligible?	Firefighters, peace officers and emergency rescue personnel, whether volunteers or partly/fully paid while providing emergency services.
How does this start?	Your employee notifies you as soon as he/she learns of the need for volunteer civil service duty.

Table 26. Time Off for Volunteer Civil Service Duty *(continued)*

Question	Response
How long does it last?	For the duration of the civil or required service.
What's the process like?	Ask employees to give as much notice as possible.
What if the employment relationship ends?	If the employee decides to leave the company (voluntary quit), the leave ends. If you need to fire an employee on volunteer civil service leave, consult legal counsel. If you need to lay off an employee on volunteer civil service leave, remember that the employee enjoys the same rights and seniority that he/she would have earned if he/she had been at work. See "Layoff" in Chapter 8, page 288 for more information.
What other benefits are related/can be affected?	If the employee takes company paid leave, then sick pay, vacation and PTO continue to accrue. If on unpaid leave, they only accrue if your other policies require.

Table 27. Time Off for Civil Air Patrol Leave

Question	Response
Do I have to provide this benefit?	Yes. All employers with more than 15 employees must provide this leave.
Is this time off paid?	No.
Who's eligible?	Any employee who is a volunteer member of the California Wing of the civilian auxiliary of the U.S. Air Force (Civil Air Patrol), responding to an emergency operation mission. The employee must have been employed by the employer for at least a 90-day period before the start of the leave.
How does this start?	Your employee notifies you as soon as he/she learns of the need for volunteer Civil Air Patrol duty.
How long does it last?	An employee is entitled up to 10 days of leave per year. The leave for a single emergency mission can't exceed three days, unless the emergency is extended by the entity in charge of the operation and the extension of leave is approved by the employer.
What's the process like?	Ask employees to give as much notice as possible.

Table 27. Time Off for Civil Air Patrol Leave

Question	Response
What if the employment relationship ends?	If the employee decided to leave the company (voluntary quit), the leave ends. If you need to fire an employee on Civil Air Patrol leave, consult legal counsel.
	If you need to lay off an employee on volunteer Civil Air Patrol leave, remember that the employee enjoys the same rights and seniority that he/she would have earned if he/she had been at work. See "Layoff" in Chapter 8, page 288, for more information.
What other benefits are related/can be affected?	Employees who take leave under this law can't be required to exhaust all accrued vacation, personal, sick, disability, CTO or other leave available to the employee.
	The employer and employee can negotiate for the employer to maintain the benefits of the employee at the expense of the employer during the leave. The leave can't result in a loss of benefits accrued before the date on which the leave began.

What Do I Need to Know About Time Off for Voting?

Registered voters have a right to vote in local, statewide and national elections.

Table 28. Time Off for Voting

Question	Response
Do I have to provide this benefit?	Yes. All employers must comply.
Is this time off paid?	Yes.
Who's eligible?	Any registered voter without sufficient time outside of working hours to vote in a statewide election.
How does this start?	Your employee notifies you as soon as he/she learns of the need for time off to vote.
How long does it last?	Up to two hours on election days.

Table 28. Time Off for Voting *(continued)*

Question	Response
What's the process like?	1. The employee notifies you at least two working days in advance to arrange a voting time. 2. You grant time at the beginning or end of the regular working shift, whichever allows the most free time for voting and the least time off from work.
What if the employment relationship ends?	Nothing. This is not an accrued benefit.
What other benefits are related/can be affected?	None.

What Do I Need to Know About SDI?

State Disability Insurance (SDI) is not a leave of absence. It's a partial wage-replacement plan for California workers *during* a leave of absence. SDI provides short-term benefits to eligible workers who suffer a loss of wages when unable to work due to a non-work-related illness or injury, or when medically disabled due to pregnancy or childbirth.

Table 29. State Disability Insurance

Question	Response
Do I have to provide this benefit?	Yes, almost every employer must comply. You must withhold part of an employee's pay and send it to the SDI program, which is administered by the EDD. You face steep penalties for failing to comply. When you register with the EDD, you will receive a registration number and information concerning your tax and reporting requirements. You can rely on the EDD's regulations and advice; its Web site is at *www.edd.ca.gov/*.
Is this time off paid?	The time off is governed by applicable leave of absence laws or your company policy, not the SDI program. Any benefits get paid through SDI in an amount equaling approximately 55 percent of the employee's weekly wages. The employee may choose to take accrued vacation or PTO, or you may require that the employee do so. Payment of vacation or PTO does not affect the employee's SDI benefits. If you pay out accrued sick leave, the employee's SDI benefits get reduced by the amount of sick pay. To avoid reduction of SDI benefits, you may coordinate the payment of sick leave with SDI benefits.
Who's eligible?	Everyone is eligible. The EDD administers the benefit uniformly.
How does this start?	Your employee becomes disabled. He/she will notify you in some way.
How long does it last?	SDI benefit payments can't exceed 52 times the employee's weekly benefit amount or the total wages subject to SDI tax paid in the base period, whichever is less.
What's the process like?	1. Provide the employee with a copy of the *State Disability Insurance Provisions* pamphlet (located in the **Required Notices Kit** available at *www.calbizcentral.com*). 2. Keep records of employee pay as required by state and federal law. 3. When an employee files an SDI claim, the EDD will contact you and provide you with the appropriate paperwork. You fill out the employer portion of the form. The EDD does the rest.

Table 29. State Disability Insurance *(continued)*

Question	Response
What if the employment relationship ends?	The law doesn't require you to hold the employee's job merely because he/she collects SDI benefits. However, laws that do protect the employee's job (such as family leave, PDL, workers' compensation or the ADA) may apply.
What other benefits are related/can be affected?	SDI covers loss of earnings not covered by workers' compensation. If someone receives workers' compensation, then he/she is only eligible for SDI benefits in the amount of the difference between normal wages and workers' compensation.
	If a person receives Unemployment Insurance (UI) benefits, he/she can't receive SDI benefits for the same period.
	When employees receive full pay, they are ineligible for SDI benefits during that time. Employers can coordinate sick leave, PTO benefits or other pay (excluding vacation) with the EDD to maximize SDI payments. An employee receiving vacation pay doesn't affect SDI payments.
	For information about specific leave benefits, see: • "How Do Different Types of Leave Interact?" on page 113; • "What Do I Need to Know About PDL?" on page 101; • "What Do I Need to Know About Family and Medical Leaves?" on page 105; • "What Do I Need to Know About Disability Leave?" on page 112; and • "What Do I Need to Know About Workers' Compensation?" on page 133.

What Do I Need to Know About Paid Family Leave?

Paid Family Leave (PFL) is not a leave of absence. It's a partial wage-replacement plan for California workers during an absence. PFL provides short-term benefits to eligible workers who suffer a wage loss when unable to work because of the need to:

- Care for a seriously ill child, spouse, parent, domestic partner, grandparent, grandchild, parent-in-law or sibling;

- Bond with the employee's new child or the new child of the employee's spouse or domestic partner; or

- Bond with a child in connection with the adoption or foster care placement of the child with the employee, the employee's spouse or domestic partner.

Table 30. Paid Family Leave

Question	Response
Do I have to provide this benefit?	Yes. If you pay into the SDI program, you also pay into the PFL program. You must withhold part of an employee's pay and send it to the PFL program, which is administered by the EDD. You face steep penalties for failing to comply. When you register with the EDD, you will receive a registration number and information concerning your tax and reporting requirements.
Is this time off paid?	Benefit payments represent approximately 55 percent of the employee's regular wages and may be used for a maximum of six weeks in a 12-month period.
Who's eligible?	Everyone is eligible. The EDD administers the benefit uniformly.
How does this start?	Your employee will be absent for a reason that qualifies for PFL benefits. He/she will notify you in some way.
How long does it last?	Employees are eligible for benefit payments for a maximum of six weeks in a 12-month period.
What's the process like?	1. Provide all new employees and employees absent for a qualifying reason with a copy of the *Paid Family Leave* pamphlet (located in the **Required Notices Kit** available from **www.calbizcentral.com**). 2. Keep records of employee pay as required by state and federal law. 3. When an employee files a PFL claim, the EDD will contact you and provide you with any paperwork required from you. The EDD does the rest.

Table 30. Paid Family Leave *(continued)*

Question	Response
What if the employment relationship ends?	The law doesn't require you to hold the employee's job merely because he/she collects PFL benefits. However, laws that do protect the employee's job (such as FMLA and CFRA) may apply.
What other benefits are related/can be affected?	PFL covers loss of earnings not covered by workers' compensation and SDI benefits. If a person receives Unemployment Insurance benefits, he/she can't receive PFL benefits for the same period. If the employee receives full replacement wages, such as sick leave and PTO, then he/she is ineligible for PFL benefits during that time. Employers can coordinate sick leave and PTO benefits with the EDD to maximize PFL payments. An employee receiving vacation pay doesn't affect PFL benefits. However, employers may require that employees take up to two weeks of accrued, unused vacation before PFL payments begin. The first week of vacation would be the seven-day waiting period for PFL payments. For information about specific leave benefits, see Table 15 on page 101.

What Do I Need to Know About Unemployment Insurance?

The Unemployment Insurance (UI) system is a state program required by federal law. Typically funded by funds from employers, UI payments are sometimes extended by federal law, particularly during times of high unemployment.

Table 31. Unemployment Insurance

Question	Response
Do I have to provide this benefit?	Yes. Almost all California employers must pay the tax. You face steep penalties for failing to pay your share. If your employees work in multiple states, contact legal counsel or the EDD to determine how to file. For more information, visit the EDD's Web site ***www.edd.ca.gov.***
Is this time off paid?	This is not time off from work. Employees must be unemployed or going through a reduction in hours to receive UI benefits.
Who's eligible?	To be eligible for UI, a claimant must: • Make a claim for benefits in accordance with the regulations; • Be unemployed through no fault of his/her own; • Have earned $1,300 in one quarter, or have high quarter wages of $900 and total base period earnings of 1.25 times that amount; • Be able to work and available for work (including part-time work, if appropriate); • Be actively looking for work; and • Register for work and conduct a search for suitable work, as directed. A claimant is ineligible if he/she is out of work for one of the following reasons: • Voluntarily quitting without just cause; • Termination for willful misconduct; and • Refusing to perform suitable work. See Chapter 8, "Ending the Employment Relationship" for further information.
How does this start?	The EDD will notify you of your tax rate, and you will pay quarterly into your reserve account. The EDD sets an initial rate of 3.4 percent of payroll. After three years in business, your rate goes up or down depending on the cost of the claims submitted.
How long does it last?	UI benefits may be paid for a maximum of 26 weeks. However, this time is often extended, depending on the unemployment situation.

Table 31. Unemployment Insurance *(continued)*

Question	Response
What's the process like?	An employee may file for UI benefits when he/she is out of work or when his/her hours get significantly reduced. Respond to the EDD's request for information. You face penalties for providing false information in connection with a UI claim as to the reason for an employee's termination. See "What Do I Need to Know About the Basic Process for Ending the Employment Relationship?" in Chapter 8, page 285 for the steps to follow when the employment relationship ends. UI benefits get paid every two weeks (after a one-week waiting period) for up to 26 weeks. Keep records of employee pay as required by state and federal law. See "What Sort of Records Must I Retain?" in Chapter 5, page 196 for more information. If you disagree with EDD's determination, you can protest the claim. You must appeal in a timely manner. You can use *Responding to a Claim for Unemployment Insurance, Appealing a UI Claim to an Administrative Law Judge* and *Appealing a UI Claim to the UI Appeals Board*, described in Table 75 on page 301.
What if the employment relationship ends?	N/A
What other benefits are related/can be affected?	An unemployed person can't draw both UI and SDI or PFL benefits. See "What Do I Need to Know About SDI?" on page 128 and "What Do I Need to Know About Paid Family Leave?" on page 129" for details.

What Do I Need to Know About Workers' Compensation?

You must carry workers' compensation insurance, which provides payments, without regard to fault, for any injury or death "arising out of and in the course of employment." Injured workers must receive the necessary medical care, at no cost to them, to cure or relieve the effects of the injury. Employees generally give up their rights to sue you for civil damages in exchange for certain, though limited, benefits, which may include pay for time away from work.

For information on preventing injuries at work, see Chapter 6, "Ensuring Workplace Safety."

Table 32. Workers' Compensation

Question	Response
Do I have to provide this benefit?	Yes. You must maintain coverage at all times while your business is in operation. If you fail to provide coverage and an injury occurs, you still have to pay the employee's medical costs, in addition to penalties and possible financial damages from lawsuits. Every employer must comply, including nonprofit organizations, government entities and every person employing another person.
Is this time off paid?	The employer doesn't pay for the time off directly. The workers' compensation insurance carrier pays the injured employee.
Who's eligible?	Just about everybody, including non-U.S. Citizens, casual workers (if they work at least 52 hours in a 90-day period) and minors. Independent contractors are excluded. See Table 3 in Chapter 2, page 10 for more information about independent contractors. You can refute a claim if the employee was: • Under the influence of alcohol or drugs at the time of the injury; • Intentionally inflicting the injury or committing suicide; • Engaging in an "altercation" in which he/she was the initial physical aggressor; • Committing a felony for which he/she was convicted; • Engaging in horseplay; • Voluntarily participating in off-duty recreational, social or athletic activity not constituting his/her work-related activities (unless those activities are expected of employees); and • Going to or coming from work, unless you control the route or mode of transportation.

Table 32. Workers' Compensation *(continued)*

Question	Response
How does this start?	Employees are protected as soon as they start performing work on your behalf.
	You must provide all new employees with the current **Workers' Compensation Rights and Benefits** pamphlet, described in Table 8 in Chapter 2, page 40, and located in the **Required Notices Kit** available from **www.calbizcentral.com**.
	Workers' compensation law covers four types of injuries:
	• Specific physical injury;
	• Cumulative physical injury;
	• Specific mental/psychiatric injury; and
	• Cumulative mental/psychiatric injury.
	Workers' compensation law covers any one of these injuries, regardless of whether first aid or surgery is required or if the injury is work-disabling, even if no medical treatment is required.
	An injury is deemed job-related when:
	• It arises out of and in the course of employment;
	• The job played an "active" role and was a "positive" factor in the injury;
	• The injury was caused only by something to which the employee was exposed in his/her employment period;
	• The employment brought the employee to the place where the accident occurred; or
	• The injury happened at home, if the employee's work duties require tasks at home.
	Typically, courts will resolve any reasonable doubt about whether an injury occurred in the course of employment in favor of the injured claimant.
	NEW for 2010 If an employee suffers from a specific injury and a cumulative injury, regardless of when the injury occurred, the employee is entitled to two separate awards — one for each injury — but not a combined award with a longer payout period. [*]
	Psychiatric injuries fall under slightly different standards. Work-related stress must be "predominant as to all causes of the psychiatric injury combined." Unless a "sudden and extraordinary" employment condition is involved, the employee must have worked for you for at least six months.

Table 32. Workers' Compensation *(continued)*

Question	Response
How does this start? (continued)	Work-related stress (not stress from the employee's family, health or other issues) must account for more than half of the employee's injury. Psychiatric injuries must meet *all* of the following criteria: • Diagnosis as a mental disorder, based on the published criteria of the American Psychiatric Association; • Determination that the mental disorder results in disability or requires medical treatment; and • Proof that the "actual events of employment were predominant as to all causes combined," except in situations involving a significant violent act. As soon as you get workers' compensation insurance, you should identify health care providers and hospital facilities designated by the insurance company and/or are familiar with occupational injuries and the workers' compensation system. In most circumstances, you may designate the treating physician for at least the first 30 days following an injury. For more on designating physicians, see "Choice of Physician, Chiropractor or Acupuncturist" on page 140. **TIP** Regulatory activity continues in the area of workers' compensation. For up-to-date information on this and other employment-related issues, subscribe to the CalChamber's free newsletter, *HR California Extra* at *www.calbizcentral.com/HRC/Pages/FreeNewslettersSignup.aspx*
How long does it last?	This is determined by the workers' compensation carrier and the treating physician.
What's the process like? **TIP** Need help finding a medical provider? Check out *www.scif.com/mpn/MPNhome.html*	1. Should a work-related injury or illness occur, your company's first duty is to provide the employee with first aid or emergency medical care, if needed. Even if your company designated a medical provider and the employee didn't predesignate his/her own physician, you can lose the right to control the medical care if you fail to promptly provide medical care when requested. For more on designating physicians, see "Choice of Physician, Chiropractor or Acupuncturist" on page 140.

Table 32. Workers' Compensation *(continued)*

Question	Response
What's the process like? (continued)	**2.** If the injury requires more than first aid, give the employee the *Employee's Claim for Workers' Compensation Benefits (DWC 1)* as soon as possible after the incident.
	Although you can postpone acceptance of a workers' compensation claim for up to 90 days, pending an investigation to determine if the injury is work-related, you must provide all appropriate medical care immediately upon learning of the injury. Your potential liability for medical care costs is limited to $10,000 for treatment prior to the decision to accept or reject the claim.
	3. File the *Employer's Report of Occupational Injury or Illness* with your insurance company.
	4. Conduct an investigation into the circumstances surrounding the injury. Document any findings and use this information to prevent future injuries.
	5. If you must record and report injuries on the Cal/OSHA *Log 300* forms, do so. See "How Do I Report and Record Work-Related Injuries and Illnesses?" in Chapter 6, page 226, to find out if these requirements apply to you.
	6. Communicate with your injured employee and focus on his/her recovery and return to work. Make sure the employee knows about available benefits and when the benefit services will be furnished. Make sure that employees receive the benefit checks they're entitled to. Stay informed.
	7. Take corrective action to eliminate any workplace hazards discovered during the injury investigation.
	8. Respect employee confidentiality. Like most types of medical information, workers' compensation claim information must be kept private.

Table 32. Workers' Compensation *(continued)*

Question	Response
What if the employment relationship ends?	Don't take adverse action against an employee involved in a workers' compensation claim, unless you consulted an attorney. The law explicitly prohibits you from discharging, threatening or discriminating in any way against an employee because he/she received an award from, filed or intends to file a workers' compensation claim. If the employee decides to leave the company (voluntary quit), workers' compensation leave ends. The workers' compensation carrier handles medical treatment and disability benefits, which may continue even if the employee no longer works for you. If you need to fire an employee on workers' compensation leave, consult legal counsel. If you need to lay off an employee on workers' compensation leave, remember that the employee enjoys the same rights and seniority that he/she would have earned if he/she was at work. See "Layoff" in Chapter 8, page 288, for more information.

Table 32. Workers' Compensation *(continued)*

Question	Response
What other benefits are related/can be affected?	Workers' compensation leave may run concurrently with family and medical leave for eligible employees. During the time workers' compensation leave runs concurrently with family and medical leave, the employee may receive the following health benefits: • The same access to participation in health and benefits plans as with any other unpaid disability leave. If you provide health insurance during other disability leaves, you must do so for workers' compensation; and • COBRA coverage, if triggered by absences related to the workers' compensation injury. Contact your insurance provider for information. Workers' compensation covers the following employee benefits: • Seniority — employees continue to accrue seniority as defined by your paid and unpaid leave policies; • Holidays — you determine whether an employee on workers' compensation leave receives holiday pay. Treat the employee on workers' compensation the same as you treat employees on other types of disability leave; and • Sick leave, vacation and PTO — if the employee takes company-paid leave, these benefits continue to accrue. If unpaid leave, they only accrue if your other disability policies allow. You may allow the use of sick pay (page 145), vacation (page 141) or PTO (page 147) to supplement workers' compensation benefits. The employee may now be a "qualified person with a disability" requiring reasonable accommodation. See "What Is Reasonable Accommodation?" in Chapter 7, page 252.

*Benson v. Workers' Compensation Appeals Board, 170 Cal. App. 4th 1535 (2009)

Choice of Physician, Chiropractor or Acupuncturist

Although employees have the right to notify you that they have a personal medical doctor (MD), doctor of osteopathic medicine (DO) or medical group, specific rules govern this predesignation. Employees make a valid physician pre-designation if:

- The employer offers group health coverage;

- The doctor is the employee's regular physician; either a physician who limited his or her practice of medicine to general practice or a board-certified or board-eligible internist, pediatrician, obstetrician-gynecologist or family practitioner, and previously directed the employee's medical treatment and retains the employee's medical records;

- The employee's "personal physician" may be a medical group if it is a single corporation or partnership composed of licensed doctors of medicine or osteopathy, which operates an integrated, multi-specialty medical group providing comprehensive medical services predominantly for non-occupational illnesses and injuries;

- Prior to the injury, the employee's doctor agrees to treat the employee for work injuries or illnesses;

- Prior to the injury, the employee provided his/her employer the following in writing:

  - Notice that the employee wants his/her personal doctor to treat him/her for a work-related injury or illness; and

  - The employee's personal doctor's name and business address.

- A physician pre-designation made before March 14, 2006, is valid if all of the above conditions are met.

Employers must notify employees of the right to pre-designate a personal physician and provide new employees with a physician pre-designation form upon hire or by the end of the first pay period. Employees that properly pre-designated a personal physician are entitled to be treated by that physician regardless of whether the employee would otherwise be treated within a medical provider network. If emergency or first aid treatment is required, you must provide it, but employees can get follow-up treatment with their pre-designated personal physician.

The rules also require employers whose employees are not treated by a medical provider network to provide their employees with a form for pre-designating a chiropractor or acupuncturist, upon hire or by the end of the first pay period. A valid personal chiropractor or personal acupuncturist pre-designation requires the chiropractor or acupuncturist to have previously directed treatment of the employee and retain the employee's treatment records and history. The chiropractor or acupuncturist must also be licensed under the Business and Professions Code. There is no requirement for acceptance by the health care provider as there is with the personal physician.

Employers must notify employees in writing of their right to request a change to a treating physician of their choice 30 days after reporting an injury if the original treating physician was selected by the employer or its insurer.

What Do I Need to Know About Vacation?

Vacation is paid time away from work that is typically planned in advance. Many employers offer two or three weeks of paid vacation per year.

Table 33. Vacation

Question	Response
Do I have to provide this benefit?	No. If you choose to offer paid vacation, you must follow important rules. Vacation can accrue or vest on an hourly, daily, weekly or monthly basis.
	Example: If your employees earn three weeks of vacation a year (120 hours), then vacation accrues at a rate of approximately 0.45 hours daily.
	Any employer who offers vacation must offer it in accordance with these requirements.
Is this time off paid?	Vacation can be paid or unpaid. If it's paid, vacation is treated like wages. Once it is earned, it can't be taken away.
	You can't maintain a "use it or lose it" policy, but you can require that your employees cash out their unused vacation once a year or that they stop accruing vacation after reaching a certain cap. For more information about vacation policies, see "Vacation" in Table 12 in Chapter 3, page 69.
Who's eligible?	You decide who is eligible to accrue vacation. Be consistent. Similarly situated employees should accrue vacation at the same rate.

Table 33. Vacation *(continued)*

Question	Response
How does this start?	You can allow your employees to start accruing vacation from the day they start work. Or you can choose to make your employees wait a reasonable period (30 days or 90 days, for example) before vacation begins to accrue.
How long does it last?	You get to decide. Your policy may offer an employee three weeks of vacation per year, and may forbid employees from taking it all at once. You can approve or deny any given vacation schedule. For nonexempt employees, you can decide whether vacation is taken in days, hours or half hours. For exempt employees, you may decide whether vacation is taken in four hour increments or more, or in full day increments only.
What's the process like?	1. Your employee will notify you that he/she wants to take vacation. You might want to create a form for this that your employees can use. 2. You either approve the requested day(s) or ask the employee to reschedule. 3. When the employee takes the day(s), be sure to subtract the time from the amount of his/her accrued vacation.
What if the employment relationship ends?	If you offer paid vacation, when an employee leaves you must include any accrued but unused vacation at the same time as the final paycheck, See "How Do I Calculate a Final Paycheck?" in Chapter 5, page 187.
What other benefits are related/can be affected?	You can require employees to use their accrued vacation for some types of leave. For other leaves, you can't require employees to use vacation, but they can choose to do so. See: • "Pregnancy Disability Leave" on page 101; • "Family and Medical Leave" on page 105; • "Disability Leave" on page 112; • "Paid Family Leave" on page 129; and • "Workers' Compensation" on page 133.

What Do I Need to Know About Holidays?

Common holidays include New Year's Day, Presidents' Day, Memorial Day, the Fourth of July, Labor Day, Thanksgiving and the Friday after, and Christmas.

Table 34. Holidays

Question	Response
Do I have to provide this benefit?	No. However, you may need to accommodate religious holidays in certain circumstances. See "Religion" in Chapter 7, page 249. If you maintain a policy of giving paid days off for holidays, courts will construe that as an obligation.
Is this time off paid?	Not necessarily. For nonexempt employees, the law doesn't require you to pay for holiday time, although many employers do. For exempt employees, you must pay them their full weekly salary for any week in which they perform any work. For more information about holiday policies, see "Holidays" in Table 12 in Chapter 3, page 69.
Who's eligible?	You decide who is eligible for holidays. All similarly situated employees should receive the same holiday benefits.
How does this start?	N/A
How long does it last?	Typically, one day at a time.
What's the process like?	Create a holiday policy and provide it to your employees. See "Holidays" in Table 12 in Chapter 3, page 69. Tell employees at the beginning of each year which holidays will be granted and whether they will be paid.

Table 34. Holidays *(continued)*

Question	Response
What if the employment relationship ends?	Employees cannot accrue or vest holiday pay, like they can with vacation. You don't need to pay a departing employee for any future holidays.
What other benefits are related/can be affected?	Holidays don't directly affect other types of leave, although employees may want to take vacation or other time off on days before or after a holiday to extend their time away from work. Certain leaves may have an affect on holidays. See: • "Pregnancy Disability Leave" on page 101; • "Family and Medical Leave" on page 105; • "Disability Leave" on page 112; and • "Workers' Compensation" on page 133.

What Do I Need to Know About Floating Holidays/Personal Holidays/ Personal Days?

The way your policy defines floating holidays/personal days determines how you need to treat the time off.

- You must treat time off associated with an event as a holiday. See "What Do I Need to Know About Holidays?" on page 143; and

- You must treat time off that an employee may take any time and for any reason as vacation. See "What Do I Need to Know About Vacation?" on page 141.

As with vacation, you may place a cap on the accrual of these days off. But you must give employees reasonable opportunity to take the days off so that they can stay below the cap.

What Do I Need to Know About Sick Leave?

Sick leave is an optional benefit many employers provide to their employees to take care of themselves and family members during illness.

Table 35. Sick Leave

Question	Response
Do I have to provide this benefit?	No. If you do, you must also allow employees to use one-half of their annual sick leave to care for family members. See the "What's the process like?" entry in this table for more information about kin care.
Is this time off paid?	For nonexempt employees, you decide. Unlike vacation, accrued but unused sick leave need not be paid out at termination. For exempt employees, you need not provide sick leave. But if you don't, you will not be able to deduct for any complete days of absence due to illness. See "Deductions from an Exempt Employee's Salary" in Chapter 5, page 192. Your policy should specify the minimum increment that sick leave may be taken (15 minute, one hour, etc.). Whatever your payroll specifies as a minimum increment is acceptable for exempt and nonexempt employees.
Who's eligible?	You decide. Make sure that similarly situated employees are similarly eligible.
How does this start?	You decide. Your policy should make clear what the employee needs to do to use a sick day.
How long does it last?	You decide. You also aren't required to allow accrual of sick leave, so unused sick leave can be forfeited at the end of a designated period (for example, annually or every quarter).

Table 35. Sick Leave *(continued)*

Question	Response
What's the process like?	If you choose to offer sick leave, document your policy and provide this information to all employees (even if not eligible).
	You should document absences for sick leave. Consider requiring a medical excuse for extended absences. Keep a copy of the excuse in the employee's medical file. Document time off for payroll purposes. For more information, see "Deductions from an Exempt Employee's Salary" in Chapter 5, page 192.
	Kin Care
TIP **Kin care** includes care of a sick child, parent, spouse, registered domestic partner, or child of a registered domestic partner.	If you offer sick leave, you must also allow employees to take up to half of their annual accrued sick leave for kin care. You should require employees to designate time off for kin care. See the *Request for Use of Kin Care*, described in Table 39 on page 156. Keep the documentation in the employee's medical file.
	Denying an employee this right or discriminating against an employee who exercises this right can cause you problems. This includes reinstating an employee to a previous position, and paying back wages, other damages and attorneys' fees. You can't discipline, discharge, demote or suspend an employee for taking time off for kin care. You also can't count time off for kin care against an employee in accordance with any absence control policy you may have.
What if the employment relationship ends?	Regardless of how the relationship ends, you aren't required to pay an employee for unused sick leave.
What other benefits are related/can be affected?	If you offer sick leave, you must also provide kin care benefits.
	If you offer sick leave as part of a PTO policy, allow your employees to take up to half of their annual accrued PTO as kin care leave.
	Any sick leave payment you provide your employees can reduce the amount of SDI benefits they receive. For more information, see "What Do I Need to Know About SDI?" on page 128.
	Pregnant employees must be allowed to use accrued sick leave during PDL. For more information, see "What Do I Need to Know About PDL?" on page 101.

What Do I Need to Know About PTO?

Paid time off (PTO) may be a combination of sick pay, holiday pay and/or vacation. Employees can take planned and unplanned days off. California law treats PTO like vacation. See "What Do I Need to Know About Vacation?" on page 141. If you offer PTO, you must allow employees to use half of their annual PTO accrual for kin care. See "Paid Time Off (PTO)" in Chapter 3, page 71, for more information.

What Do I Need to Know About CTO?

If you are a private employer, never offer compensatory time off (CTO) as a benefit.

CTO (or "comp time") is time off given in exchange for extra hours worked, in the public sector only.

> **Example:** An employee might work an extra two hours and ask for "comp time" of three hours off at a later date.

> ❶ It is illegal for all private sector employers to provide CTO not only in California, but nationwide. Private-sector employers can't provide it under any circumstances.

Do not confuse CTO with makeup time, which California law permits. See "How Can I Use Makeup Time?" in Chapter 5, page 178.

What Do I Need to Know About Bereavement Leave?

When an employee experiences the death of a family member or friend, he/she may request time off for a funeral or for mourning.

Table 36. Bereavement Leave

Question	Response
Do I have to provide this benefit?	No. This is entirely a matter of company policy.
Is this time off paid?	For nonexempt employees, you decide. Many employees want to take the time off even if unpaid. For exempt employees, you need not pay the employee for time missed if it was a complete day of absence for personal reasons.

Table 36. Bereavement Leave *(continued)*

Question	Response
Who's eligible?	You can determine eligibility requirements for this leave. You might designate bereavement leave as applicable only to family deaths, or you might extend it for other circumstances.
How does this start?	Your employee notifies you as soon as he/she learns of the need for bereavement leave.
How long does it last?	You can determine how much time you want to give for this type of leave.
What's the process like?	A request for this type of leave may come up suddenly. 1. Document the circumstances and how much leave you grant. You may want to have the employee fill out a request for time off form. 2. Make the necessary adjustments to the work schedule and paycheck of the affected employee.
What if the employment relationship ends?	Nothing. This is not an accrued benefit.
What other benefits are related/can be affected?	You may require nonexempt employees to use sick leave, vacation or PTO for this purpose. For exempt employees, see "Deductions from an Exempt Employee's Salary" in Chapter 5, page 192.

What Do I Need to Know About Personal Leaves of Absence?

An employee may wish to take a leave of absence for personal reasons.

Table 37. Personal Leaves of Absence

Question	Response
Do I have to provide this benefit?	No. This is entirely a matter of company policy. However, a personal leave may constitute a form of reasonable accommodation. See "What Is Reasonable Accommodation?" in Chapter 7, page 252, for more information.
Is this time off paid?	For nonexempt employees, you decide. Many employees want to take the time off, even if unpaid. For exempt employees, see "Deductions from an Exempt Employee's Salary" in Chapter 5, page 192.

Table 37. Personal Leaves of Absence *(continued)*

Question	Response
Who's eligible?	You can determine eligibility requirements for this leave. ❗ If you provide this benefit for one employee, you set a precedent for other employees and could create a potential for discrimination claims if you deny another employee's request for the same type of leave.
How does this start?	An employee requests time off.
How long does it last?	You can determine how much time you want to give for this type of leave.
What's the process like?	A request for this type of leave may come up suddenly. 1. Document the circumstances and how much leave you grant. You may want to have the employee fill out a request for time off form. 2. Make the necessary adjustments to the work schedule and paycheck of the affected employee.
What if the employment relationship ends?	Nothing. This is not an accrued benefit.
What other benefits are related/can be affected?	Depending on the reason for the leave, it may qualify as family leave, sick leave or some other type, therefore placing it under the regulations for those types of leave. When your employee requests the time off, inquire about the reason to determine if the leave qualifies as some other leave.

What Do I Need to Know About Domestic Partner Rights?

The California Domestic Partner Rights and Responsibilities Act of 2003 took effect in 2005. The act:

- Gives domestic partners the same rights, protections and benefits as those granted to, and imposed on, spouses;

- Subjects domestic partners to the same responsibilities, obligations and duties under law, whether they derive from statutes, administrative regulations, court rules, government policies, common law or any other provisions or sources of law, as those granted to and imposed on spouses;

- Registered domestic partners have the same rights, with respect to a child of either of them, as spouses would with respect to a child of either of the spouses; and

- Gives domestic partners the same rights for leave under the California Family Rights Act (CFRA) as that given to spouses and their children. See "Domestic Partners and CFRA" on page 110; and

 • Same sex couples who are legally married in another state will have the same rights, protections and benefits, and be subject to the same responsibilities, obligations and duties in California as spouses.[2]

Employers with state contracts for $100,000 or more must certify that they comply with legislation[3] regarding benefits. If you want to contract with the state, you must provide the same benefits to domestic partners of employees as those provided to spouses of employees. If you do business with the state, consult with your legal counsel and benefits adviser.

---

2. Family Code section 308
3. California Public Contract Code, sec. 10295.3

What Do I Need to Know About Health Care?

A health care plan is an organized way for you to help employees cover their health-related costs. Some employers offer plans covering medical, dental, vision, prescription drug and mental health care. This type of benefit is complicated so you should consult a benefits expert when setting up your plan.

Table 38. Health Care

Question	Response
Do I have to provide this benefit?	No. If you do offer it, you must offer it in accordance with the laws. See "Glossary of Terms, Laws and Agencies" on page 305 for details about COBRA, HIPAA and ERISA.
Is this time off paid?	This is a benefit and not time off.
Who's covered?	If you offer a health care plan, you may fall under ERISA regulations about notifying your employees or other duties. Check with your legal counsel. ERISA is very complicated.
Who's eligible?	You decide. Make sure that similarly situated employees are similarly eligible.
How does this start?	You decide. Your insurance carrier can offer advice and suggestions.
How long does it last?	N/A
What's the process like?	Your insurance carrier or third party benefits administrator will help you.
What if the employment relationship ends?	If you employ between two and 19 people (Cal-COBRA), or more than 20 employees (COBRA) and you offer health care, you must give ex-employees the opportunity to continue coverage by paying their own premiums. See Chapter 8, "Ending the Employment Relationship" for details.
What other benefits are related/can be affected?	During certain leaves, health care benefits must be extended to cover the leave. See "What Do I Need to Know About Family and Medical Leaves?" on page 105 and "What Do I Need to Know About PDL?" on page 101 for details.

San Francisco Health Care

Employers in San Francisco must also comply with the San Francisco Health Care Security Ordinance. The ordinance requires San Francisco employers to pay a health care tax to the City of San Francisco.

NEW 2010 Effective Jan. 1, 2010, medium employers (with 20 to 99 employees) must pay a tax of $1.31 per hour, per employee; and large employers (with 100 or more employees) must pay a tax of $1.96 per hour, per employee. Small employers with between one and 19 employees are exempt from the tax, as are nonprofit organizations with fewer than 50 employees.

Though the legality of the ordinance is being challenged in court, San Francisco employers must comply with the ordinance while the case goes through the court system.

Domestic Partners and Health Plans

The California Insurance Equality Act amended the Health and Safety Code and the Insurance Code regarding domestic partner coverage.

The carrier must provide the same coverage to domestic partners as is provided to a spouse. This law may result in carriers offering employers only plans that provide registered domestic partner and spousal benefits. The employer still has the option to offer only employee coverage, and no spouse or domestic partner coverage.

Domestic Partners and COBRA

A registered domestic partner is not a qualified beneficiary under COBRA (20 or more employees) because federal law does not treat a domestic partner the same as a spouse. The federal Defense of Marriage Act of 1996 provides that a spouse can only be a person of the opposite sex. Therefore, domestic partners have no independent rights as qualified beneficiaries.

A former employee's domestic partner may be enrolled as a dependent at open enrollment time, but the duration of that coverage is determined by that of the former employee. However, the child of a domestic partner has COBRA rights independent of the former employee if the child was covered as a dependent under the former employee's plan on the day before the COBRA qualifying event.

> **Example:** If an employee in your health plan terminates, the employee is eligible for COBRA, followed by Cal-COBRA, for a total of 36 months. The employee's domestic partner is not eligible for COBRA. If the employee was married, his/her spouse would have an independent right to COBRA.
>
> However, at open enrollment, the employee on COBRA may choose to add his/her domestic partner as a dependent. This does not give the domestic partner any COBRA rights. The domestic partner is entitled to dependent coverage only

for the remaining length of time that your former employee is entitled to COBRA coverage. If the former employee and his/her domestic partner end their relationship, the dependent coverage for the domestic partner also ends.

Domestic Partners and Cal-COBRA

Registered domestic partners are qualified beneficiaries under Cal-COBRA (between two and 19 employees). If a registered domestic partner was a health plan participant on the day before a qualifying event, he or she would be entitled to continuation benefits.

The Cal-COBRA extension of federal COBRA continuation benefits does not apply to a registered domestic partner. A person must have been a COBRA-qualified beneficiary to be entitled to this extension, and COBRA doesn't cover domestic partners. Once COBRA benefits are exhausted, a domestic partner may be eligible to continue benefits by converting to an individual policy.

Mental Health and Substance Abuse

 The federal Mental Health Parity and Addiction Equity Act of 2008 went into effect for health plan years beginning on Oct. 3, 2009. The act does not apply to group plans for 50 or fewer employees. The act requires covered group health plans to offer mental health plan parity with health and surgical benefits. A similar California law has been in effect for some time. Consult with your benefits adviser if you employ more than 50 staff and want to know how the act applies to the health plans you offer as employee benefits.

What Do I Need to Know About Life Insurance Plans?

Many employers include life insurance among the benefits they offer to their employees. This type of benefit is complicated, so you should consult a benefits expert when setting up your plan.

What Do I Need to Know About a Voluntary Disability Plan?

Most employers must contribute to the SDI program. Employers can establish their own program with the EDD and employee approval. Your plan must offer coverage, benefits and rights equal to the state program in all aspects, and better in at least one.

Your employees can still opt into the state program. See "What Do I Need to Know About SDI?" on page 128. Check with your legal counsel if you want to set up a voluntary program.

What Do I Need to Know About Providing Bonuses?

See Table 45 in Chapter 5, page 179. This type of benefit is complicated, so you should consult a benefits expert when setting up your plan.

What Do I Need to Know About Retirement or Pension Plans?

Although not required by law, a company-sponsored qualified retirement plan (one that meets IRS specifications) is an excellent benefit that can attract and reward employees and provide you with tax advantages. You can choose from a wide range of options, from complex plans requiring advice from experts to simple plans that you can establish without any outside consultants. Some examples include Individual Retirement Accounts (IRAs), Simplified Employee Pensions (SEPs), profit-sharing plans (including 401(k) plans) and Employee Stock Ownership Plans (ESOPs).

Although many different types of retirement plans exist, they fall into two general categories:

- Defined benefit plans — a predetermined formula determines the benefits received, tied to the employee's salary, length of service or both. You bear the responsibility for funding and investment risks; and

- Defined contribution plans — a specified amount is placed in a participant's account. The amount of funds accumulated and the investment gains or losses determine the benefit received at retirement. You bear no responsibility for investment returns, but you must provide a good selection of sound investment options.

Retirement plans are regulated by ERISA. See "Glossary of Terms, Laws and Agencies" on page 305 for details about ERISA. You should consult with competent legal counsel to make sure you establish and maintain your plans according to this complex and technical area of the law.

What Do I Need to Know About Commuter Benefits?

Offering commuter benefits is voluntary in California, unless your business is located in San Francisco.

All employers in San Francisco with 20 or more persons performing work for compensation on a full-time, part-time or temporary basis and who work an average of at least 10 hours a week while working for the same employer within the previous calendar month, must offer one of the following options:

- Pre-tax Transit: Employer sets up a deduction program under existing Federal Tax Law 132(f), which allows employees to use an amount each month in pretax wages to purchase transit passes or vanpool rides.

- Employer Paid Transit Benefits: Employer pays for workers' transit fares on any of the San Francisco Bay Area mass transit systems or reimburses workers for their vanpool expenses. Reimbursements for transportation expenses must be of at least an equivalent value to the purchase price of a San Francisco MUNI Fast Pass, which is presently $45.

- Employer Provided Transit: Employer offers workers free shuttle service on a company-funded bus or van between home and place of business.

Any Other Benefits?

Many small businesses offer their employees other benefits and perquisites, often called perks. A clothing store might offer employees a significant discount on purchases. A restaurant might give employees a free meal for every shift they work. An information technology company might offer memberships to professional organizations, training and certification to add value to employees and the work they do. Company cars, designated parking spaces, picnics, parties, etc., are all ways for employers to offer competitive compensation packages and motivate employees.

The law doesn't address these creative types of benefits. Remember, if you make a promise (i.e., create a contract), you will be obligated to keep it. Also consult with a tax professional to understand potential tax liabilities for you and your employees.

The Hitches, Glitches and Pitfalls of Providing Benefits

Make sure that you offer benefits evenly. Don't discriminate amongst your employees.

When an employee goes on leave, make sure you know (and the employee knows) which type of leave it is. If you fail to establish that the employee is taking FMLA/CFRA leave, for example, then the leave taken doesn't count toward the enforceable limit.

What Forms and Checklists Do I Use To Provide Benefits?

The following table describes forms associated with leaves of absence and other benefits.

 You can find these forms in your online formspack, described in detail in"Online Forms" on page 4.

Table 39. Forms and Checklists

Form Name	What do I use it for?	When do I use it?	Who fills it out?	Where does it go?
Certification of Physician or Practitioner for Employee Return to Work	To obtain physician or medical practitioner approval for the employee to return to work.	Just before the employee returns to work.	The employee's physician or medical practitioner.	Keep a copy in the employee's confidential medical file, separate from his/her personnel file.
Certification of Physician or Practitioner for PDL or PDL/FMLA	To obtain physician or medical practitioner certification that the employee is disabled due to pregnancy.	At the time of, or just before, PDL leave.	The employee's physician or medical practitioner.	Keep a copy in the employee's confidential medical file, separate from her personnel file.

Table 39. Forms and Checklists

Form Name	What do I use it for?	When do I use it?	Who fills it out?	Where does it go?
COBRA Administration Guide	To ensure you use the proper, required forms relating to COBRA (20 or more employees) and Cal-COBRA (2 to 19 employees), as applicable.	Use when an employee is hired and refer back to it when a qualifying event occurs.	N/A	N/A
Family Medical Leave - Approval/ Conditional Approval	To notify the employee of the type of leave granted.	At the beginning of the leave.	The employer.	Send a copy to the employee and keep a copy in the employee's confidential medical file, separate from his/her personnel file.
FMLA/PDL - Approval	To notify the employee of the type of leave granted.	At the beginning of the leave.	The employer.	Send a copy to the employee and keep a copy in the employee's confidential medical file, separate from her personnel file.

Table 39. Forms and Checklists

Form Name	What do I use it for?	When do I use it?	Who fills it out?	Where does it go?
FMLA/CFRA Application - English	Give to employees who request or may need a leave of absence under FMLA/CFRA.	Provide this form when an employee requests a leave of absence or you recognize the need.	The employee.	The employee's personnel file - medical file if the request for leave is for the employee's own medical condition.
FMLA/CFRA Application - Spanish	Give to employees who request or may need a leave of absence under FMLA/CFRA.	Provide this form when an employee requests a leave of absence or you recognize the need.	The employee.	The employee's personnel file - medical file if the request for leave is for the employee's own medical condition.
FMLA/CFRA/PDL - Form Usage Chart	For information on which forms to use when an employee needs family or medical leave.	When an employee requests a leave of absence or your recognize the need.	N/A	N/A
FMLA-CFRA-PDL Timeline	For information about relationships among various state-mandated leaves of absence and benefits during the time off.	When an employee considers a leave.	N/A	Your employee would also benefit from this information.
Leave Interaction	Use this form to determine the relationships among the various state-mandated leaves of absence and benefits during the time off.	When an employee considers a leave.	N/A	Your employee would also benefit from this information.

Table 39. Forms and Checklists

Form Name	What do I use it for?	When do I use it?	Who fills it out?	Where does it go?
Medical Certification – FMLA/CFRA	To obtain physician or medical practitioner certification that the employee is disabled due to "a serious health condition."	At the time of the medical leave.	The patient's health care provider. (The patient could be either the employee or a family member.)	Keep a copy in the employee's confidential medical file, separate from his/her personnel file.
Military Spouse Leave Policy (25 or more employees)	To notify employees of their rights under the military spouse leave law.	Add to your employee handbook and distribute to employees upon hire.	N/A	In your employee handbook or with your other leave policies.
Military Spouse Request for Leave (25 or more employees)	For employees to request military spouse leave in writing.	At the time an employee requests military spouse leave.	The employee.	In the employee's personnel file.
PDL Timeline	For information about relationships among various state-mandated leaves of absence and benefits during the time off.	When an employee considers a leave.	N/A	Your employee would also benefit from this information.

Table 39. Forms and Checklists

Form Name	What do I use it for?	When do I use it?	Who fills it out?	Where does it go?
Personal Physician or Personal Chiropractor Predesignation Form **TIP** This form is also a tear-out in the **Workers' Compensation Rights and Benefits** pamphlet (in the **Required Notices Kit** associated with this product).	To notify employees of their right to choose medical treatment by their personal physician or chiropractor.	Give it to the employee at the time of hire.	The employee.	Keep a copy in the employee's personnel file, and send a copy to your contact at your insurer or claims administrator.
Request for Use of Kin Care - English	To notify the employee of the type of leave granted to him/her.	At the beginning of the leave.	The employee.	Keep a copy in the employee's confidential medical file, separate from his/her personnel file.
Request for Use of Kin Care - Spanish	To notify the employee of the type of leave granted to him/her.	At the beginning of the leave.	The employee.	Keep a copy in the employee's confidential medical file, separate from his/her personnel file.

Table 39. Forms and Checklists

Form Name	What do I use it for?	When do I use it?	Who fills it out?	Where does it go?
Temporary Modified Duty Agreement	To document a temporary modified duty assignment.	When an employee can't perform the essential functions of a job without accommodation.	The employee.	Keep a copy in the employee's confidential medical file, separate from his/her personnel file.
Workers' Compensation Insurance Shoppers Checklist	Use this form to ask potential brokers and carriers important questions as you shop for a workers' compensation policy.	When shopping for a workers' compensation insurance policy.	N/A	In your files.

Where Do I Go for More Information?

CalBizCentral and federal and state government agencies offer a variety of resources to help you develop written employee policies.

Table 40. Additional Resources

For information on	Check out these resources
General	From CalBizCentral: • *2010 California Labor Law Digest*; • *2010 California Labor Law Administration*; • *2010 Employee Handbook Software*; • *Required Notices Kit*; • *www.hrcalifornia.com*; and • *www.calbizcentral.com*
Paid family leave	*www.edd.ca.gov*

Table 40. Additional Resources *(continued)*

For information on	Check out these resources
Military leave	• Veterans' Employment and Training Service "eLaws Advisor" *www.dol.gov/elaws/userra.htm*;
	• The National Committee for Employer Support of the Guard and Reserve (ESGR) at *www.esgr.org/*; or National Committee for Employer Support of the Guard and Reserve 1555 Wilson Boulevard, Suite 200 Arlington, VA 22209-2405 800-336-4590;
	• Non-technical Resource Guide to the USERRA at *www.dol.gov/vets/whatsnew/userraguide0903.rtf*;
	• HRCalifornia at *www.calbizcentral.com/HRC/LawLibrary/TimeOff/MilitaryServiceLeave/Pages/EligibilityNoticeand-DocumentationofMilitaryLeave.aspx*; and
	• *www.dol.gov/osbp/sbrefa/poster/userra.htm*.
San Francisco-specific benefits	• For current information on San Francisco's Health Care Security Ordinance, visit *www.healthysanfrancisco.org/employers/HCSO_Compliance.aspx*
	• For information on commuter benefits, please visit *http://commuterbenefits.org/*
Self-insured employers	• Department of Industrial Relations Office of Self Insurance Plans 2265 Watt Avenue, Suite 1 Sacramento, CA 95825 916-483-3392; and
	• The Department of Industrial Relations Web site *www.dir.ca.gov/*.
State Disability Insurance	• *www.edd.ca.gov/taxrep/taxrte9x.htm*;
	• *www.edd.ca.gov/Disability/For_Employers.htm*;
	• California Employer's Guide 2010 at *www.edd.ca.gov/pdf_pub_ctr/de44.pdf*; and
Unemployment Insurance	• The California EDD Web site at *www.edd.ca.gov/UIBDG/*;
	• *www.edd.ca.gov/employer.htm*; and
	• California Employer's Guide 2010 at *www.edd.ca.gov/pdf_pub_ctr/de44.pdf*.

Table 40. Additional Resources *(continued)*

For information on	Check out these resources
Work Sharing	EDD Special Claims Office P.O. Box 269058 Sacramento, CA 95826-9058 (916) 464-3300

Workers' Compensation	• From CalBizCentral:
	  – ***2010 Labor Law Digest***;
	• The Division of Workers' Compensation within the Department of Industrial Relations will provide assistance and advice;
	• The Equal Employment Opportunity Commission (EEOC) at ***www.eeoc.gov/policy/docs/workcomp.html***;
	• State Compensation Insurance Fund at ***www.scif.com***; and
	• Workers' Compensation Offices
	  455 Golden Gate Avenue, 9th Floor
	  San Francisco, CA 94102-3660
	  (415) 703-4600
	  (800) 736-7401

CalBizCentral also provides many ongoing and comprehensive educational opportunities for small business owners, HR beginners and experienced HR professionals alike. These include online sexual harassment training, DVDs and special HR seminars. For more information, please visit our Web site at ***www.calbizcentral.com***.

Providing Benefits Frequently Asked Questions

How long can a person take to decide whether to choose COBRA coverage?

After being notified of Consolidated Omnibus Budget Reconciliation Act (COBRA) rights, the qualified beneficiary can take up to 60 days to choose or waive COBRA coverage.

The initial premium is then due within 45 days of the date COBRA coverage was chosen, retroactively paying for time elapsed during the election period.

When do I have to give my employees information about COBRA?

Notification of COBRA rights is required both at the time an employee becomes covered by a plan subject to COBRA and at the time of a qualifying event.

Employers and employees have certain notification obligations when qualifying events occur. Failure to notify qualified beneficiaries of their COBRA rights can subject the employer to penalties.

Is a pregnant employee entitled to SDI? Yes. Under the State Disability Insurance (SDI) program, disabilities arising from pregnancy, childbirth and related medical conditions receive the same classification as any other temporary disability.

The usual disability period for a normal pregnancy is up to four weeks before the expected delivery date and up to six weeks after the actual delivery. However, a woman's doctor may certify that she is disabled for a longer period before or after the expected delivery if the delivery is a Cesarean section, if medical complications arise or if she is unable to perform her regular or customary job duties.

The period of actual disability is covered by the Pregnancy Disability Act, and for eligible employees, the PDL leave will run concurrently with FMLA.

I employ fewer than 50 people. Do I have to comply with federal and state family leave laws? Can my employees take paid family leave? And do I need to distribute Paid Family Leave pamphlets to new employees? Employers with fewer than 50 employees do not have to comply with the federal Family and Medical Leave Act (FMLA) or the California Family Rights Act (CFRA), which provide up to 12 weeks of job protection when an employee needs time off for a serious health condition or that of a family member, or for baby bonding. Smaller employers must comply with California's paid family leave (PFL) law, and must provide a copy of the PFL brochure to all new hires, and another copy to any employee who leaves work to bond with a new baby or to care for a seriously ill spouse, parent, child or registered domestic partner.

Can an employee quit and still receive Unemployment Insurance? Yes. There are times when an employee may still qualify for unemployment benefits (UI) even though she/he quits work. Normally, to qualify for benefits, a claimant must have "good cause" for leaving work.

"Good cause" exists when a reasonable person genuinely desirous of retaining employment chooses to leave work because of a substantial motivating factor, such as:

- Being needed to care for an ill spouse, child or parent;

- An employer not addressing serious harassment or safety issues;

- A change in travel time or distance;

- Moving beyond reasonable commuting distance to be with a spouse; or

- Going to school.

Must employers offer health insurance to registered domestic partners?
Yes. California law requires the same civil rights, legal status and benefits for registered domestic partners as for spouses. Insurance companies operating in California are required to provide coverage, and companies that offer dependent coverage must offer it to dependent registered domestic partners. You can't require documented proof of registered domestic partner status unless you also require documented proof of marriage.

The California Secretary of State created a registry of domestic partners conferring on them the same legal status as marriage. Only individuals of the same sex living together in the same household or opposite sex individuals with one partner over the age of 62, living together in the same household, may register as domestic partners.

Even though registered domestic partners may be added as a dependent on a group health insurance plan, federal law has not been amended to include the term domestic partners. Since COBRA is federal law, insurance companies are not required to provide domestic partners with COBRA coverage. However, insurance companies operating in California are extending coverage on the basis of the state law requiring equal benefits for domestic partners

Am I required to provide sick leave for employees? Employers are not required to provide paid sick leave for their employees.

However, you may be required to grant unpaid time off work in the form of reasonable accommodation under the federal Americans with Disabilities Act (covers employers with 15 or more employees) and state disability discrimination laws (covers employers with five or more employees), and to provide family/medical leave under state and federal law (employers with 50 or more employees and public-sector employers).

Must I allow an employee to use sick time when his/her children are sick?
Employees may use up to half of their sick leave to care for a sick child, spouse or domestic partner. This is called "kin care."

If an employee needs to care for a sick family member, the employer must allow that employee to use accrued and available sick leave in an amount not less than what would accrue in six months of employment.

For example, an employee who earns one week of sick leave per year could use two-and-one-half days to care for a child with an ear infection, but only after actually earning those days. An employee who earns two weeks of sick leave per year could use one week of that leave if his mother needed help during a bout with the flu.

Nothing in the law requires that the amount of days available for kin care carry over from year to year. An employer may limit the amount of kin care leave to one-half of that year's allotment of sick leave regardless of what was or was not taken the year before.

Does the law require me to provide time off for victims of domestic violence? Victims of domestic violence must be allowed to take time off for certain purposes, depending on the size of their employer.

All employers, regardless of size, must allow an employee who is a victim of domestic violence to take time off from work to obtain a temporary restraining order. An employer with 25 or more employees must allow time off related to domestic violence for medical/psychological care, crisis counseling, safety planning or relocation.

A victim of domestic violence must give an employer reasonable advance notice of the intention to take time off for any of the above purposes, unless such notice is not feasible. When an unscheduled absence occurs, the employer may not take any action against the employee if the employee, within a reasonable time after the absence, provides documentation of the reason for the absence to the employer. Acceptable documentation includes a police report, court order or other evidence from the court, or a note from a medical professional, domestic violence advocate, health care provider or counselor.

What rules apply to personal days or floating holidays? The way an employer's policy defines personal days or floating holidays is critical to the issue of whether those days are defined as vacation, and whether unused days must be paid out at the end of the employment relationship:

- Time off tied to a specific event, such as a birthday or employee anniversary date, is treated as a holiday; and

- Time off not tied to a specific event (even if the employer requires previous notification of the time off) must be treated the same as vacation time.

This means that a personal day or floating holiday an employee may take at any time for any reason must be treated as vacation which accrues and vests, and must be paid out at termination. A personal day or holiday that can only be taken in relation to a specific event need not be paid out at termination.

Must I reinstate employees returning from military leave? An employer must allow an employee to report for military service and reinstate the employee to his/her former position if the employee requests reinstatement, in a timely manner, after his/her military service is completed.

The Uniformed Services Employment and Re-employment Rights Act (USERRA) governs the employment rights of veterans (38 U.S.C. 4301–4333). USERRA covers every individual who serves, or who has served, in the uniformed services and applies to any employer in the public or private sector.

Reinstatement

USERRA provides that returning service members must be re-employed in the job that they would have retained had they not been absent for military service, with the same seniority, status and pay, and other rights and benefits determined by seniority.

The period within which an employee must apply for reinstatement is based on the length of military service. If the service lasted fewer than 31 days, the employee must return on the next regularly scheduled work day after release from service (taking into account travel time and a minimum of eight hours rest time). If the service lasted longer than 30 days but fewer than 181 days, the employee must submit an application for re-employment within 14 days of release from service. For a service of more than 180 days, the employee must submit an application for re-employment within 90 days of release from service.

Employee Benefits

USERRA mandates that while an individual performs military service, he/she is deemed to be on a furlough or leave of absence and is entitled to the rights accorded other employees on nonmilitary leaves of absence. Under USERRA, employees are allowed, but not required, to use accrued vacation or annual leave while performing military duty.

USERRA amends COBRA and allows employees performing military duty of more than 30 days to choose to continue employer-sponsored health insurance for as many as 24 months. For military service of fewer than 31 days, health insurance coverage is provided as if the employee had remained employed.

Does the law require me to give an employee a personal leave of absence? The law doesn't require employers to provide time off for employees wishing to take leaves of absence for personal reasons. However, when an employee requests a personal leave, an employer who is covered by family medical leave laws should always inquire further about the reason for the leave to determine whether it would qualify as family leave (for example, leave to care for an ill parent).

Can I ask a potential new hire to tell me that she is pregnant before I hire her? No, you can't ask a potential or new employee whether she is pregnant or is planning to become pregnant.

In addition, you can't make an employment decision based upon her pregnancy or intention to become pregnant without violating California and federal laws.

Can I create a waiting period before an employee starts earning vacation?
An employer may create a policy under which employees do not begin earning vacation immediately upon hire. The typical policy of this type requires an employee to work 90 days before vacation begins to accrue, and the employee doesn't earn any vacation until the 91st day of employment.

The policy may not delay the earning of vacation for 90 days but then retroactively grant that amount of accrued vacation once the 90 days are up.

Chapter 5

Paying Employees

In California, an exhaustive set of rules governs employee pay. This can be more complicated than it sounds, but it doesn't have to be painful.

In this chapter you can find answers to questions about:

- Work schedules;
- The minimum wage;
- Overtime;
- Payroll deductions; and
- Much more.

Minimum Compliance Elements

1. Hang your **Employment Notices Poster** (available from **www.calbizcentral.com**), which includes mandatory postings that all employees and applicants must be able to see, in a prominent place (such as a break room).

2. Require your nonexempt (hourly) employees to keep accurate records of time worked.

3. Calculate overtime for nonexempt employees after eight hours worked in a day and after 40 hours in a workweek (see "What Is Overtime and How Does It Affect Me?" on page 183).

4. Make sure you don't treat your exempt employees like nonexempt workers — remember, your exempt employees get paid to get the job done, not to work a set number of hours.

5. Get to know the Wage Order for your industry (see the tip on page 171).

The Basics of Paying Employees

Within the protective laws and regulations, it's up to you to determine how and how much to pay your employees. The basic process looks like this:

1. **Classify** — determine the worker's classification (exempt, nonexempt, independent contractor, full-time, part-time, temporary). See "How Do I Know Which Type of Worker to Hire?" in Chapter 2, page 9.

2. **Work** — your employee works for a certain wage, either per amount of time (hourly or salary), or per item (piece rate or flat rate). See "What Do I Pay My Workers?" on page 179. The work is done for a defined duration of time according to a work schedule. See the sections starting with "How Do I Set Up Work Schedules?" on page 170.

3. **Calculate** — calculate the amount he/she earned, adding up the wages earned (regular and overtime), plus any other compensation earned (such as tips, commissions or, in the case of a final paycheck, accrued vacation or PTO). This is the gross amount. See the sections starting with "What Do I Pay My Workers?" on page 179.

4. **Deduct** — make deductions from that amount for benefits, garnishments, taxes and the like. This is the net amount. See the sections starting with "What Deductions Must I Make?" on page 187.

5. **Pay** — create a paycheck for that amount and deliver it to the employee in the appropriate manner at the appropriate time (according to your established workweek and payday schedules), with a statement of how wages and deductions were calculated. See the sections starting with "When Do I Pay My Workers?" on page 193.

6. **Record** — keep records of everything from basic employee identification information to the hours actually worked and not worked by nonexempt employees, and what deductions you made from employee earnings. See the sections on record keeping, starting with "Do I Need to Report any Payroll Information?" on page 196.

How Do I Set Up Work Schedules?

You can set up a work schedule that suits your company or a particular job in your company if your schedule complies with the day and hour limits and overtime regulations for your industry.

Base your work schedule(s) on workdays and workweeks. You can start the workday and workweek at a specific date and time of your choosing, but from then on you must follow this schedule as a uniform rule.

TIP See "What Scheduling Options can I Choose From?" on page 172 for examples of schedules you can use.

TIP The **California Labor Commissioner** oversees investigations to ensure compliance with, and to resolve disputes arising under, state labor laws and Industrial Welfare Commission (IWC) Wage Orders.

Table 41. Workdays and Workweeks

Workday	Any consecutive 24-hour period starting at the same time each calendar day.
	If you don't define the workday, the California Labor Commissioner will presume a workday of 12:01 a.m. to midnight.
Workweek	Any seven consecutive 24-hour periods, starting on the same calendar day and at the same time each week.
	If you don't define the workweek, the California Labor Commissioner will presume a workweek of Sunday through Saturday.

Why Do I Need to Define Workdays and Workweeks?

Despite the freedom to set up your own work schedule, you must make sure to follow regulations that govern day and hour limits, overtime, paydays and meal and rest breaks.

TIP A **Wage Order** is an IWC regulation that defines minimum wages, hours and working conditions for nonexempt employees in a specific industry. Currently, California law contains 17 Wage Orders, plus a Wage Order Summary and a Minimum Wage Order. The purpose of your business determines which Wage Order applies to you.

For help determining the correct wage order for your business, use CalChamber's Web-based wizard at ***www.calbizcentral.com/HRC/LawLibrary/Posters/Pages/iwcwageorders.aspx***.

Table 42. Effects of Workday/Workweek Definitions

Limits	Generally, every employee is entitled to at least one day off in a seven-day workweek or, under some circumstances, the equivalent to one day's rest in seven during each calendar month. You can't require employees who work under Wage Orders 4 and 13 to work more than 72 hours per week. Other limits are placed on daily and weekly hours of work for certain types of employees such as minors, truck drivers, pharmacists, train crews and health care employees.
Overtime	The definition of workweek becomes extremely important when calculating overtime under the "seventh-day" rule, because this rule applies only on the last day of your defined workweek, not simply any time an employee works seven days in a row. ***Example:*** In a Sunday through Saturday workweek, the seventh day rule applies only if an employee works each day, Sunday through Saturday. Consequently, even if the employee works each day beginning on Monday of the first workweek and ending on Sunday of the next workweek (7 consecutive days), Sunday does not count as the seventh consecutive day in that "workweek"— Sunday starts the new workweek. In the first workweek, the employee worked only six days — Monday through Saturday. For more information, see "What Is Overtime and How Does It Affect Me?" on page 183.
Paydays	See "When Do I Pay My Workers?" on page 193.
Meals & rest breaks	See "How Do I Handle Time Spent Traveling, on Rest Breaks or Between Shifts?" on page 176.

What Scheduling Options can I Choose From?

You can choose from a variety of scheduling options for your employees. You may define different workdays or workweeks for different groups of employees if all the employees in the group follow the same schedule. Also, make sure to observe rest and meal break requirements, whatever schedule you choose. See "What Meal and Rest Break Requirements Must I Comply With?" on page 174.

Table 43. Scheduling Options

Type of schedule	What it means
"Regular" workweek	A seven-day workweek where anything over eight hours in a workday or 40 hours in a workweek is considered overtime. See "Why Do I Need to Define Workdays and Workweeks?" on page 171.
Flexible schedule	A workweek schedule of eight hours per day where some employees begin the shift early in the day and others begin their work later in the day.
Split shift	Any two distinct work periods, established by the employer, separated by more than a one-hour unpaid break. You must pay the employee at least one hour's pay, at no less than minimum wage, for the time between shifts. Any hourly amount the employee earns above minimum wage can be used to partially or fully offset the split shift requirement.
Alternative work-week	Any regularly scheduled workweek requiring an employee to work more than eight hours in a 24-hour period. Common schedules: • 4/10 — a four-day workweek of 10 hours per day; and • 9/80 — a two-week schedule of nine-hour days with every other Friday off. Employees on an alternative workweek earn overtime differently than those employees eligible for overtime after eight hours per day. **Use extreme caution when setting up an alternative workweek.** Consult your industry's Wage Order to learn the specific steps you must follow to create, implement, follow and repeal an alternative workweek. See *www.calbizcentral.com/HRC/LawLibrary/Posters/Pages/iwcwageorders.aspx* for more information. *California Labor Law Administration*, published by CalBizCentral, contains detailed, step-by-step guidance on implementing alternative workweeks. To order, visit *www.calbizcentral.com*.

Can I Require My Employees to Work Overtime?

With a couple of limited exceptions, employees can use no statutory or regulatory basis to refuse your request that they work overtime. You can often find employees who will voluntarily work overtime.

A good approach is to first request volunteers among qualified employees, and then require overtime only in the absence of such volunteers. You can enforce overtime requests with disciplinary action if the employee refuses.

For more information, see "What Is Overtime and How Does It Affect Me?" on page 183.

Wage Orders 3, 4, 8, 13 and 16 contain special provisions regarding required overtime:

- Wage Order 3 — an employee may work up to a maximum of 72 hours in seven consecutive days, after which the employee must receive a 24-hour period off duty.

- Wage Order 4 — no employee shall be terminated or otherwise disciplined for refusing to work more than 72 hours in any workweek, except in an emergency.

- Wage Order 8 — an employee may work up to a maximum of 72 hours in any workweek, after which the employee must receive a 24-hour period off duty. The wage order contains some exceptions. All employers who permit any employees to work more than 72 hours in a workweek must give each employee a copy of the applicable provision for exemption, in English and in Spanish, and post it at all times in a prominently visible place.

- Wage Order 13 — any work by an employee in excess of 72 hours in any one workweek must be on a voluntary basis. No employee can be discharged or in any other manner discriminated against for refusing to work in excess of 72 hours in any one workweek.

- Wage Order 16 — no employee can be terminated, disciplined or otherwise discriminated against for refusing to work more than 72 hours in any workweek, except in an emergency.

What Meal and Rest Break Requirements Must I Comply With?

You must provide nonexempt employees a 30 minute meal period no later than 4:59 into their shift. However, if six hours of work will complete the day's work, the employee and employer can mutually agree, in writing, to waive the meal period.

Meal periods may be unpaid only if:

- They last at least 30 minutes;

- The employee is relieved of all duty; and

- The employee is free to leave the premises.

You must provide a second meal period of at least 30 minutes for all workdays on which an employee works more than 10 hours. Refer to the Wage Order for your industry for any exceptions, especially if your employees work shifts between 10-12 hours long.

You must provide rest periods or "breaks" at the rate of 10 consecutive minutes for each four (or major portion thereof) hours worked. The breaks should occur as near as possible to the middle of the work period.

Rest breaks can't be combined with or added on to meal breaks, even at the employee's request, and employees can't use them to come in 10 minutes late or leave 10 minutes early. Since you pay for rest breaks as time worked, you control them. You may require employees to remain on the premises during the 10-minute rest period.

Make sure you comply with these rules, because you can end up paying the employee for any time not provided. See "What Happens if I Fail to Give Nonexempt Employees Meal and Rest Breaks?" on page 200. In addition, if employees miss any part of their meal break, start it later than 4:59 into their shift or miss it altogether (even if they do so voluntarily), you will owe the employee one hour of pay equal to one hour's wage no later than their next paycheck.

 Meal periods may go longer than a half-hour at the employer's discretion. However, any employer-scheduled break longer than one hour may raise issues of a split shift. See Table 43 on page 173.

How Do I Handle Time Spent Traveling, on Rest Breaks or Between Shifts?

At times, you need to pay a nonexempt employee for time not spent working. If you will pay a special rate for travel time or other special circumstances, you must establish and communicate the rate to employees in advance of the event. The amount and duration depends on what he/she does during that time.

Table 44. Types of Paid Non-Working Time

Type of time	Must be paid if	Amount/duration of pay	Included in overtime calculation?
On-duty meals	You require the employee to remain on the premises.	Hourly wage for the meal time.	Yes.
Time spent between split shifts	The time between shifts is more than one hour.	No less than minimum wage for at least one hour of time between shifts.	No, because the time wasn't actually spent working.
Reporting time Not paid for on-call employees or when disrupted by: • Threats to the employer's property; • Utility failure; and • Acts of God.	You require the employee to report to work at his/her normal work time, and: • Do not put him/her to work; or • Give him/her less than half the hours he/she was scheduled to work.	Hourly wage for at least half of the employee's scheduled hours, which must be paid for no less than two hours, and no more than four.	No.
	You require the employee to report to work a second time in any one workday and give him/her less than two hours of work.	Hourly wage for at least two hours.	Only the time actually worked.
Call-in	You call the employee in on a day other than normal.	For employees not regularly scheduled to work, employee must be paid at least one-half of his/her usual/scheduled workday.	Only the time actually worked.

Table 44. Types of Paid Non-Working Time *(continued)*

Type of time	Must be paid if	Amount/duration of pay	Included in overtime calculation?
On call (standby)	The time spent on call can't be used for the employee's benefit. You must also pay for: • Time spent on call-backs; and • Time spent traveling from the point summoned to the work-site and the return trip.	Applicable rate (straight time or overtime).	Yes.
Travel time — general	The employee reports to the regular site and then has to go to another site.	At least minimum wage, for the time between sites	Yes, see "How Do I Calculate Overtime for Nonexempt Employees?" on page 184.
	The employee has to work at another site.	At least minimum wage, for the time in excess of the employee's normal commute.	
	The employee must travel to a distant place, like another city.	At least minimum wage, for the time spent in transit from home/office to the first destination (for example, to the hotel).	
Travel time — mandatory mode of transportation	You require your employees to travel to the worksite on employer-provided transportation.	At least minimum wage for duration of travel.	Yes.
Uniform changing and washing up	You require the employee to do so at work.	Applicable rate (straight time or overtime).	Yes.
Employee meetings	You require attendance.	At least minimum wage	Yes.
Employer-sponsored: • Training; • Lectures; and • Work courses.	You require attendance or if the training relates to the employee's regular job.	At least minimum wage.	Yes.

Table 44. Types of Paid Non-Working Time *(continued)*

Type of time	Must be paid if	Amount/duration of pay	Included in overtime calculation?
Time spent on physical fitness maintenance	You require remedial fitness training for the employee's regular job.	At least minimum wage.	Yes.
Additional wage owed due to missed meal or rest break	One additional hour of wages owed if employees miss any part of their unpaid meal break, or the break starts later than 4:59 into the shift. One additional hour of wages owed if the employer restricts employees' ability to take the 10-minute, paid rest break.	Amount is equal to employee's hourly rate of pay, up to a maximum of two hours a day (one for any missed meal breaks and one for any rest breaks the employee was not allowed to take.)	No.

How Can I Use Makeup Time?

You can choose to offer makeup time to your nonexempt employees if they want to request time off for a personal obligation and make up the time without receiving overtime pay. The law doesn't require you to offer this option, but if you offer it, you must abide by these rules:

- You can't ask or encourage employees to use makeup time;

- The time must be made up within the same workweek;

- The employee is limited to 11 hours per day and 40 hours per week when working makeup time; and

- Before taking off or making up the time, the employee must provide you with a signed, written request for each occasion that makeup time is desired, unless the time off is for a recurring event, such as a college course.

Make sure to have a time-recording system that shows which hours you will pay at an overtime rate and which hours you will pay at a normal rate as makeup time.

Don't confuse makeup time with compensatory time off (CTO), which is illegal for private employers. For more on CTO, see "What Do I Need to Know About CTO?" in Chapter 4, page 147. The sample *Makeup Time Checklist* and *Makeup Time Request* forms are described in Table 54 on page 203.

What Do I Pay My Workers?

What you pay your worker depends on what type of worker he/she is (see "How Do I Know Which Type of Worker to Hire?" in Chapter 2, page 9) and what type of earnings you designate for the job (Table 45). California law creates minimum wage and overtime requirements for nonexempt employees and minimum salary requirements for exempt employees that you must meet. See "What Is the Minimum Wage?" on page 181 and "What Is the Minimum Salary?" on page 180.

For nonexempt employees, Wage Orders govern pay by industry. Get to know the Wage Order for your industry. You can find this information at ***www.calbizcentral.com/HRC/LawLibrary/Posters/Pages/iwcwageorders.aspx.*** As long as you comply with these regulations, you can choose from a variety of compensation scenarios.

Table 45. Types of Earnings

What kind	What it means
Salary (exempt)	Employees paid on a salary receive a fixed amount for each payroll period, whether weekly, bi-weekly, semi-monthly or monthly.
Hourly (nonexempt)	Workers paid an hourly rate receive a fixed amount for each hour they work.
Piece rate (nonexempt)	A piece rate is based on a figure paid for completing a particular task or making a particular piece of goods. Compensation must add up to at least minimum wage for all hours worked. Piece-rate employees are entitled to overtime wages. To determine the regular rate of pay, divide total earnings by total hours (even if more than 40 hours).
Flat rate (nonexempt)	Employee pay is based on the job completed, not the number of hours spent completing it. (Basically, a flat rate is a piece rate where there is only one piece.) Auto mechanics often receive flat-rate pay. Compensation must add up to at least minimum wage for all hours worked. Flat rate employees are entitled to overtime wages. To determine the regular rate of pay, divide total earnings by total hours (even if more than 40 hours).
Meals and lodging (nonexempt)	Employer-provided food and lodging counts as wages and can help you meet minimum wage requirements. Meals must be varied and nutritious, and lodging must meet sanitary standards. Employees can't be required to share beds. Meals or lodging can't be credited against the minimum wage without a voluntary written agreement between the employer and the employee.

Table 45. Types of Earnings

What kind	What it means
Tips and gratuities	Any money left by patrons for an employee is for employees only. You can't count tips against minimum wage requirements. If tips get paid by credit card, payment can be delayed only until the next payday.
Commissions	Compensation based on a proportional amount of sales of the employer's property or services. Employees' main task must be selling a product or service, not making the product or rendering the service. NEW 2010 — When a compensation package includes commission payments, employers should create a written agreement, specifying when commissions are earned, paid out and how the employee's termination impacts the commission payment.[*] This amount is part of the worker's regular rate of pay, used to calculate overtime. Divide total earnings by total hours (even if more than 40 hours).
Bonuses	A bonus is money promised to an employee in addition to the salary or hourly rate usually due as compensation. Bonuses must be included in an employee's regular rate of pay for purposes of determining overtime rates. Divide total earnings by total hours (even if more than 40 hours).

[*] *Nein v. HostPro, Inc.*, 174 Cal. App. 4th 833 (2009)

What Is the Minimum Salary?

To be considered exempt, employees must perform job duties defined as exempt in California and federal law and be paid the minimum salary, which is $2,733.33 per month. This amount is arrived at by multiplying the state minimum wage of $8.00 by 2,080 hours, multiplying by two and dividing by 12 months:

$$\$8.00 \times 2,080 = \$16,640 \times 2 = \$33,280/12 = \$2,733.33$$

Salary is limited to cash wages. It may not include payments "in kind," such as the value of meals and lodging.

Exempt Computer Professionals

Exempt computer professionals may be paid on a salaried basis, either monthly or annually. This new law allows for salaried pay without having to break down the payment by hour. These rates usually change annually, based on the California Consumer Price Index for Urban Wage Earners and Clerical Workers. Because there was no increase in the index for 2009, the minimum rates will remain the same for 2010. The minimum hourly wage is $37.94; the minimum monthly salary to meet the exemption is $6,587.50; and the minimum annual salary to meet the exemption is $79,050. Computer professionals must meet separate exemption requirements regarding their job duties (see *Exempt Analysis Worksheet – Computer Professional Exemption* in Table 8 in Chapter 2, page 40).

Computer professionals who meet the job duties and minimum wage requirements are exempt from overtime pursuant to Labor Code sec. 515.5; they must still take mandatory meal and rest breaks. For more information see, "What Meal and Rest Break Requirements Must I Comply With?" on page 174.

Licensed Physicians and Surgeons

A licensed physician or surgeon primarily engaged in performing duties that require a license is exempt from overtime if paid $69.13 or more per hour. This exemption doesn't apply to employees in medical internships or resident programs, physician employees covered by collective bargaining agreements or veterinarians.

What Is the Minimum Wage?

California's minimum wage is $8.00 an hour. Even though the federal minimum wage is lower, you must pay at least the state minimum wage. Not paying the minimum wage can get you in trouble. For more information, see "What Happens If I Fail to Pay the Minimum Wage?" on page 198.

You may be required to pay more than the minimum wage in some cities and counties because of local living wage ordinances. You can use information in Table 55 on page 208 to check if a living wage ordinance applies to your city or community.

A **living wage** is a wage sufficient to provide the necessities and comforts essential to an acceptable standard of living.

Can I Ever Pay Less Than Minimum Wage?

The IWC, which creates and monitors the Wage Orders in California, and the federal FLSA, which is the governing law for most wages and hours issues, both contain provisions for paying less than the minimum wage under certain circumstances. For more information about the IWC and the FLSA, see "Glossary of Terms, Laws and Agencies" on page 305.

> **TIP** **Indentured apprentices** are workers committed to a particular company for a specified period of time to learn a trade.

Table 46. Exceptions to the Minimum Wage Requirements

Type of employee	Conditions
Learners	Employee must have no previous experience.
Indentured apprentices	Applies only to the first 90 days of work.
	Must be indentured under the state Division of Apprenticeship Standards.
"Opportunity wage" earners	Applies only to persons under 20 years of age during the first 90 days of work.
People with certain disabilities	Employee productivity must be affected.
	Requires a license from the state Labor Commissioner to pay less than minimum wage.
Your parent, spouse or child	No minimum wage laws apply.
Outside sales staff	Must spend more than one-half of work time away from the employer's place of business.
	No minimum wage laws apply.
	For more information, see *Exempt Analysis Worksheet – Salesperson Exemption*, described in Table 8 in Chapter 2, page 40.

Must I Reimburse My Employees for Their Expenses?

You must reimburse all employees (exempt and nonexempt) for all the expenses they incur in performing their duties, such as mileage, travel and dining expenses.

The mileage reimbursement rate considered most reasonable in California is set by the IRS. At the time of this book's publication, the 2010 rate has not been set by the IRS. However, the 2009 rate was 55.0 cents per mile. Readers will find the updated rate, as soon as it becomes available, at *www.calchamber.typepad.com/hrwatchdog*.

What Is Overtime and How Does It Affect Me?

When your nonexempt employees work beyond a "normal" number of hours, you must compensate them at a higher rate. In most cases this means you pay overtime to a nonexempt employee who works more than eight hours a day or 40 hours in a week. Failing to pay overtime can get you into trouble. For more information, see "What Happens if I Fail to Pay Overtime?" on page 199.

Remember — exempt employees do not receive overtime pay.

Employees with an alternative workweek schedule earn overtime differently (see "Alternative Workweek" in Table 43 on page 173).

Sometimes a collective bargaining agreement can affect overtime rules, so check yours if you have one.

In California, nonexempt employees must be paid overtime at the following rates:

Table 47. Overtime Rates

For these types of hours	Pay the employee's regular rate of pay, multiplied by this factor
Hours beyond eight in a workday	1.5 (time-and-one-half)
Hours beyond 12 in a workday	2.0 (double-time)
Up to eight hours on the seventh consecutive day of the workweek	1.5 (time-and-one-half)

Table 47. Overtime Rates *(continued)*

For these types of hours	Pay the employee's regular rate of pay, multiplied by this factor
Hours beyond eight on the seventh consecutive day of the workweek	2.0 (double-time)
Hours beyond 40 straight-time hours in a work-week	1.5 (time-and-one-half)

How Do I Calculate Overtime for Nonexempt Employees?

1. Determine the employee's regular rate of pay:

- For hourly workers, total the amount earned for each hour worked plus any bonuses and commissions, and divide that by the total number of actual hours worked; and

- For piece workers, total the amount earned for units produced and divide that by the total number of actual hours worked, even if it's more than 40.

TIP The **regular rate of pay** equals an employee's actual earnings, which may include an hourly rate, commission, bonuses, piece work and the value of meals and lodging. See Table 45 on page 179 for examples of different types of compensation.

Though you need to include bonuses and commissions in the regular rate of pay, you don't need to include:

- Hours paid but not worked (vacation, reporting time, etc.) (see "How Do I Handle Time Spent Traveling, on Rest Breaks or Between Shifts?" on page 176);

- Reimbursement of expenses (see "Must I Reimburse My Employees for Their Expenses?" on page 183);

- Gifts or discretionary bonuses (in recognition of services performed during a given period); and

- Benefits payments (profit sharing plan, health care plan, etc.).

 See "How Do I Calculate Overtime for Nonexempt Employees with More Than One Rate of Pay?" on page 185 for a sample calculation.

2. Determine how many straight-time hours the employee worked for that workweek. For information on defining your workweek, see "How Do I Set Up Work Schedules?" on page 170.

TIP **Straight-time hours** are hours that the employees would usually work (the first eight hours of their workday.)

Only hours worked at straight time apply to the weekly 40-hour limit. (This prevents "pyramiding" of overtime, where an employee earns overtime on top of overtime already paid.) Once an employee has been paid overtime for hours over eight in a day, those overtime hours do not count toward the weekly 40-hour limit.

Example: Assume the workweek is Monday through Sunday. An employee works 10 hours each day Monday through Thursday, and therefore is owed eight hours of straight time and two hours of overtime for each of those days. When that employee comes in on Friday morning, although he/she actually has worked 40 hours already in the workweek, he/she has worked only 32 hours of straight time and does not begin earning weekly overtime until after he/she works eight more hours.

The employee works 10 hours on Friday. So far, the employee earned straight time hours for the 8 hours worked on each of the five days, and earned overtime at the rate of time and a half for two hours on each of the five days. If the employee works on Saturday, those hours will exceed 40 straight time hours in the workweek and the employee will be entitled to overtime for up to 12 hours of work on Saturday.

3. For any overtime hours, pay the appropriate rate listed in Table 48 on page 186.

How Do I Calculate Overtime for Nonexempt Employees with More Than One Rate of Pay?

Different rates may be paid for different jobs, so long as the work involved is objectively different. For example, travel time pay may be paid at a lower rate than the employee's regular rate of pay, as long as it is at least the minimum wage. Accurate record keeping is imperative in such scenarios. Especially with travel time, employers should communicate with nonexempt employees regarding these obligations.

In this case, there's a difference between the hourly rate and the regular rate of pay when an employee works overtime and earns:

- Time-and-one-half: you must pay him/her the hourly rate for the job he/she does, plus one-half of the regular rate of pay; or

- Double-time: you must pay him/her two times the regular rate of pay.

When employees travel to a different time zone, be sure to ask them track all hours based on California time — it will make the math much easier and your payroll people will sincerely appreciate it. Consistent communication by e-mail or phone can also cut down on later disputes regarding hours actually worked.

If your employee works an alternative workweek, you must use different calculations. See "What Scheduling Options can I Choose From?" on page 172.

Table 48. Regular Rate of Pay for Multiple Hourly Rates

An employee normally earns $10 per hour working at trade shows for his/her employer and $8.00 per hour for travel time. In one week, the employee works 40 hours at the trade show and spends 10 hours traveling.	
Total rate 1	$10/hour x 40 hours = $400
Total rate 2	$8.00/hour x 10 hours = $80
Total weekly wages before overtime premiums	$400 + $80 = $480
Regular rate of pay	$480 divided by 50 hours = $9.60
Overtime premium for time-and-one-half	$9.60 divided by 2 = $4.80

For more than two rates, multiply the additional rates by the number of hours worked at those rates and include them in the total weekly compensation; and

If the employee earned commissions or bonuses in addition to his/her hourly rates, include those amounts in the total weekly compensation.

How Do I Calculate a Final Paycheck?

When you're ready to prepare a final paycheck, gather all timecards and documentation regarding the employee's unpaid work period or outstanding advances or expenses. Calculate the paycheck through the final day of work, based on the employee's:

- Regular rate of pay (see "What Do I Pay My Workers?" on page 179);

- Hours worked;

- Earned bonuses or commissions; and

- Accrued vacation.

 If you can't determine commission wages owed at the time of termination, you must pay the commission owed as soon as the amount is determined — follow your policy regarding the payout of commissions, even after employees leave your employment.

You can use the *Final Paycheck Worksheet*, described in Table 54 on page 203 to help you.

After determining the amount due to the employee, make proper calculations for any deductions, following the guidelines in "What Deductions Must I Make?" on page 187.

 You can't make deductions from an employee's final paycheck if the employee doesn't return property to you. You face fines if you do so.

To document that the last paycheck deadline was met as required (see Table 52 on page 193), ask employees to sign an acknowledgement that they received the final paycheck. Use this opportunity to verify that the employee received proper payment. You can use the *Final Paycheck Acknowledgment*, described in Table 54 on page 203.

What Deductions Must I Make?

You must make certain deductions from the total compensation of both exempt and nonexempt employees. You must take out taxes and wage garnishments, if any. Special rules apply to deductions for salaried employees.

Deductions for Federal and State Government

You must make certain tax deductions from employee paychecks.

Table 49. Standard Deductions — Taxes

Tax	Deductions
Federal income tax	Use the employee's *W-4 Form – Employee's Withholding Allowance Certificate* (described in Table 8 in Chapter 2, page 40) and the withholding methods described in Publication 15 from the IRS. You can download Publication 15 at the IRS's Web site at ***www.irs.gov***.
State income tax	Use the employee's Form DE-4, State Withholding Allowance Certificate (described in Table 8 on page 40). For information about rates, forms, exemptions and withholdings, contact the EDD or visit its Web site at ***www.edd.ca.gov***.
	NEW 2010 Employees may want to change their withholding for state income tax because the state withholding on wages increased by 10 percent, effective Nov. 1, 2009.
Social Security (FICA) and medicare	Both you and your employee must pay Social Security and Medicare taxes.
	You must withhold and deposit the employee's withheld taxes and pay a matching amount at the following rates:
	• Social Security — 6.2 percent (wage base limit for 2010 is $106,800); and
	• Medicare — 1.45 percent (no wage base limit).
State Disability Insurance (SDI) tax and Paid Family Leave (PFL) tax	SDI provides temporary disability benefits for employees disabled by a non-work-related illness or injury. You must withhold monies from each paycheck.
	PFL provides temporary disability benefits for employees who can't work because of the need to care for a family member or bond with a child. You must withhold monies from each paycheck.
	The 2008 SDI withholding rate for 2008 is 0.8 percent, with a taxable wage limit of $86,698 per employee and an annual maximum withholding of $693.58.

Deductions for a Third Party

A public agency or court judgment may require you to withhold money from an employee's paycheck. This is a wage garnishment. Make these deductions after taking out taxes.

The Consumer Credit Protection Act prohibits you from terminating an employee for having his/her wages garnished.

Table 50. Wage Garnishments and Back Taxes

Child support/ alimony	Court orders for child support take precedence over all other garnishments. If the employee has multiple child support garnishments, current support takes priority over past due support.
	Regardless of the number of garnishments, you can't deduct more of the employee's disposable income than:
	• 50 percent if the employee has current spouse/child dependents; or
	• 60 percent if the employee has no dependents.
	An additional 5 percent may be garnished for support payments that are more than 12 weeks behind.
	California law imposes a penalty on an employer that helps an employee or contractor with child support obligations to evade meeting those obligations, including failure to file reports upon hiring.
	This law imposes liability upon any person or business entity that knowingly helps a child support obligor with an unpaid child support obligation to escape, evade or avoid current payment of those unpaid child support obligations. The penalty is three times the value of the assistance to have been provided, up to the total amount of the entire child support obligation due. The penalty will not apply if the unpaid obligation is satisfied. Prohibited actions, when an individual or entity knows or should have known of the child support obligation, include:
	• Hiring or employing a child support obligor without timely reporting to the EDD's New Employee Registry;
	• Retaining an independent contractor who is a child support obligor and failing to file a timely report of such engagement with the EDD; or
	• Paying wages or other forms of compensation, (including cash, barter or trade) not reported to the EDD.
Debt repayment	This includes loans, credit collections and other debts. These are secondary to child support garnishments.
	Regardless of the number of garnishments, you can't deduct more than 25 percent of the employee's disposable income.
Back taxes	The amount deducted depends on how many dependents the employee has. The more dependents, the less the IRS can deduct.

 You must notify the appropriate agency if an employee subject to wage garnishment leaves your company.

You must comply with garnishment orders as written until directed otherwise by the issuing agency or the court, stopping the withholdings only when ordered to do so. When you receive the court order:

- Mark the date received on the notice and retain the postmarked envelope in case you need to prove timely compliance;

- Keep a copy of the court order in the employee's personnel file as the legal basis for making the payroll deduction; and

- Advise the employee of the court order within 10 days of receiving the order, as well as the date you will make the first deduction. The first deduction must be made within 10 days of you receiving the order, unless the order specifies otherwise.

Employers can withhold $1.50 for each payment made, in compliance with an earnings withholding order that enforces payment of support obligations.

Deductions for Items That Benefit the Employee

You can make deductions from an employee's paycheck for certain items, such as meals, lodging or other facilities. These deductions are for the employee's benefit. You can consider it part of his/her wages and include it in your calculations to ensure that you're meeting minimum wage requirements if:

- The employee entered into a voluntary agreement; and

- The amounts credited do not exceed the limits specified in the applicable Wage Order.

As a result of updates to the DLSE's manual, consider the following before deducting from an employee's paycheck:

- If you loan money to employees, ask them to sign a promissory note guaranteeing repayment and get the repayment by personal check or other form of payment — never through a payroll deduction;

- Discuss automatic enrollment in your 401(k) or other retirement plan with your benefits provider. Not all providers follow the automatic enrollment process; and

- Review your policies and procedures regarding loans or advances, including advances on vacation and PTO, to ensure you aren't repaid by payroll deduction.

See Table 45 on page 179 for more information.

Deductions for Your Benefit

You can't deduct from wages for any cash shortages (for example, if a cashier's drawer doesn't match the record), breakage or loss of equipment. You can't make deductions for ordinary wear and tear to uniforms and equipment. You can't deduct the cost of a uniform from employees' wages.

You also can't require them to purchase the uniform on their own, unless it would be generally worn in an occupation — for example, a nurse's white uniform, or basic wardrobe items, such as white shirts, dark pants and black shoes and belts (of an unspecified design) for waitstaff.

If you require tools and equipment, you must furnish and maintain them, except for customary hand tools required of employees making at least twice the minimum wage.

Deductions "Paid" to the Employee

The employee can volunteer to have other monies deducted from his/her paycheck, such as:

- Charitable contributions;

- 401(k)/IRA contributions;

- Health insurance plans; and

- Union dues.

Some voluntary deductions can be taken out before taxes, thus reducing the employee's taxable income. For more information, visit **www.irs.gov.**

Deductions for Exempt Employees

Exempt employees receive a full week's salary for any week in which they perform any work, except in the following situations:

- If the employee is hired and begins work in the middle of the week;

- If the employee is terminated in the middle of the week; or

- If the employee's absence meets the criteria in Table 51 on page 192.

Deductions may be made from an exempt employee's accrued vacation or paid time off (PTO) bank for partial-day absences of four or more hours. Never make a partial day deduction from an exempt employee's salary. Different rules apply to partial day absences due to illness.

If you have a policy permitting partial day deductions from vested benefits, or you wish to implement a policy that complies with current case law, you should consult with your legal counsel before making such deductions.

Table 51. Deductions from an Exempt Employee's Salary

Type of pay	Can I deduct for:	
	Complete day of absence	**Partial day of absence**
Sick pay (bona fide sick leave plan) *		
Sick pay accrued	Yes, deduct from paid sick leave plan.	Yes, deduct only from accrued paid sick leave. You can never deduct from an exempt employee's salary for a partial day's absence.
No sick pay accrued or all sick pay used	Yes, you can deduct from salary for a full day if no work was performed.	No, you can never deduct from an exempt employee's salary for a partial day's absence.
Vacation pay		
Vacation pay accrued	Yes† You can't require employees to use vacation for a partial week's absence for convenience only (for example, for a plant shutdown).	No, you can't deduct from salary. but you may deduct from accrued vacation pay provided the absence is for four or more hours in a workday.
No vacation accrued or all vacation pay used	Yes, you may deduct from salary if the employee is absent for personal reasons and no accrued benefit or all accrued time has been used.	No, you can never deduct from an exempt employee's salary for a partial day's absence.
Paid time off (PTO)		
PTO accrued	Yes, you can deduct from the accrued PTO‡ You can't require employees to use vacation for a partial week's absence for convenience only (for example, for a plant shutdown).	You may deduct from accrued PTO pay if the absence is for four or more hours in a workday.

Table 51. Deductions from an Exempt Employee's Salary *(continued)*

Type of pay	Can I deduct for:	
	Complete day of absence	**Partial day of absence**
No PTO accrued or all PTO used	Yes, if for personal reasons; or No, if sick.	No, you can never deduct from an exempt employee's salary for a partial day's absence

* The sick pay plan must not give the employee a vested right to wages in lieu of sick pay or at termination.

† The Labor Commissioner recommends that you give reasonable notice, as far in advance as possible, to exempt employees before you require them to take paid time off or vacation during a business closure or plant shutdown, but generally no less than 90 days or a full fiscal quarter (whichever is greater).

‡ The Labor Commissioner recommends that you give reasonable notice, as far in advance as possible, to exempt employees before you require them to take paid time off or vacation during a business closure or plant shutdown, but generally no less than 90 days or a full fiscal quarter (whichever is greater).

When Do I Pay My Workers?

Not paying your workers in a timely manner can get you into trouble (see "What Happens if I Fail to Pay Wages Due an Employee?" on page 199). You must pay employees according to guidelines that apply to the type of payment.

Table 52. Payday Rules

Type of payment	Must be paid

Regular wages (nonexempt)	At least twice each calendar month on days designated in advance (see "How Do I Notify Employees About Paydays?" on page 195).
	
	• Twice-monthly (semi-monthly)
	  – For hours worked between the 1st and the 15th day of the month (no later than the 26th day of the same month)
	  – For hours worked between the 16th and the last day of the month (no later than the 10th day of next month)
	• Weekly or bi-weekly
	  – Within seven days of the end of the pay period

Regular wages (exempt)	At least once a month by the 26th day of the month for all wages, including those yet unearned for the month.

Table 52. Payday Rules *(continued)*

Type of payment	Must be paid
Overtime	No later than the next work period's payday.
Tips/gratuities paid by patron's credit card	No later than the next scheduled payday following the date the patron authorized the credit card payment.
Expense reimbursements	On any reasonable schedule. Expense reimbursements to terminated employees are not subject to final paycheck deadlines and can be paid at the same time as reimbursements to active employees.
Final paycheck: • Termination	Immediately. **You may not** require the employee to wait until the next regular payday. **You may not** withhold a final paycheck.
• Voluntary quit (less than 72 clock hours notice)	No later than 72 hours after the employee gives notice. If the employee requests to receive his/her final paycheck by mail and designates a mailing address, the date of mailing is considered the date of payment. Be sure to get this authorization in writing, along with the employee's statement of where the check should be mailed.
• Voluntary quit (more than 72 clock hours notice)	On the employee's last day of work.
Vehicle sales people commission wages	Once a month.
Farm labor contractor employees	At least once every week on a day designated in advance. Payment must include all wages earned up to and including the fourth day.
Temporary Service Employees	At least weekly. Daily if employee is assigned to a client on a day-to-day basis or to a client engaged in a trade dispute. Exception to these pay rules: employees assigned to a client for more than 90 consecutive calendar days unless the employer pays the employee weekly.

Under certain circumstances, you can make exceptions to the payday requirements.

Table 53. Exceptions to Payday Rules

Type of employee	May be paid	Under these circumstances
Agriculture workers	Once a month	If you lodge and board them
Domestics	Once a month	If you lodge and board them
Striking employees	Next regularly scheduled payday	When they come back to work

What if a Payday Falls on a Sunday or Holiday?

If your business is closed on a payday that falls on a Sunday or a legal holiday, you must pay wages no later than the next business day. Make sure you state your policy in your employee handbook. For more information, see "Payment of Wages" in Table 12 in Chapter 3, page 69.

What if My Employee Fails to Turn in a Time Card?

Even when a nonexempt employee fails to turn in a record of time worked, the law requires you to pay him/her on the established payday.

Since you have no time record to verify actual hours worked, pay all wages that would normally be due for the employee's work period and defer payment of overtime until the next pay period. If the payment results in an overpayment of wages, deducting the wages from the next payroll is not without risk. Consult legal counsel before taking such action.

 Exempt employees should not turn in time cards for pay purposes.

How Do I Notify Employees About Paydays?

You must post the day, time and place of the regular payday in a way that your employees can understand. As a convenience, the state provides a small form for this purpose, which CalBizCentral includes as part of the **Employment Notices Poster** (located in the **Required Notices Kit** available from **www.calbizcentral.com**).

If you change the payday schedule, notify your employees of the change at least one full payroll cycle in advance.

What Form Can a Paycheck Take?

All paychecks must be payable in cash, on demand and without discount, at a bank that does business in California. The bank's name and address must appear on the paycheck.

At the time the paycheck is issued, and for at least 30 days after, you must maintain sufficient funds in the payroll account, or credit, for payment. Paying any wage with a check that is backed by insufficient funds is unlawful. See "What Happens if I Issue a Paycheck that Is Returned for Insufficient Funds?" on page 202.

You can also use an electronic transfer system (direct deposit) to transfer wages to a bank, savings and loan or credit union if the employee chooses to do so. You may not force employees to use a direct deposit system. Even though the money is transferred electronically, you must still provide a written statement of wages and deductions to the employee. See "How Do I Record Deductions from Wages?" on page 197.

You may deposit final wages by direct deposit if the payment complies with existing laws concerning final payment and the employee authorized the payment via direct deposit. For more information on payday rules, see Table 52 on page 193.

Do I Need to Report any Payroll Information?

You must provide information to assist district attorneys with the enforcement of garnishments for child support. In an effort to collect child support, federal law requires all employers to report certain information on their newly hired employees to the EDD within 20 days of hire. All businesses and government entities that hire independent contractors must file similar reports. See "What if I Use Independent Contractors?" in Chapter 2, page 32 for more details.

What Sort of Records Must I Retain?

You must maintain an accurate record of employees' hours of work and compensation. The basic record keeping obligation includes the employee's:

- Name;
- Home address;
- Date of birth (if under 18 years of age);
- Occupation/job title; and

- Total wages and other compensation paid during each payroll period.

And for nonexempt employees:

- Clock time when each work period and off-duty meal period begins and ends;

- Total hours worked in each payroll period and applicable rates of pay; and

- Number of piece rate units earned, if applicable, and any piece rate paid.

How Do I Record Deductions from Wages?

You must keep an indelible record of payments and deductions for each employee for at least three years. The employee, upon reasonable request, can inspect and/or copy these records.

Indelible records are records that can't be erased or deleted.

At the time wages are paid, you must provide each employee an itemized statement, in writing, that contains the following information:

- Gross wages earned;

- All hourly rates in effect during the pay period and the corresponding number of hours worked at each hourly rate (nonexempt employees);

- Piece rate units and piece rate, if applicable;

- All deductions, including:

  - Taxes;

  - Disability insurance; and

  - Health and welfare payments.

- Net wages earned;

- Employer's name and address;

- Inclusive dates of the pay period;

- Employee's name; and

- Employee's Social Security number.

Permitted deductions authorized by the employee may be combined and shown as one item.

Only the last four digits of the employee's Social Security number, or an employee identification number, may appear on the itemized statement.

You must comply within 21 calendar days to a request by an employee or ex-employee to review or receive copies of the payments and deductions listed on page 197. You may charge the individual for the actual cost of reproducing the requested information.

The penalty (for actual damages) for failure to comply may be up to $4,000 plus costs and attorneys' fees for the employee. The Labor Commissioner may also impose a penalty of up to $750.

Labor Code 206.5 has been amended making null and void the execution of any release on account of wages due. Employers who violate this law are guilty of a misdemeanor. "Execution of a release" includes requiring an employee, as a condition of being paid, to execute a statement of the hours he or she worked during a pay period which the employer knows to be false.

Follow the law, keep accurate time records, don't force employees to work off the clock or miss meal and rest breaks, and pay employees on time.

For more information, see "What Happens if I Fail to Provide a Statement of Wage Deductions?" on page 201.

The Hitches, Glitches and Pitfalls of Paying Employees

Employee pay is serious business. You face steep penalties cheating your employees and government agencies out of money due to them.

What Happens If I Fail to Pay the Minimum Wage?

The California Labor Commissioner can:

- Assess fines
  - First offense — $100 per employee per pay period
  - Subsequent offenses — $250 per employee per pay period; and
- File charges with the district attorney.

TIP A **misdemeanor** is a criminal offense that's less serious than a felony.

If found guilty of a misdemeanor, you will have to:

- Pay the difference between the minimum wage and the wage paid during the period of violation; and

- Pay the court costs.

You may also have to:

- Pay a fine of $100 or more;

- Go to jail for 30 days; or

- Both.

 If you fail to pay an exempt employee the minimum salary, or misclassify an exempt employee who should be nonexempt, the employee's exempt status can change, and force you to pay for overtime worked and any missed meal and rest breaks.

What Happens if I Fail to Pay Overtime?

The California Labor Commissioner can assess civil penalties against you or any other person acting on your behalf.

- First offense — $50 fine per underpaid employee plus the amount of underpaid wages; and

- Subsequent offenses — $100 fine per underpaid employee plus the amount of underpaid wages.

The term "other person acting on behalf of the employer" means that payroll personnel, other employees who perform payroll functions (for example, human resources) and contracted payroll services could potentially be liable to pay fines out of their own pockets for miscalculating overtime under California law. However, the Labor Commissioner clarified that individual employees won't be fined unless they formulate policies that lead to nonpayment of required overtime.

What Happens if I Fail to Pay Wages Due an Employee?

This is a misdemeanor, and can bring about court cases and court costs. The Labor Commissioner can assess fines of up to $200 per employee per pay period plus 25 percent of the wages not paid to each employee each pay period. All awards made by the Labor Commissioner accrue interest on all due and unpaid wages.

When employees file complaints with the Labor Commissioner to recover unpaid wages, the Labor Commissioner will:

- Investigate these complaints;

- Hold hearings and take action to recover wages; and

- Assess penalties and make demands for compensation.

The Labor Commissioner will notify the parties whether a hearing will be held within 30 days after a complaint was filed.

In the event of a dispute over wages, you must pay, without condition, all of the undisputed wages. If you don't pay the disputed wages within 10 days after the dispute is resolved by the Labor Commissioner, you will have to pay triple the amount due to the employee.

If you must comply with the federal FLSA, employees may initiate claims with the United States Department of Labor (DOL). Employers should contact legal counsel if a DOL investigation commences.

For details about the FLSA and the DOL, see "Glossary of Terms, Laws and Agencies" on page 305.

What Happens if I Fail to Give Nonexempt Employees Meal and Rest Breaks?

For each workday you fail to provide an employee (or if the employee fails to take) a meal period, you must pay the employee one additional hour of pay at his/her regular rate.

For each workday you fail to provide an employee a rest period, you must pay the employee one additional hour of pay at his/her regular rate. Penalty pay for missed meal or rest breaks can raise your payroll costs by as much as 25 percent.

You are only liable for one hour of pay, even if the employee fails to take both rest periods. However, if the employee does not receive one or more meal breaks and one or more rest breaks, you owe two hours of pay at the regular rate of pay. Failure to pay the wages due may result in a civil penalties. For more information, see "What Happens if I Fail to Pay Wages Due an Employee?" on page 199.

A three-year statute of limitations, not one year, applies to the "one additional hour of pay" employers must pay employees when meal and/or rest breaks aren't provided.

The issue of whether employers must ensure that employees take the unpaid 30-minute meal break or simply provide the break is before the California Supreme Court as of the publication date of this book.[4] A concrete answer to this question will not be available until the status of that case is resolved.

Federal courts ruled that employers must only provide the breaks, as did two recent California Court of Appeals cases. Although the California DLSE updated its Policies and Enforcement manual to reflect the court of appeal holding that employers must only provide the meal break, CalChamber recommends enforcing your current policies ensuring nonexempt employees take their meal breaks.

What can go Wrong with an Alternative Workweek Schedule?

The Labor Commissioner can invalidate an alternative workweek schedule for a number of reasons, including improper implementation, improper payment of overtime and changing the schedule without the required procedure, among others. In addition, employees on public works and those in agricultural occupations under Wage Order 14 may not work alternative workweeks. Employees covered by collective bargaining agreements that pay premium rates for overtime hours and at least 30 percent more than the state minimum wage are not required to comply with the alternative workweek regulations.

What Happens if I Fail to Provide a Statement of Wage Deductions?

If you don't provide the paycheck information, the employee can recover:

- $50 per employee for the initial violation; and
- $100 per employee for subsequent violations, up to $4,000.

If you don't provide the statements in writing or fail to keep the records for three years, you must pay a civil penalty of:

- $250 per employee for the first violation; and
- $1,000 per employee for each subsequent violation.

If you make a clerical error or inadvertent mistake on the first violation, the Labor Commissioner has discretionary power not to penalize you.

---

4. *Brinker v. Superior Court* 165 Cal. App. 4th 25 (2008)

What Happens if I Issue a Paycheck that Is Returned for Insufficient Funds?

The penalty for issuing a nonsufficient (NSF) check is one day's pay for each day the wages remain unpaid, not to exceed 30 days of wages.

- The penalty applies to any wages paid with an nonsufficient funds instrument.

- If the NSF check is provided for payment of final wages owed, the employer would face penalties both for payment by NSF check and for late payment of final wages.

- The penalty provided for NSF is not applicable if the employee recovers the service charge authorized by law.

What Happens If I Don't Issue a Final Paycheck in a Timely Manner?

You are liable for a penalty of one day's wages for each day the check is late, up to a maximum of 30 days. Any penalty awarded by the Labor Commissioner is paid to the employee who was not paid on time.

Could I Be Liable for a Civil Claim?

Employees who believe they have not been paid correctly may file a wage claim with the state Labor Commissioner or pursue a civil claim. When a claim is filed with the Labor Commissioner and a decision rendered, either party can file an appeal to the trial court. If the party seeking the review is not successful, the court could award the non-appealing party monetary damages for court costs and attorneys' fees. The party that appealed would have to pay these costs.

An employee's claim is considered successful if he/she recovers a judgment in any amount greater than zero.

The Labor Code Private Attorneys General Act of 2004 permits employees to bring a civil action for labor code violations. Employees must comply with specific procedural and notice requirements before filing a civil suit. Employers have the opportunity to "cure" violations before the lawsuit proceeds.

The law includes civil penalties of:

- $100 per aggrieved employee per pay period for the initial violation; and

- $200 per aggrieved employee per pay period for subsequent violations.

Twenty-five percent of the penalties goes to the employee(s). If the employee prevails in the civil action, he/she is also entitled to an award of reasonable attorneys' fees and costs.

What Forms and Checklists Do I Use to Help Me Pay Employees?

The following table describes forms and checklists associated with paying employees.

 You can find these forms in your online formspack, described in detail in "Online Forms" on page 4.

Table 54. Forms and Checklists

Form name	What do I use it for?	When do I use it?	Who fills it out?	Where does it go?
Absence Request - English	Give this form to employees when requesting future time off or reporting previous time off. This form also gives your employees the opportunity to indicate a Family and Medical Leave absence, although it is not required.	When an employee requests time off or reports time off taken.	The employee.	In the employee's personnel file; and a copy should go to payroll.

Table 54. Forms and Checklists *(continued)*

Form name	What do I use it for?	When do I use it?	Who fills it out?	Where does it go?
Absence Request - Spanish	Give this form to employees when requesting future time off or reporting previous time off. This form also gives your employees the opportunity to indicate a Family and Medical Leave absence, although it is not required.	When an employee requests time off or reports time off taken.	The employee.	In the employee's personnel file; and a copy should go to payroll.
Final Paycheck Acknowledgment	Recommended for ALL types of separation.	When the final paycheck is issued to the employee.	The employee signs the form.	Keep it in your personnel records.
Final Paycheck Worksheet	Recommended for ALL types of separation.	When preparing the employee's final paycheck. (For more information about how to calculate an employee's final paycheck, see "How Do I Calculate a Final Paycheck?" on page 187.)	The employer.	Keep the worksheet in your personnel records.
Makeup Time Checklist	To help you figure out if, when and how to offer the time.	When you plan your pay policies.	The employer.	Keep the checklist in your own employee pay records.
Makeup Time Request	To document requests for the time.	When an employee requests the time.	The employee.	Keep it in the employee's personnel file.

Table 54. Forms and Checklists *(continued)*

Form name	What do I use it for?	When do I use it?	Who fills it out?	Where does it go?
Makeup Time Request - Spanish	To document requests for the time.	When an employee requests the time.	The employee.	Keep it in the employee's personnel file.
Meal and Rest Periods Policy	Use this policy to remind employees of legally required meal and rest breaks to ensure employees understand that your obligation to provide such breaks is met.	Not required by law, but should be part of your employee handbook or distributed to employees upon hire.	N/A	Employees keep their own copies. You should keep a copy as part of your employee handbook or personnel policies file.
Meal Break Waiver - English	Written documentation of a worker's waiver of the 30-minute meal break.	When a nonexempt employee works a shift of six hours or less; use this form when both you and the worker wish to waive the required 30-minute meal break.	You and the employee.	In the employee's file; a copy to payroll.
Meal Break Waiver - Spanish	Written documentation of a worker's waiver of the 30-minute meal break.	When a nonexempt employee works a shift of six hours or less; use this form when both you and the worker wish to waive the required 30-minute meal break.	You and the employee.	In the employee's file; a copy to payroll.

Table 54. Forms and Checklists *(continued)*

Form name	What do I use it for?	When do I use it?	Who fills it out?	Where does it go?
Meal Break - On Duty	Written documentation of an on-duty meal break.	When a nonexempt employee's work prevents him/her from being able to take a meal break; use this form when both you and the worker wish to have the worker work through the required 30-minute meal break. ❗ On-duty meal breaks are enforceable in very limited circumstances. Please consult with legal counsel before using this form.	You and the employee.	In the employee's file; a copy to payroll.
Meal Break Waiver - Second Meal	Written documentation of a second meal break waiver.	When a nonexempt employee's shift will be more than 10 hours but less than 12 hours, the worker has not waived his first meal break, and both you and the worker wish to waive the second required 30-minute meal break, use this form.	You and the employee.	In the employee's file; a copy to payroll.

Table 54. Forms and Checklists *(continued)*

Form name	What do I use it for?	When do I use it?	Who fills it out?	Where does it go?
Overtime Request - English	To document in writing employee requests to work overtime hours.	Provide these forms to supervisors, managers and employees and train all employees in using this form whenever overtime work is needed or performed.	You and the employee.	In the employee's file; a copy to payroll.
Overtime Request - Spanish	To document in writing employee requests to work overtime hours.	Provide these forms to supervisors, managers and employees and train all employees in using this form whenever overtime work is needed or performed.	You and the employee.	In the employee's file; a copy to payroll.

Where Do I Go for More Information?

CalBizCentral and federal and state government agencies offer a variety of resources to help you learn the ins and outs of wages and hours.

Table 55. Additional Resources

For information on	Check out these resources
General	From CalBizCentral: • The *2010 California Labor Law Digest*, the most comprehensive, California-specific resource to help employers comply with complex federal and state labor laws and regulations; • *2010 California Labor Law Administration*; • *2010 Employee Handbook Software*; • *www.hrcalifornia.com*; and • *www.calbizcentral.com*.
Child support wage garnishments	• State Department of Social Services, Office of Child Support 916-654-1532 at *www.childsup.ca.gov*; and • Franchise Tax Board at *www.ftb.ca.gov/aboutFTB/manuals/arm/cpm/*
Living wage	• Living Wage Resource Center at *www.livingwagecampaign.org*; and • Communities with Living Wage Ordinances at *www.epionline.org/lw_proposal.cfm?state=CA*

TIP CalBizCentral also provides many ongoing and comprehensive educational opportunities for small business owners, HR beginners and experienced HR professionals alike. These include online sexual harassment training, DVDs and special HR seminars. For more information, please visit our Web site at *www.calbizcentral.com*.

Paying Employees Frequently Asked Questions

What's the difference between "flexible scheduling" and "flex time"? In general, flexible scheduling allows an employer to vary the work schedule, and flex time allows an employee to work flexible hours. With flexible scheduling, the employer may have an employee start one day at 8:00 a.m. and another day at 9:00 a.m., or work on different days of the week to meet business demands.

Flex time allows employees to control when they report to work and, in some cases, the hours and days that they work. For example, an employer may allow employees to report to work any time between the hours of 8:00 a.m. and 9:00 a.m.

By allowing employees the ability to fluctuate hours of work, commute and child care issues can be lessened. In either case, daily and weekly overtime rules must be observed.

Flexible scheduling should not be confused with an alternative workweek, which requires a regular schedule of work and strict compliance with state requirements both in implementing the alternative workweek and when employees work during the alternative workweek.

If a nonexempt employee begins a meal break after working 5.5 hours, does that violate state laws on meal breaks? Yes. The meal break must begin not later than 4 hours and 59 minutes into the shift.

Can an employee make up time missed in one day by working extra time during another day without earning overtime pay for that extra time? Employers can choose to allow employees to request time off for a personal obligation on one day of the week, and then make up that time by working extra hours on another day or days in that workweek without incurring overtime pay for the make up time.

An employer who chooses to offer makeup time must comply with the following:

- An employee may work no more than 11 hours on another workday, and no more than 40 hours in a workweek, to make up the time off;

- The time must be made up within the same workweek;

- The employee must provide a signed, written request to the employer for each occasion that makeup time is desired. (There is an exception if an employee knows in advance that he or she will be requesting make up time for a personal obligation that will recur at a fixed time over a succession of weeks. In that case the employee may request to make up work time for up to four weeks in advance, but the makeup work must be performed in the same workweek that the work time was lost.); and

- Though an employer may inform an employee of the make up time option, the employer can't encourage or otherwise solicit an employee to request the employer's approval for make up time.

How do I know which IWC Wage Order applies to my business? An industry, business, or establishment generally is classified according to the main purpose of the business.

Distinctly separate units of multi-purpose companies may be classified separately by division or establishment if the units are different, operating for distinctly different business purposes and the operational management is organized separately at all levels.

Must I pay wages to employees who serve on jury duty? The law doesn't require you to pay wages to nonexempt employees who serve on jury duty, but exempt employees must be paid their full salary for any week in which they perform any work. This is just another reason it is so important to properly classify your employees.

Can an employee choose to waive his or her 10-minute rest break? No, rest breaks cannot be waived. The mandate for rest breaks appears in the Industrial Welfare Commission (IWC) orders. The orders don't provide for a waiver of the rest break similar to that authorized for meal periods.

Although a rest-break waiver is not available, some exceptions to the usual rest break provisions exist in IWC Order 16, covering on-site construction, drilling, logging and mining industries, and in IWC Order 5, covering specific residential care employees.

Chapter 6

Ensuring Workplace Safety

You must provide a safe working environment for all your workers. By keeping safety a top priority, this doesn't have to be difficult. Employees who can concentrate on their jobs without constant fear of work-related injury will be more productive and less inclined to complain to Cal/OSHA.

The law requires you to reasonably protect your employees from:

- Work-related illness and injuries; and
- Workplace violence.

In this chapter, you can find answers to questions about:

- Preventing injuries;
- Workplace violence;
- OSHA inspections;
- Ergonomics; and
- Much more.

Minimum Compliance Elements

1. Hang your **Employment Notices Poster** (available from **www.calbizcentral.com**), which includes mandatory postings and Cal/OSHA postings that all employees and applicants must be able to see, in a prominent place (such as a break room).

2. Create and follow an Injury and Illness Prevention Program (IIPP) (see "Injury and Illness Prevention Program" on page 213), and make sure your employees know about the workplace safety practices it covers (see "The Basics of Ensuring Workplace Safety" on page 212).

The Basics of Ensuring Workplace Safety

Every employer must follow the regulations created by OSHA and Cal/OSHA (see "Glossary of Terms, Laws and Agencies" on page 305) that set standards for workplace safety. The general standard that every company must comply with requires you to establish an overall plan, an Injury and Illness Prevention Program (IIPP), for keeping your workforce free from work-related injuries and illnesses. The individual standards require more detailed plans, such as the Emergency Action Plan, that describe how you will help your employees stay safe on the job.

Knowing which safety standards apply to your company and communicating them clearly to your employees is essential for avoiding inspections and, more importantly, preserving the welfare and safety of your workplace and employees.

You can get copies of the exact standards from the California Department of Occupational Safety and Health (DOSH). See "Where Do I Go for More Information?" on page 241.

How do I Know Which Standards Apply to Me?

The Cal/OSHA standards you must comply with vary on the size of your company and whether your company is deemed high- or low-hazard.

Five basic standards apply to just about every company:

- IIPP (see page 213);

- Emergency Action Plan (see page 215);

- Fire Prevention Plan (see page 216);

- Hazard Communication Program (HAZCOM) (see page 218); and

- Repetitive Motion Injuries (Ergonomics) (see page 219).

Even in cases where your company is exempt from complying with part or all of a standard, consider establishing a plan or program for handling potential situations, especially if the information can be added to your employee handbook or employee manual. See "The Basics of Developing Policies" in Chapter 3, page 58, for more information.

Injury and Illness Prevention Program

Every company in California must create an IIPP, which essentially contains a generalized plan for keeping the workforce free from work-related injuries and illnesses. For companies with more than 10 employees, the plan must be in writing.

The formspack that comes with this book contains an approved *Injury and Illness Prevention Program*. The following table provides information about developing an IIPP.

Table 56. IIPP

Question	Response
Do I need to comply with this standard?	Yes, every employer must have a program. You are exempt from the record keeping requirements if you: • Employ 10 or fewer staff; • Employ 20 or fewer staff and are in a designated low-hazard industry; or • Are a local government entity, seasonal employer or a licensed contractor. See "How do I Know if I Must Report an Incident?" on page 227 for more information about recrudescing requirements.
Do I have to create a written program?	Yes, if you employ more than 10 staff. You can use the *Injury and Illness Prevention Program*, described in Table 65 on page 234, to help you get started. Your plan must specify: • Management approval of the plan and the person(s) responsible for implementing it; • A company safety policy statement; • A system to identify workplace hazards; • A plan for periodic scheduled inspections; • A plan for investigating injuries; • A plan for safety training; • How you will communicate with employees about safety; and • The recrudescing and posting requirements and any exceptions to these.

Table 56. IIPP *(continued)*

Question	Response
Do I have to provide training?	Yes. Training is required when you: • Implement your IIPP; • Assign a new employee to a position; • Transfer an existing employee to a new position; and • Make changes to workplace conditions. Provide refresher training as necessary. You can use the *Individual Training Certificate, Individual Employee Training Documentation – Initial Safety Training,* and *Training Sign-in Sheet,* described in Table 65 on page 234, to document training sessions.
Do I have to provide PPE? **TIP** **PPE**, or Personal Protective Equipment, includes items such as gloves, masks and special clothing used to protect against hazardous, toxic or infectious materials.	Only if other standards, such as those governing chemical use or certain types of machinery, require you to supply equipment to protect your employees.
Do I have to perform inspections?	Yes. You can choose the frequency, depending on how hazardous your work environment is.
Do I have to record and/ or report anything?	Yes. Any injury that requires medical treatment beyond first aid and all occupational illnesses must be investigated, recorded and reported. You can use the *Accident, Injury and Illness Investigation Form,* described in Table 65 on page 234, to help you document the incident. For more information on knowing what to record and when, see "How Do I Report and Record Work-Related Injuries and Illnesses?" on page 226.

Emergency Action Plan

The Emergency Action Plan standard requires you to create and follow a plan for handling emergencies, including evacuating employees, providing emergency medical attention and reporting emergencies to employees and community agencies.

Table 57. Emergency Action Plan

Question	Response
Do I need to comply with this standard?	Yes, every employer must have a program. You are exempt from the recrudescing requirements if you: • Employ 10 or fewer staff; • Employ 20 or fewer staff and are in a designated low-hazard industry; and • Are a local government entity, seasonal employer or a licensed contractor. See "How Do I Report and Record Work-Related Injuries and Illnesses?" on page 226 for more information about recrudescing requirements.
Do I have to create a written program?	Yes. You can use the *Emergency Action Plan*, described in Table 65 on page 234, to help you document your program. Your plan must specify: • Person(s) responsible for implementing the plan or portions of the plan; • How to communicate emergencies to employees; • Fire and emergency evacuation policies; and • Personnel assigned to provide first aid and emergency medical attention.
Do I have to provide training?	Yes. Train employees when you establish or change your plan, and when you hire new employees. Conduct emergency training and drills periodically. You can use the *Individual Training Certificate, Individual Employee Training Documentation – Initial Safety Training, and Training Sign-in Sheet*, described in Table 65 on page 234, to document training sessions.
Do I have to provide PPE?	Yes. You must comply with blood-borne pathogens exposure regulations, exposure prevention requirements for any employee who provides emergency first aid and provide any other equipment employees need to handle emergencies. See "Where Do I Go for More Information?" on page 241 for links to helpful Web sites.

Table 57. Emergency Action Plan *(continued)*

Question	Response
Do I have to perform inspections?	No, but you should cover this as part of your periodic IIPP inspections.
Do I have to record and/ or report anything?	Not for the Emergency Action Plan, but recrudescing is required for your IIPP. Follow those requirements in case of an incident.

Fire Prevention Plan

The Fire Prevention Plan standard requires you to know what fire hazards your employees are exposed to and to create and follow a plan for handling fires. For companies with more than 10 employees, the plan must be in writing.

Table 58. Fire Prevention Plan

Question	Response
Do I need to comply with this standard?	Yes, every employer must have a plan.
Do I have to create a written program?	Yes, if you employ more than 10 staff. You can use the *Fire Prevention Plan,* described in Table 65 on page 234, to help you document your program. Your plan must specify: • Person(s) responsible for implementing the fire prevention program; • Known fire hazards in the area; • Your fire prevention practices; • What fire control measures you put in place (i.e. sprinkler systems); • The frequencies of inspection and maintenance of fire control devices; • Alarm systems; and • Special employee responsibilities.
Do I have to provide training?	Yes. Train employees on fire prevention and safe work practices, either as part of your IIPP training or as a separate fire prevention program. You can use the *Individual Training Certificate, Individual Employee Training Documentation – Initial Safety Training, and Training Sign-in Sheet,* described in Table 65 on page 234, to document training sessions.
Do I have to provide PPE?	No PPE is required, but standard fire protection equipment, such as fire extinguishers, sprinkler systems and alarms, is required.

Table 58. Fire Prevention Plan *(continued)*

Question	Response
Do I have to perform inspections?	Yes. Use the *Fire Prevention Checklist,* described in Table 65 on page 234, to help you determine what and when you should inspect.
Do I have to record and/or report anything?	Yes. Record employee training in fire prevention, and document periodic inspections and fire protection equipment maintenance.

Work Surfaces, Control Devices and Emergency Equipment

The Work Surfaces, Control Devices and Emergency Equipment standards cover employee-occupied areas and set minimum safety limits for lighting, flooring, housekeeping, entrances and exits.

Table 59. Work Surfaces, Control Devices and Emergency Equipment

Question	Response
Do I need to comply with this standard?	Yes, every employer must comply with the standards. Use the *Inspection Checklist for Work Spaces and Surfaces,* described in Table 65 on page 234, to help you comply.
Do I have to create a written program?	No. Include general information about potential hazards in your written IIPP.
Do I have to provide training?	Only if you use engineered controls, such as guard rails. Include the training as part of your IIPP training.
Do I have to provide PPE?	Not unless another standard also applies, such as working with chemicals, projectiles or machinery.
Do I have to perform inspections?	Not required. IIPP inspections cover most situations.
Do I have to record and/or report anything?	Yes. Record employee training and document any inspections.

HAZCOM

The Hazard Communication Program (HAZCOM) standard requires all employers to communicate workplace hazards to employees, particularly when employees handle, or may be exposed to, hazardous substances during normal work or foreseeable emergencies.

Table 60. HAZCOM

Question	Response
Do I need to comply with this standard?	Everyone must comply, except for in a few, limited situations. See "Where Do I Go for More Information?" on page 241 for a link to the federal Standard Industry Code (SIC) Web site.
Do I have to create a written program?	Yes. Use the *Hazard Communication Program* form, described in Table 65 on page 234, to help you document the program, and the *Hazard Communication Information Summary*, described in Table 65 on page 234, to inventory hazardous substances in the workplace. You are also required to obtain MSDSs from manufacturers for all labeled containers and items on your inventory of hazardous substances. These sheets must be those provided by suppliers. **TIP** **MSDSs** — Material Safety Data Sheets — information provided by the manufacturer of a product that describes the product's chemical properties, potential hazards and instruction on safe handling.
Do I have to provide training?	Yes. Train all new employees, and provide refresher training when you receive new information on hazards and standards. In addition, provide Proposition 65 warnings in the training. You can use the *Individual Training Certificate* and *Training Sign-in Sheet*, described in Table 65 on page 234, to document training sessions. **TIP** **Proposition 65** requires that employers with 10 or more employees warn any person prior to their exposure to a chemical known to California state government to cause cancer, birth defects or other reproductive harm.
Do I have to provide PPE?	Not unless another standard also applies, such as working with chemicals, projectiles or machinery.
Do I have to perform inspections?	Inspections are optional as long as you properly maintain all standard documents, such as MSDSs, labels and warnings.
Do I have to record and/ or report anything?	Yes. You must develop and maintain an inventory of all hazardous substances, and document employee training and compliance with the standard.

Repetitive Motion Injuries (Ergonomics)

The Repetitive Motion Injuries Standard, commonly referred to as the Ergonomics standard, requires employers to address workplace injuries due to repetitive motion. Repetitive motion hazards are work tasks that require repeated actions with the additional stress of improper ergonomics or work-station design.

> **TIP**
>
> **Ergonomics** is the scientific study of the relationship between people and their work environments.

Table 61. Ergonomics

Question	Response
Do I need to comply with this standard?	Technically, all employers must do what they can to prevent repetitive motion injuries (RMIs).
	The formal requirements of the standard only apply when:
	• More than one employee suffers an RMI;
	• The RMIs are musculoskeletal injuries diagnosed by a licensed physician;
	• The RMIs were predominantly caused by a repetitive job, process or operation;
	• The employees were performing a job, process or operation of identical work activity; and
	• The reports of the two RMIs occurred within 12 months of each other.
Do I have to create a written program?	No. But a written procedure can assist you in properly implementing the standard. You can use the *Hazard Prevention Data Sheet – Ergonomics Safety* form, described in Table 65 on page 234, as a guide. Your written program should describe:
	• How the standard applies and step-by-step instructions for compliance;
	• Any interim actions to prevent RMIs;
	• How to verify the diagnosis of an RMI;
	• How to conduct worksite evaluations; and
	• How to implement controls of RMI hazards.

Table 61. Ergonomics (continued)

Question	Response
Do I have to provide training?	Yes, you must provide initial training. But refresher training is not required. The standard itself specifies training program content and implementation. See the *Hazard Prevention Data Sheet – Ergonomics Safety* form, described in Table 65 on page 234, for an example of the required training elements.
Do I have to provide PPE?	Only as a supplement to engineering controls (workstation redesign, adjustable fixtures, etc.) and administrative controls (job rotation and work pacing).
Do I have to perform inspections?	You need to evaluate a representative number of jobs, processes or operations for proper ergonomic design and to determine if they involve certain motions, positions or other bodily movements hazardous to muscles and joints.
Do I have to record and/ or report anything?	You must keep records of all worksite evaluations conducted, control measures taken, training provided and Cal/OSHA *Log 300* reporting completed.

Heat Illness

Cal/OSHA's heat illness regulations mandate training for all outdoor workers and their supervisors. Training must be provided to all outdoor employees as follows, and employees must understand:

- The environmental and personal risk factors of heat illness, including high air temperature, high relative humidity, radiant heat from the sun and other sources, conductive heat sources such as the ground, air movement, workload severity and duration, and protective clothing and personal protective equipment worn by employees;

- The risk factors for heat illness unique to individuals, such as age, degree of acclimatization, health, water consumption, alcohol consumption, caffeine consumption and use of prescription medications that affect the body's water retention or other physiological responses to heat;

- The employer's procedures for complying with the requirements that adequate water, shade and first aid be provided;

- The importance of frequent consumption of small quantities of water, up to four cups per hour, when the work environment is hot and employees will likely sweat more than usual while working;

- The importance of temporarily adapting the body (acclimatization) to work in the heat through gradual initial exposure to it. Acclimatization peaks in most people occur within four to 14 days of regular work in the heat for at least two hours per day;

- The different types of heat illness and the common signs and symptoms of heat illness;

- The importance to employees of immediately reporting symptoms or signs of heat illness in themselves or in co-workers, to the employer directly or to the employee's supervisor;

- The employer's specific procedures for responding to symptoms of possible heat illness, including how emergency medical services will be provided should they become necessary;

- The employer's procedures for contacting emergency medical services and, if necessary, for transporting employees to a point where they can be reached by an emergency medical service provider; and

- The employer's procedures for ensuring that clear and precise directions to the work site can and will be provided as needed to emergency responders.

Heat Illness Training for Supervisors

Supervisors must receive additional training prior to managing outdoor workers. Supervisors must understand:

- The procedures to follow to implement the regulation requirements and the employer's procedures; and

- The specific steps to follow when an employee exhibits symptoms consistent with possible heat illness, including emergency response procedures.

TIP
CalBizCentral's *Heat Illness Prevention Kit* includes five "mini-books" with removable wallet cards, a prevention plan and one poster. Give your employees the tools necessary to stay healthy on the job. Use the poster, books and wallet cards as staff-training tools to avoid, identify and, if necessary, take action to treat employees' heat illness symptoms. Hang the poster in high traffic areas at your office or job location and be sure all outdoor worker have their own mini-book and carry a wallet card as a constant reference. To order, visit *www.calbizcentral.com*.

Do I Need to Consider any Other Standards?

Other specific Cal/OSHA standards may apply to your company, especially if you belong to a designated high-hazard industry. The following table will help you determine which standards may apply.

Table 62. Other Standards

If employees	This standard applies
May be exposed to an airborne contaminant.	Permissible Exposure Limits
Use or are exposed to a certain level or concentration of hazardous chemicals, such as lead, benzene, formaldehyde and other carcinogens.	Chemical Protection
Use any respirator, except for voluntary filtering dust masks.	Respiratory Protection
Are exposed to hazardous substances in a laboratory operation, except for test kits, and manufacturing and process simulations.	Exposure to Hazardous Substances in Laboratories
Are assigned to provide an emergency medical response, or may potentially be exposed to blood borne pathogens.	Blood Borne Pathogens
Must work in a facility that contains a confined space, such as a tunnel, underground storage tank or utility vault, that presents or contains a hazard.	Permit Required Confined Space Entry
May be exposed to hazardous machinery motion during normal operations or servicing.	Lockout/Tagout and Machinery Guarding
Operate a forklift or industrial truck, or if onsite materials are handled in volume.	Forklifts and Material Handling
Are exposed to noise averages over 85 dBA during a work shift.	Occupational Exposure to Noise
Are exposed to certain highly dangerous chemicals at or above the specified threshold quantities.	Process Safety Management (PSM) of Acutely Hazardous Materials (also known as the "Access Standard")
Work outdoors and/or are exposed to extreme heat and the possibility of heat illness.	Final regulations are available at *www.dir.ca.gov/ DOSH/HeatIllness- Info.html*.

For additional information on high-hazard industries, visit the Department of Industrial Relations (DIR) Model IIPP Web site at *www.dir.ca.gov/dosh/ dosh_publications/iiphihzemp.html*.

Why Do I Need to Create and Follow All These Plans?

If you don't create and follow these plans, Cal/OSHA can cite you for violating the applicable standard. In addition, documenting your plans for compliance can help you prove your intentions of complying if you receive a citation, which can help reduce the citation.

Sharing the information in these standards with your employees also helps you provide the knowledge they need to avoid or respond to potential dangers. For example, advise them on the best escape route in case of a fire, where you store the first aid kit, what health dangers they might be exposed to at work and how they can communicate their safety concerns to you.

How Do I Create a Written Program?

When you create a written program, either for your IIPP or for any other standard, base it on processes and policies you put in place for your company. The following table guides you through the process of developing a written program.

Table 63. Written Program

Research/ Prepare	1. Gather any existing documents you have that can help you fill in the information (such as a fire escape plan, local emergency contact information, MSDSs or workplace violence policies).
	2. Find out if your company is considered to belong to a high-hazard industry by the DIR. For general guidelines on high hazard employers, see the DIR's Model IIPP Web site at ***www.dir.ca.gov/dosh/ dosh_publications/IIphlhzemp.html***.
	3. Find out if Cal/OSHA considers your workplace to be at-risk for workplace violence. For workplace violence guidelines, visit the DIR's Workplace Security Web site at ***www.dir.ca.gov/dosh/dosh_publications/worksecurity.html***.
	4. Identify lacking or missing processes or policies, and what else you need to implement.
	5. Create two levels of information: general and detailed. The general information will go in your IIPP and your employee handbook. The detailed information will go in the appropriate document for each specific standard.

Table 63. Written Program *(continued)*

Compile	1. Use the *Injury and Illness Prevention Program*, described in Table 65 on page 234, to create your IIPP, and to figure out what information you need to supply. Keep in mind that your IIPP doesn't need to cover every detail; the IIPP is only an outline of your entire compliance plan. 2. Use the detailed information to complete the written programs for all other standards. 3. Consider adding text for standards that don't require written programs to your employee handbook or safety manual. For an example of a safety policy, see the sample *Employee Handbook* in your online formspack.
Maintain	The easiest way to help your company avoid violations, injuries and lawsuits is to keep your compliance information up-to-date and to communicate changes to your employees. See "How Should I Cover Safety Training?" on page 224 for more information.

How Should I Cover Safety Training?

Most Cal/OSHA standards require training, which is an effective way for you to keep employees informed of your policies and procedures. The regulations don't specify the type of training or the frequency. The following table shows you the essentials of developing a training program.

Table 64. Safety Training

Question	Response
What	1. Determine which standards require you to train your employees. You can also refer to the *Training Requirements* form, described in Table 65 on page 234, for information on training requirements for all Cal/OSHA standards. Keep in mind that even when a particular standard doesn't require training, the IIPP often does. 2. Compile all the subjects into a list to determine if you can combine subjects to cover multiple standards. You can use this list as a foundation for selecting your method of training.
Who	Designate an internal or external resource qualified to provide training, based on the requirements of the standard. Remember that you must also provide training to independent contractors.

Table 64. Safety Training *(continued)*

Question	Response
When	Provide the training: • To all new employees and existing employees who transfer to new positions; • After an incident or change of process (e.g., when you install new equipment or move to a new site); and • As an annual refresher.
How	The method you use to provide training is up to you, depending on how complex the training needs to be, the number of employees you need to train and your budget. Keep in mind that supervisors may need separate training. In addition, always document the training employees receive to show your compliance with the IIPP and that you take safety seriously.

How Do I Properly Provide PPE to My Employees?

Providing PPE (e.g., gloves, lead aprons, hard hats and keyboard wrist rests) for your employees, if required, helps prevent injuries and illnesses. Use the following guidelines to help you determine what your employees need to work safely.

1. Evaluate your workplace for the need for PPE; consider all the jobs, processes and operations (day-to-day and emergency) employees will perform. Some examples of evaluation questions might be:

   • Do your employees handle, or are they exposed to, chemicals or blood borne pathogens?

   • Do your employees perform tasks that require the same bodily motions to be repeated?

   • Do your employees work in areas with falling items, flying projectiles or heavy machinery?

   • Do your employees lift heavy or cumbersome objects, or work in areas that require forceful exertion to perform tasks?

2. Document the situations that require your employees to use PPE, and identify which PPE items you will supply.

You can't charge employees for the use and cost of PPE.

3. Provide and maintain PPE for all employees exposed to hazards.

4. Perform periodic inspections:

- Make sure the PPE is in good working order and is readily accessible; and

- Verify that employees use PPE properly and consistently.

How Do I Report and Record Work-Related Injuries and Illnesses?

Recording and reporting are two separate processes required by Cal/OSHA's *Log 300* regulation, though you don't always have to do both.

The *Log 300* regulation requires employers to record and report work-related fatalities, injuries and illnesses.

- **Reporting** includes notifying Cal/OSHA of a serious work-related injury or death. See "What Qualifies As a "Serious" Injury?" on page 226 for more information. All employers must report fatal or serious incidents within eight hours of the incident or fatality. Report fatal or serious incidents to the Cal/OSHA district office nearest to your business. To find the nearest Cal/OSHA district office, go to ***www.dir.ca.gov/DOSH/DistrictOffices.htm***.

- **Recording** involves creating and maintaining records of work-related injuries, both to keep documents as references, and to prepare in case an inspection requires you to present your records. You are exempt from recording if you employ 10 or fewer staff or if your company is classified in a specific low hazard Standard Industry Code (SIC) category. SICs classify businesses by their primary activity, and get used for a variety of statistical purposes.

  To find out if you must record incidents using the *Log 300* forms, go to ***www.hrcalifornia.com/log300*** and click the Log 300 Exempt Wizard link.

What Qualifies As a "Serious" Injury?

A work-related incident that results in the:

- Death of an employee;

- Hospitalization of an employee for more than 24 hours for treatment other than observation; or

- Loss or serious disfigurement of any body part.

How do I Know if I Must Report an Incident?

You must submit incident reports in two situations:

- When an employee is seriously or fatally injured; or

- When you receive an annual survey form from the Bureau of Labor Statistics or a specific request from Cal/OSHA.

California law mandates a fine of $5,000 for employers who don't report a serious injury or death. Individual employees serving in supervisory, management or similar roles may be individually liable for up to one year in jail and/or a $15,000 fine. Corporations face fines up to $150,000.

How Long do I Need to Keep These Records?

You must save the *Log 300* forms for five years following the end of the calendar year the records cover.

During the storage period, you must update the *Log 300* forms to include newly discovered recordable injuries or illnesses and to show changes that occurred in the classification of previously recorded injuries and illnesses.

The *Log 300* forms are available to CalChamber members at **www.hrcalifornia.com/log300**.

Why Must I Perform Inspections?

Many benefits can come from performing your own inspections of your site and equipment, your employees' safety practices and safety documents:

- Internal inspections present the best defense against and preparation for inspections by outside agencies;

- Many OSHA standards require you to document periodic inspections for compliance;

- During an inspection, you may identify a potential hazard, find a broken safety guard or determine that your employees need refresher safety training; and

- Inspections keep you familiarized with your site, processes and operations so you can evaluate your workplace's efficiency and productivity.

What Should I Expect From the Cal/OSHA Inspection Process?

Cal/OSHA inspections follow a process governed by the Labor Code and the Cal/OSHA Policy and Procedure Manual:

1. **Surprise!** You receive no advance notice, except:

   - When apparent imminent danger requires prompt correction;

   - To ensure availability of essential personnel or access to the site, equipment or specific process; and

   - When the Cal/OSHA chief or his/her designee decides that giving advance notice would help achieve a thorough inspection.

2. **Opening conference**. The Cal/OSHA inspector presents credentials and provides the reason for the inspection to someone with the authority to consent to the inspection.

   You can ask for a postponement of the inspection but only for a good reason, such as:

   - All essential personnel are not available; or

   - The inspector's stated reason for the inspection or credentials lack credibility.

   The inspector can obtain a search warrant if you refuse the inspection.

3. **Document request.** The inspector usually requests the following documents to review:

   - Cal/OSHA *Log 300* forms for the current year and for the six previous years;

   - Your written IIPP;

   - Any written programs required by a standard that your business must follow;

   - Codes of safe practice at a construction site; and

   - A copy of any permit issued by Cal/OSHA.

4. **Walk-through**. The inspector conducts a walk-through of the premises subject to the inspection, accompanied by key personnel from your company.

   This can take the form of a wall-to-wall inspection or involve only the limited area defined by the inspector's represented reasons for the inspection (such as an employee complaint about the warehouse). It's good practice to restrict the inspector's access to the areas specifically designated for inspection.

During a wall-to-wall inspection, the inspector may stop to examine machinery, interview employees and observe working situations. Your personnel accompanying the inspector may be asked to explain an operation or answer questions.

5. **Exit and closing conferences.** When the inspection is over, the inspector:

- Summarizes the results of the inspection;

- Makes any pertinent observations;

- Discusses findings and conclusions; and

- Requests information, documents or further inspections.

If no citations get issued, this is considered an exit conference and nothing else follows. If the inspection results in a citation or another action (such as a Special Order), the exit conference is followed by a formal closing conference scheduled after the issuance of citations that comes approximately one month later.

The Hitches, Glitches and Pitfalls of Ensuring Workplace Safety

Safety in the workplace is a very serious topic. You face inspections, citations and compliance schedules. A limited appeals process does exist, but your best bet is simply to maintain a safe workplace.

When Does Cal/OSHA Perform Inspections?

The Cal/OSHA inspection program targets workplaces with a likelihood of health and safety hazards and/or violations of standards. Due to constitutional limitations on government searches and seizures, the agency must have reasonable cause to conduct an inspection. However, courts granted Cal/OSHA broad discretion in determining what is reasonable cause. Cal/OSHA inspects when:

- An employer reports a fatality or serious injury or illness;

- An employee complains;

- The issuance of a permit requires a follow-up inspection;

- The Cal/OSHA general administrative plan calls for inspections for a certain type of employer (the targeted group shifts periodically based on injury/illness statistics for that industrial classification); and

- An industry has been selected as part of the TICP.

TIP The **TICP**, or Targeted Inspection and Consultation Program, is a Cal/OSHA program that identifies certain high-hazard employers and requires them to pay a fee to fund a special inspection unit. Cal/OSHA also offers other consultation services to help businesses avoid investigations and costly fines. You can find more information on these programs at *www.dir.ca.gov/dosh/consultation.html.*

How Can I Prepare for an Inspection?

You should develop policies for handling an inspection, designate key personnel to participate, train them in procedures to follow and advise them on handling potential issues that may emerge as the inspection progresses. Your policy can be formal or informal but should cover the key phases of an inspection. See "What Should I Expect From the Cal/OSHA Inspection Process?" on page 228.

To find resources that can help you develop these procedures, check out "Where Do I Go for More Information?" on page 241.

What Happens If the Inspector Finds a Violation?

You could receive a citation with civil penalties based on the violation's severity, extent, likelihood and size of your business. These penalties include:

- Non-serious or minor violations, such as not hanging the required posting included on the *Employment Notices Poster* (available at *www.calbizcentral.com*)— up to $7,000 per violation;

    - Repeat or willful violations — from $5,000 to $70,000;

    - Serious violations — up to $25,000;

    - Failure to correct or abate a violation — up to $15,000 for each day the failure continues; and

    - Substantial if you fail to report a fatal or serious incident. See the note on page 227 for details.

- You could receive a Special Order to remedy any unsafe condition, device or other workplace hazard to employee safety and health not covered by any existing standard. In a sense, this creates a special standard for you;

- If the violation is a general or regulatory offense and doesn't immediately relate to employee safety and health, you may receive a Notice to Comply;

- You could receive an Information Memorandum to direct your attention to a workplace condition with the potential of becoming a hazard to the safety or health of employees;

- In situations where an unsafe workplace condition, covered by an existing standard, requires specific instruction, you may receive an Order to Take Special Action; and

- When any condition, equipment or practice poses an imminent hazard to employees that could cause death or serious physical harm immediately or before you can eliminate the hazard, Cal/OSHA issues an Order Prohibiting Use ("Yellow Tagging").

Whatever the result of your violation, you must:

- Post the citation, order or notice of violation in a place where employees working nearby can easily read it; and

- Correct the problem within a specified amount of time and notify Cal/OSHA of the correction.

Make sure to review the content of the citation or order for accuracy in terms of its statement of the violated standard's requirements, your observations of the inspection and your understanding of the inspector's findings. If you object to the citation and can produce enough evidence, you can appeal. See "What Can I Do If I Disagree with the Results of an Inspection or with a Citation?" on page 231 for more information.

What Can I Do If I Disagree with the Results of an Inspection or with a Citation?

You can appeal to the Occupational Safety and Health Appeals Board within 15 working days of receipt of a citation or order.

How Does the Appeals Process Work?

1. Because the time allotted to appeal is so short (15 days), you should start the decision-making process immediately upon receiving an order or citation.

   You should identify issues that you can appeal, and consider:

   - The size of the penalty, and the cost and time allowed for correction compared to appeal;

   - The potential for a repeat citation; and

   - Your likelihood of success, given the strength of your defenses.

2. Communicate your desire to appeal to the Board by hand delivery, mail, FAX or telephone.

   The Board provides you an appeal form and other information on the appeal process. If you return the form to the Board within 10 working days, the appeal is considered perfected.

   The appeal is in progress. The Board assignment of a docket may take up to six months. When docketed, the Board sends a copy of the form to you with a docket number and Board stamp affixed.

You must post a copy of the docketed appeal form at or near the site of the already posted citation. The posting must remain in place until the appeal hearing begins or you receive an order disposing of the appeal.

3. Since notification of docketing can be a lengthy process, begin preparing your defense for the hearing while the incident/inspection/facts are current and fresh.

   Hearings typically happen no more than six months from the docketing of the appeal. You can investigate Cal/OSHA's information by filing a discovery letter on the agency, with copies sent to the Board and any other interested party. You can subpoena witnesses or physical evidence.

   You can't communicate with the Board unless all parties to the appeal receive notification. You may serve a document on another party by personal delivery, first-class mail, overnight delivery or FAX. You can do this by a declaration, a written statement or by a letter of transmittal.

4. You can request an informal conference.

   This meeting between you, your representatives, Cal/OSHA's district manager and the inspector responsible for the citation allows you to discuss any evidence in an attempt to resolve any disputes and avoid the need for an appeal.

   District managers must hold the conference no more than 10 working days after issuing citations. If you already filed an appeal, the conference can occur any time up to the date of the hearing.

You must notify employees of the conference, its date and location, usually by posting this information near the already posted citation and a copy of the conference confirmation issued by Cal/OSHA.

At this stage, the district manager, based on new evidence or interpretation, can withdraw or amend citations, including the existence of the violations, proposed penalties and correction methods and schedules.

5. If you don't reach a settlement, you will make your defense in an official hearing before an Administrative Law Judge (ALJ).

At least 30 days prior to a hearing, the Board will send the parties a notice of hearing, advising them of the location, date and time. A hearing is postponed only if an emergency arises, or if a party or witness has a pre-existing scheduling conflict. If either party fails to appear at the hearing, the Board will send a notice of intent to dismiss. To reinstate the matter, the absent party must establish just cause within 10 days for the failure to appear.

 You must notify employees of the pending hearing, usually by posting this information near the already posted citation.

6. At the close of the hearing, all the proceedings are considered submitted for decision. Within 30 days, the ALJ summarizes the evidence received, makes findings and files a proposed decision along with his/her reasons for the decision.

The Board may confirm, adopt, modify or set aside the proposed decision. The Board then sends copies of the decision to each party. If no one files a petition for consideration, the decision is final and can't be reviewed by any court or agency.

7. Either party can take up to 30 days to file a petition for reconsideration. The petition must set forth, specifically and in full detail, every issue to be considered by the Board. Anything not raised in the petition is waived and can't be re-examined. If the Board does not act upon a petition within 45 days, it's considered denied.

Upon reconsideration, the Board can make another decision or let the original one stand. If no one requests a judicial review, the decision is final.

8. Any party that disagrees with a decision after reconsideration or the denial of a petition must apply to the Superior Court for a writ of mandate within 30 days of the Board's decision or denial.

What Forms and Checklists Do I Use for Ensuring Workplace Safety?

The following table describes forms and checklists associated with workplace safety.

 TIP You can find these forms in your online formspack, described in detail in "Online Forms" on page 4.

Table 65. Forms and Checklists

Form Name	What do I use it for?	When do I use it?	Who fills it out?	Where does it go?
Accident, Injury and Illness Investigation Form	To help you document information about a workplace incident that involves an accident, injury or both.	As soon as possible after an incident occurs.	The employer.	If you don't have to report the incident, keep the document for at least one year (longer if you are documenting compliance). If you must record the incident on the *Log 300* form, keep the document for five years.
Code for Safe Practices for Construction Workplaces	The sample code in this form was developed by the California Department of Occupational Safety and Health. It is a suggested code, general in nature and is intended as a basis for preparing a code that fits the specific contractor's operations more exactly.	Use this form to assist you in preparing a code of safe practices.	N/A	N/A

Table 65. Forms and Checklists *(continued)*

Form Name	What do I use it for?	When do I use it?	Who fills it out?	Where does it go?
Ergonomics Checklist - Computer and Keyboard Issues	As an inspection tool to help you identify potential ergonomic problems related to computers and keyboards.	Annually and as needed.	The employer.	N/A
Ergonomics Checklist - Hand Tool Use	As an inspection tool to help you identify potential ergonomic problems related to hand tool use.	Annually and as needed.	The employer.	N/A
Ergonomics Checklist - Manual Handling	As an inspection tool to help you identify potential ergonomic problems related to manual handling.	Annually and as needed.	The employer.	N/A
Ergonomics Checklist - Task-Work Methods	As an inspection tool to help you identify potential ergonomic problems related to task/work methods.	Annually and as needed.	The employer.	N/A
Ergonomics Checklist - Work-station Layout	As an inspection tool to help you identify potential ergonomic problems related to workstation layout.	Annually and as needed.	The employer.	N/A

Table 65. Forms and Checklists *(continued)*

Form Name	What do I use it for?	When do I use it?	Who fills it out?	Where does it go?
Emergency Action Plan	To help you create a written plan for handling emergency situations, and to satisfy Cal/OSHA compliance.	Before your business opens, or as soon after as possible.	The employer.	Make the information in your plan available to your employees through training and in your employee handbook or safety manual. Keep and maintain the document as long as the company operates.
Hazard Assessment and Correction Record	To document hazard identification and correction, and to assure compliance with applicable Cal/OSHA standards.	When an unsafe working condition is brought to your attention.	The employer.	In your files.
Hazard Prevention Data Sheet – Ergonomics Safety	To help you identify and prevent repetitive motion injuries, and to satisfy Cal/OSHA standard compliance.	Before your business opens, or as soon after as possible.	N/A; this form is for reference only.	Make the information in your plan available to your employees through training and in your employee handbook or safety manual. Keep and maintain the document as long as the company operates.

Table 65. Forms and Checklists *(continued)*

Form Name	What do I use it for?	When do I use it?	Who fills it out?	Where does it go?
Heat Illness Prevention Plan (Outdoor Employees)	To develop your company's plan and procedures for complying with Cal/OSHA regulations on heat illness prevention for outdoor workers.	Before your business opens, or as soon after as possible.	The employer.	Make the information in your plan available to your employees through training and in your employee handbook or safety manual. Keep and maintain the document as long as the company operates.
Fire Prevention Checklist	To determine which fire hazards are present in your workplace so you can create and maintain a written plan for preventing and handling workplace fires.	Before your business opens, or as soon after as possible.	The employer.	Use the checklist as an inspection tool. Keep and maintain the document as long as the company operates.
Fire Prevention Plan	To help you create a written plan for preventing and handling workplace fires and to satisfy Cal/OSHA standard compliance.	Before your business opens, or as soon after as possible.	The employer.	Make the information in your plan available to your employees through training and in your employee handbook or safety manual. Keep and maintain the document as long as the company operates.

Table 65. Forms and Checklists *(continued)*

Form Name	What do I use it for?	When do I use it?	Who fills it out?	Where does It go?
Hazard Communication Information Summary	To document the inventory of hazards in your workplace and to satisfy Cal/OSHA standard compliance.	Before your business opens, or as soon after as possible.	The employer.	Make the information in your plan available to your employees through training and in your employee handbook or safety manual. Keep and maintain the document as long as the company operates.
Hazard Communication Program	To document training provided to an employee and to satisfy Cal/OSHA standard compliance.	Before your business opens, or as soon after as possible.	The employer.	Make the information in your plan available to your employees through training and in your employee handbook or safety manual. Keep and maintain the document as long as the company operates.
Individual Employee Training Documentation – Initial Safety Training	To document the first training provided to an employee.	When you hire someone, reassign someone or identify a previously unknown hazard.	The employer.	Keep this document in the employee's personnel file. Provide a copy of this document to the employee if requested.

Table 65. Forms and Checklists *(continued)*

Form Name	What do I use it for?	When do I use it?	Who fills it out?	Where does it go?
Individual Training Certificate	To document training provided to an employee and to satisfy Cal/OSHA standard compliance.	When the employee successfully completes the training.	The employee does.	Keep the certificate in the employee's personnel file. Provide a copy of the certificate to the employee if requested.
Injury and Illness Prevention Program	To outline your plan for compliance with all OSHA standards, including a detailed plan for: • Handling emergency situations; • Preventing and handling workplace fires; • Addressing ergonomic issues; and • Documenting information about workplace hazards.	Before your business opens, or as soon after as possible.	The employer.	Make the information in your plan available to your employees through training and in your employee handbook or safety manual. Keep and maintain the document as long as the company operates.
Inspection Checklist for Work Spaces and Surfaces	To help you identify and prevent work space and surface hazards in your workplace and to satisfy Cal/OSHA standard compliance.	During periodic inspections, and after incidents or a change in process.	The employer.	Keep the checklist as a record of periodic inspections for five years after you fill it out.

Table 65. Forms and Checklists *(continued)*

Form Name	What do I use it for?	When do I use it?	Who fills it out?	Where does it go?
Safety Program Self Audit Checklist	To help ensure that your workplace safety program complies with state requirements and is well tailored to reducing risks and claims in your workplace.	Before your business opens, or as soon after as possible.	The employer.	Keep and maintain the document as long as the company operates.
Training Requirements	To determine which standards require you to provide safety training for your employees.	Use the form for reference when planning your safety training program.	No filling out needed.	Incorporate the information in the document into your training program.
Training Sign-in Sheet - English	To record and track employee attendance at training courses.	Before or after completing a training course.	You prepare the form and employees sign it.	Keep the documents as proof that an employee attended mandatory training for five years after the training.
Training Sign-In Sheet - Spanish	To record and track employee attendance at training courses.	Before or after completing a training course.	You prepare the form and employees sign it.	Keep the documents as proof that an employee attended mandatory training for five years after the training.
Worker Training and Instruction Record	To document and track all training provided to an employee.	Whenever an employee attends or completes training.	The employer.	Maintain in your training files and a copy in the employee's personnel file.

Where Do I Go for More Information?

CalBizCentral and federal and state government agencies offer a variety of resources to help you ensure safety in your workplace.

Table 66. Additional Resources

For information on	Check out these resources
General	From CalBizCentral: • *www.calbizcentral.com*; and • *www.hrcalifornia.com*.
Workers' compensation	From CalBizCentral: • *2010 California Labor Law Digest*.
State government	• California Department of Industrial Relations at *www.dir.ca.gov*; • California Division of Occupational Safety and Health at *www.dir.ca.gov/DOSH/dosh1.html*; • California's Occupational Safety and Health Standards Board at *www.dir.ca.gov/oshsb/oshsb.html*; • Model Injury and Illness Prevention Program for High Hazard Employers at *www.dir.ca.gov/dosh/dosh_publications/iiphihzemp.html*; • Cal/OSHA guidelines for Workplace Security at *www.dir.ca.gov/dosh/dosh_publications/worksecurity.html*; • User's Guide to Cal/OSHA at *www.dir.ca.gov/dosh/dosh_publications/osha_userguide.pdf*; and • For contact information for various Cal/OSHA offices, see the *Cal/OSHA Poster* (located in the *2010 Employment Notices Poster* and the *Required Notices Kit* associated with this product).
Federal government	OSHA's SIC manual at *www.osha.gov/oshstats/sicser.html*

TIP CalBizCentral also provides many ongoing and comprehensive educational opportunities for small business owners, HR beginners and experienced HR professionals alike. These include online sexual harassment training, DVDs and special HR seminars. For more information, please visit our Web site at *www.calbizcentral.com*.

Ensuring Workplace Safety Frequently Asked Questions

Do I need to create a written plan to address workplace violence? Depending on the risk factors in a particular workplace, an Injury and Illness Prevention Program (IIPP) may be required by law to address workplace violence. An assessment of the risk of workplace violence must include several relevant factors, such as the industry, location and workforce involved, and previous incidents of violence.

Employers with employees who are known to be at-risk for Type I events must address workplace security hazards to satisfy the regulatory requirement of establishing, implementing, and maintaining an effective IIPP. Type I events are those where the person committing the violent act has no legitimate relationship to the workplace and usually enters the workplace to commit a robbery or other criminal act.

Examples of employees at-risk of Type I events include taxicab drivers, clerks in liquor stores, convenience stores, grocery stores or gas stations who handle cash late at night, clerks in hotels or motels open late at night, jewelry store employees and security guards. An increasing number of workplace assaults involve an employee who provides a service to a client, patient, customer or passenger. Service employers whose employees are at-risk must also integrate an effective workplace security component into their IIPP.

What am I required to do with regard to ergonomics? California's ergonomics regulation, aimed at minimizing work-related repetitive motion injuries (RMIs), requires employers whose employees report RMIs to implement a program designed to minimize RMIs. The program must include performing worksite evaluations, controlling exposures causing RMIs and employee training. The employer must also evaluate for exposures that have caused the reported RMIs and correct them in a timely manner.

Once an employer is subject to the ergonomics regulation, all the employer's employees must be provided with ergonomics training.

Can you define 'reasonable suspicion' with respect to drug or alcohol testing based on reasonable suspicion? One court defined "reasonable suspicion" as something less than probable cause but more than mere suspicion. It's suspicion that requires further investigation and which has some factual foundation in the surrounding circumstances observed.

Specific objective facts and rational inferences drawn from those facts must justify reasonable suspicion. Evidence sufficient to justify reasonable suspicion may include alcohol on the breath, lapses in performance, inability to appropriately respond to questions and physical symptoms of alcohol or drug influence. Drug testing is a dynamic area of the law. Legal counsel should be consulted before instituting a drug testing policy or practice.

Chapter 7

Preventing Discrimination and Harassment

Discrimination and harassment can create trouble any workplace. With proper preparation, your workplace can remain healthy and you can reduce the likelihood of facing a lawsuit.

In this chapter, you can find answers to questions about:

- Sexual harassment;
- The Americans with Disabilities Act;
- California's Fair Employment and Housing Act;
- Protected classes; and
- Much more.

Minimum Compliance Elements

1. Hang your **Employment Notices Poster** (available from **www.calbizcentral.com**), which includes mandatory postings that all employees and applicants must be able to see, in a prominent place (such as a break room).

2. Pass out the mandatory **Sexual Harassment** pamphlets (located in the **Required Notices Kit** available from **www.calbizcentral.com**), forbidding unlawful harassment at your company.

3. Create and follow a written policy forbidding discrimination and harassment in your workplace, and enforce it consistently for all employees (see "Establish Policies" on page 257).

4. Take every discrimination or harassment complaint seriously — establish a complaint procedure, tell your employees about it and follow it faithfully if you learn of suspicious behavior (see "How Should I Handle a Discrimination/ Harassment Complaint?" on page 265).

5. Hold a mandatory training session so all your employees and managers can learn about discrimination and harassment (see "Provide Training" on page 259).

6. Accommodate employees with disabilities so they can work equally with their non-disabled colleagues (see "What Is Reasonable Accommodation?" on page 252).

The Basics of Preventing Discrimination and Harassment in the Workplace

One successful discrimination or harassment lawsuit could bankrupt your company. Courts awarded penalties in excess of one million dollars to employees subjected to harassment or discrimination. Even if a complaint never reaches the courts, discrimination and harassment claims can be very costly in terms of employee morale and diverted resources. You can begin to protect yourself by understanding discrimination and harassment, taking steps to avoid situations that would inspire claims and by knowing how to handle complaints when they do arise.

One court found that an employer's stated "zero tolerance" policy requiring investigation and documentation of every report of sexual harassment, posting anti-harassment posters in the workplace, requiring all employees to review training videos and consistent implementation of these requirements was sufficient to avoid liability.

What Is Discrimination?

Discrimination, legally speaking, covers only actions taken against people because of their membership, perceived membership or associated membership in certain protected classes. See "Characteristics/Activities Protected from Discrimination" on page 246.

Discrimination means treating those people differently, and disadvantageously, compared with other people not in the same class. Remember, everyone is part of a protected class; belongs to a race; has a marital status; is perceived as one gender or another; and associates with people in protected classes.

Discrimination can occur in two different ways:

- **Disparate (unequal) treatment** — when an employee or applicant is treated differently, specifically because of his/her protected class status; or

- **Disparate (unequal) impact** — an employment practice that appears neutral on its face but discriminates against protected classes in practice (for example, height and weight requirements may unequally impact women and minorities).

You commit a discriminatory employment practice if you, among other things:

- Base any employment decision regarding hiring, benefits, promotion or discipline in whole or in part on an individual's protected class status;

- Rely on stereotypes about the competence, appearance, health, interest or qualifications of individuals in protected classes;

- Engage in any employment practice that adversely impacts the hiring, training, classification, promotion or retention opportunities of individuals in a protected class;

- Engage in, or permit your employees to engage in, harassment of any member of any protected class;

- Act on the perception or assumption of a disability without evaluating the individual's fitness for the job;

- Retaliate against an employee, applicant or independent contractor for opposing sexual harassment or other unlawful discrimination, or for filing a complaint, testifying, assisting or participating in an investigation, proceeding or hearing, etc.;

- Refuse to honor an otherwise eligible employee's request for pregnancy disability leave or for leave under CFRA or FMLA (see "Glossary of Terms, Laws and Agencies" on page 305 for more details);

- Refuse to reasonably accommodate disabilities, religious requirements, etc.; and

- Inquire on a written job application (except in limited circumstances) whether a job applicant has ever been arrested.

Characteristics/Activities Protected from Discrimination

You may not discriminate against a person on the basis of:

Table 67. Protected Classes and Activities

Characteristic	Discrimination
Age	If you employ five or more staff, be careful how you treat those employees over the age of 40. Among other things, you may not: • Use age as a consideration for employment decisions, unless it is a bona fide occupational qualification (BFOQ); • Discriminate against someone who opposed, filed a charge against, testified or participated in an investigation of unlawful employment practice under the Age Discrimination in Employment Act (ADEA), (see "Glossary of Terms, Laws and Agencies" on page 305 for more information on the ADEA); • Place an employment notice or advertisement indicating a preference, limitation or specification based on age, unless it is a BFOQ; • Terminate employees based on salary if the terminations create a disproportionate impact on older workers; • Force an employee to retire because he/she reached a certain age; or • Discriminate on the basis of age with regard to the terms, conditions or privileges of employment; for example, denying an employee over 40 the educational opportunities that you give to younger employees.
AIDS/HIV+ status	These conditions are considered protected disabilities. If you employ five or more staff, you may not: • Use blood tests as a condition of employment or to determine insurability; or • Terminate, deny insurance coverage or refuse to hire individuals exposed to the AIDS virus. There may be limited exceptions in the medical field.

Table 67. Protected Classes and Activities *(continued)*

Characteristic	Discrimination
Disability	The federal ADA covers employers with 15 or more employees; California's FEHA covers employers with five or more employees. See "Glossary of Terms, Laws and Agencies" on page 305 for more information on these laws. You can't discriminate against a disabled person or someone you perceive to be disabled. In California, a **disability** is a physical or mental impairment that limits one or more of the major life activities. Disability discrimination is very complicated. See "How Is Disability Discrimination Special?" on page 251.
Domestic partner status	State law prohibits discrimination and/or harassment based on several protected classes, and registered domestic partner status is on that list. State law gives domestic partners the same rights as spouses. Conversely, you can't discriminate against someone based on marital status in favor of another person who is in a registered domestic partner relationship.
Gender	If you employ five or more staff, you can't discriminate or allow harassment on the basis of gender. Gender is defined as an employee's or applicant's actual sex or the employer's perception of the employee's/applicant's sex. This includes your perception of the employee's/applicant's identity, appearance or behavior, regardless of whether that identity, appearance or behavior is different from that traditionally associated with the employee's/applicant's sex at birth. The Lilly Ledbetter Fair Pay Act of 2009 expands the statute of limitations for federal claims of discrimination and unequal pay, expands retaliation protections and increases penalties for violations of equal pay requirements.
Genetic characteristics	This means any inherited characteristic or scientifically or medically identifiable gene or chromosome or combination or alteration thereof known to be a cause or increase the risk of a disease or disorder in a person or his/her offspring. You may not subject any person to a test for the presence of a genetic characteristic. NEW ~2010~ The EEOC poster was revised to reflect the Genetic Information Nondiscrimination Act (GINA) of 2008, which took effect November 21, 2009. More information will be available in HRCalifornia Extra when regulations relating to GINA become final.

Table 67. Protected Classes and Activities *(continued)*

Characteristic	Discrimination
Height/weight	You cannot establish height and weight standards unless you can show that such a restriction relates directly to, and is an essential function of, the job.
Language	You can't deny someone an employment opportunity because that person's accent makes him/her unable to communicate well in English, unless you can show that the ability to communicate effectively in English is necessary to the job. If you employ five or more staff, you can't enact an English-only policy unless the language restriction is justified by a business necessity and you notify your employees of the circumstances when the language restriction must be observed.
Lawful, off-duty conduct	If you employ even one person, you can't discriminate against applicants and employees for lawful conduct they engage in during nonworking hours away from the company premises, including: • Exercising free speech rights; • Engaging in political activity; • Reporting information to the government; • Moonlighting (working a second job for a different employer); and • Engaging in conduct you feel to be morally in conflict with your business.
Marital status	This is an individual's state of marriage, nonmarriage, divorce or dissolution, separation, widowhood, annulment or other marital status. If you employ even one person, you can't condition benefits or employment decisions upon whether the employee is considered a "principal wage earner" or "head of household." You also can't use job responsibilities, such as travel or customer entertainment, as justification for discrimination. You can't impose a "no employment of spouses" rule, but you can establish a policy that outlines how you situate spouses within the company. See "Employment of Relatives" in Table 12 in Chapter 3, page 69, for more details.

Table 67. Protected Classes and Activities *(continued)*

Characteristic	Discrimination
Medical condition	This includes any health impairment related to or associated with a diagnosis of cancer, or a record or history of cancer, as well as an individual's genetic characteristics. See "Genetic characteristics" in this table on page 247. If you employ even one employee, you can't: • Base employment decisions on an employee's or applicant's medical condition; or • Request any sort of medical examination until after you make an offer of employment.
National origin/ ancestry	The broad definition means the country the applicant or employee, or his/her ancestors, came from. If you employ even one person, you can't base employment decisions on an employee's or applicant's national origin.
Pregnancy	If you employ even one person, you can't discriminate in any way against an employee due to that employee's pregnancy or potential to become pregnant. The Pregnancy Discrimination Act's pregnancy discrimination protections are not retroactive before the effective date in1979.
Race/color	If you employ even one person, you can't base employment decisions on an employee's or applicant's race.
Religion	This is broadly defined to include all aspects of religious belief, observance and practice, including atheism and agnosticism. You must also accommodate the known religious creed (such as allowing the person time off for religious observance) of an applicant or employee unless you can demonstrate that such accommodation imposes undue hardship. Religious corporations and associations are generally exempt from laws governing this protected class.
Sex	If you employ even one person, you can't base employment decisions on an employee's or applicant's sex or gender. If you do more than $500,000 worth of business a year or if you are a school or educational institution, you can't pay men and women differing wages for the same work.

Table 67. Protected Classes and Activities *(continued)*

Characteristic	Discrimination
Sexual orientation	This is defined as heterosexuality, homosexuality and bisexuality. Employers of four or fewer employees and religious nonprofit organizations are exempt from laws that govern this protected class. Sexual orientation is protected from discrimination by recipients of state funds, and the definition of discrimination includes the perception that the victim is a member of a protected class. Sexual orientation is protected by law. Discrimination against any person in any program or activity conducted, operated or administered by the state or by any state agency, that the state funds directly or that receives any financial assistance from the state is prohibited. This includes unemployment insurance, disability insurance and workers' compensation. "Sex" and "sexual orientation" have the same meaning as under the FEHA. The definition of discrimination includes a perception that a person has any of these enumerated characteristics or that the person is associated with a person who has, or is perceived to have, any of these characteristics.
Union membership	Employees enjoy the right to organize and form unions, and you must bargain with unions.
Veteran status	You can't base employment decisions on an employee's or applicant's status as a veteran. Military personnel also enjoy limited protection from termination for a period of time after returning to work. See "Leave for Protected Activities" in Table 12 in Chapter 3, page 69.

Table 67. Protected Classes and Activities *(continued)*

Characteristic	Discrimination
Whistle-blowers	If you employ even one person, you can't: • Retaliate against an employee who discloses information to a government or law enforcement agency if your employee has reasonable cause to believe that the information discloses a violation of state or federal statute, or a violation of or noncompliance with a state or federal rule or regulation; • Retaliate against an employee who refuses to participate in an activity that would result in a violation of law; or • Retaliate against an employee if the employee's action occurred when he/she worked for a former employer. Fines for retaliation are up to $10,000 for each violation. The Attorney General of California is required to establish a whistle-blower hotline to receive calls from individuals with knowledge about possible violations of state or federal statutes. You must display a posting that details employees' rights and responsibilities under the whistle-blower laws and includes the telephone number of the whistle-blower hotline. The posting is included on the ***Employment Notices Poster*** (available from ***www.calbizcentral.com***).
Workers' compensation claim	If you employ even one person, you can't discharge, threaten or discriminate in any way against an employee because he/she received an award from, filed or even intends to file a workers' compensation claim.

How Is Disability Discrimination Special?

Disability discrimination law protects qualified individuals with disabilities from disparate treatment by employers. A qualified individual with a disability is a person who meets legitimate skill, experience, education or other requirements, and can perform the essential functions of the position with or without reasonable accommodation. An individual is not unqualified simply because he or she can't perform marginal or incidental job functions.

Disabilities come in all varieties. A person is considered disabled if he/she:

• Has a physical or mental impairment that limits one or more of the major life activities;

• Has a record of such an impairment;

• Is regarded as having such an impairment;

- Is regarded by the employer as having some condition that has no present disabling effect but may become a physical disability; or

- Has any health impairment that requires special education or related services.

TIP **Major life activities** include caring for oneself, sleeping, learning, walking, interacting with others, working, and other physical, mental and social activities.

California law creates a broader scope than federal law. The federal definition of disability requires that an individual be "substantially limited" in a major life activity. The California definition only requires the individual be "limited."

You can't ask questions that would be likely to lead to information about a disability unless the questions are job-related and consistent with business necessity. You can't request a medical examination until after you make an offer of employment.

Drug or alcohol abuse is not a disability. However, a person in successful recovery can be considered disabled.

A blanket prohibition on the re-employment of workers terminated for violating company drug/alcohol policy may violate the ADA. The ADA protects job applicants recovering from drug and alcohol dependencies. This protection extends to former employees terminated for alcohol or drug abuse. Consult your legal counsel before refusing to rehire someone you terminated for violating such a policy.

What Is Reasonable Accommodation?

A "reasonable accommodation" is any modification or adjustment in a job, an employment practice or the work environment that allows a qualified individual with a disability to enjoy an equal employment opportunity.

Examples of reasonable accommodations include:

- Modifying a work schedule;
- Providing an interpreter;
- Making facilities accessible; and
- Acquiring accessibility equipment.

The reasonable accommodation obligation is an ongoing duty, and may arise any time a person's disability or job changes. You must engage in a timely, good faith interactive process to determine and provide effective, reasonable accommodations. You should document this process.

When you don't know how to accommodate the disability, you can ask an employee for reasonable documentation about his/her disability, its functional limitations that require reasonable accommodation and how the disability might be accommodated.

Documentation of a disability:

- Describes:
  - The nature, severity and duration of the employee's impairment;
  - The activity or activities that the impairment limits; and
  - The extent to which the impairment limits the employee's ability to perform the activity or activities.
- Substantiates why the requested reasonable accommodation is needed.

What Should I Know About Essential Functions?

You don't have to alter the essential functions of a job — that's not considered a reasonable accommodation.

> **TIP** **Essential functions** are fundamental job duties of the position or the reason the job exists.

You need to establish the essential functions of a job to determine whether an individual with a disability is able to perform the job with or without reasonable accommodation, and as a defense against any subsequent claim of discrimination. When determining essential functions:

- Document all important job functions;
- Be accurate and realistic;
- Stay current;
- Be flexible; and
- Review job descriptions with the employee in that job.

The law doesn't require you to reasonably accommodate a qualified individual with a disability if you can prove that the accommodation would cause undue hardship. The Equal Employment Opportunity Commission (EEOC) and the California Fair Employment and Housing Commission (FEHC) determine undue hardship on a case-by-case basis, taking into consideration the size of your business and the availability of tax incentives and assistance from the government.

 The concept of **undue hardship** includes any accommodation that is unduly costly, extensive or substantial, or an accommodation that would fundamentally alter the nature of the operation of your business.

You don't need to hire or retain a person who poses a direct threat to the health and safety of co-workers. The risk must be current, not speculative, not remote, not lessened by accommodation and based on reasonable medical judgment or other objective evidence.

State employees who supervise other workers must receive additional training related to persons with disabilities. Each supervisory employee, at the time he/she is initially appointed to a supervisory position, must take a minimum of 80 hours of training. The training must be completed within the term of the probationary period or within 12 months of the appointment to supervisor. This requirement doesn't apply to private-sector employers, but such training is highly recommended.

What Constitutes Harassment?

Harassment is a pattern of unwelcome behavior. If an individual indicates that advances, attentions, remarks or visual displays are unwanted and should stop, yet the behavior continues, that constitutes harassment.

All workers in any size company are shielded from harassment. It's your duty as an employer to create a hostility-free work environment for all your workers, whatever their gender, age, race or other protected class status might be.

 Any workplace relationship can contain harassment: employee to independent contractor, vendor to employee, employee to employee, supervisor to employee, among others.

Harassment includes:

- Verbal harassment — epithets, continued requests for dates, derogatory comments, slurs, obscenities, explicit/racial jokes, graphic commentary about someone's body, verbal abuse, questions about personal practices, use of patronizing terms or remarks or threats and demands to submit to sexual advances;

- Physical harassment — assault, unwanted touching, grabbing, brushing against or interfering with a person's movement;

- Visual harassment — offensive cartoons, posters, drawings, gestures or staring; and

- Any form of retaliation for reporting or threatening to report harassment.

Though most harassment is a pattern of conduct, a single incident may constitute harassment under California law if the conduct is sufficiently severe. Harassment can take the form of:

- An employment condition (submission to harassing conduct is made a term of employment);

- An employment consequence (submission to or rejection of harassing conduct is used as the basis for employment decisions); or

- An offensive job interference (harassing conduct unreasonably interferes with an employee's work performance or creates an intimidating, hostile or offensive work environment).

If you fail to take action to stop harassment, you will be liable for damages if an employee files a complaint. Harassed employees do not need to share their complaints with a manager; they can go straight to the DFEH and file a claim against your company and against any supervisors engaging in harassing behavior. See "What do I Need to Know About the Penalties for Discrimination/Harassment?" on page 273.

The law also imposes liability on employers for harassment by a nonemployee. You're liable for acts of sexual harassment by a third party if you, your agents or supervisors knew or should have known of the conduct and failed to take immediate and appropriate action.

What Characteristics/Activities Does the Law Protect from Harassment?

All the people protected from discrimination are protected from harassment, regardless of company size. See "Characteristics/Activities Protected from Discrimination" on page 246.

Sexual harassment is the most common type of workplace harassment, and sexual harassment takes two forms:

- "Quid pro quo," which conditions job continuance, benefits, promotions, etc., on receiving sexual favors; and

- "Hostile environment," where the pattern of unwelcome sexual comments, touching or visual displays of a supervisor or co-worker creates an environment that inhibits the employee's ability to work.

California courts use a "reasonable victim" standard as a means to determine if a particular situation constitutes harassment. Though any person of any gender can be subject to unlawful harassment, courts ask whether a reasonable person in the position of the victim would consider the conduct sufficiently severe or pervasive to create a hostile or abusive working environment.

The prohibition against sexual discrimination includes protection based on "gender." You must permit employees to appear or dress consistently with the employee's gender identity. The sexual harassment policy in the sample *Employee Handbook* reflects this protection.

What Is Affirmative Action?

Affirmative action is meant to be a temporary effort designed to correct past wrongs. This remedial concept imposes the duty on employers to take positive steps to identify discrimination based on protected class status and to improve work opportunities for persons belonging to protected groups historically deprived of job opportunities.

Affirmative action involves making a specific effort to recruit individuals on the basis of membership in a protected class, and taking positive actions to ensure that such individuals, when employed, enjoy an equal opportunity for benefits and promotions.

California's Proposition 209 did create controversy, but any company with contracts with the federal government must put an affirmative action plan in place. Other companies may voluntarily put such plans in place. Check with your legal counsel.

> **TIP** **Proposition 209** bars state and local governments from granting preferential treatment on the basis of race, sex, ethnicity or national origin.

How Can I Avoid a Discrimination/Harassment Claim?

The first step in avoidance is awareness. If you're aware of the possibility of discrimination and harassment claims, you can take steps to avoid them.

Fair dealing, candid communications, objective evaluation of persons and situations, and an ongoing regard for the personal dignity of each employee present the best strategies for avoiding any appearance of discrimination.

Prepare yourself and your company for the possibility of a discrimination/harassment lawsuit:

- Develop a policy, see page 257;

- Follow the provided guidelines, see page 258;

- Train your supervisors and staff, see page 259; and

- Use the *Manager's Checklist to Avoid Discrimination* (see Table 69 on page 275).

Establish Policies

You must maintain written policies that explain your commitment to protecting your employees from discrimination and harassment. Your employee handbook should include your discrimination and harassment policies. Sample language for these important policies is available in the sample ***Employee Handbook*** (in the online formspack included with this product) and in the ***Sexual Harassment*** pamphlets (in the ***Required Notices Kit*** available from ***www.calbizcentral.com***).

Your policies need to describe the conduct that your company and the law forbid: Outline the discipline plan; point out that retaliation will not be tolerated; and explain that harassers may be held personally liable in a lawsuit. See "The Basics of Developing Policies" in Chapter 3, page 58 for tips on writing sound policies.

The fact that you maintain and follow policies and procedures isn't enough, by itself, to insulate you from litigation. The law requires you to provide information for all employees, contractors, etc., about your discrimination and harassment policies. Follow through with your policies, and update them as often as needed. You also must create an effective internal complaint procedure and an investigation procedure. See "How Should I Handle a Discrimination/Harassment Complaint?" in Chapter 7, page 265 for details.

Follow Guidelines

Any act or omission that appears unfair may be viewed as discriminatory. Follow these guidelines:

- Apply all rules and standards equally to everyone;

- Give consistent signals and honest appraisals. Mixed signals breed complaints;

- Don't delay decisions. Delay may greatly enhance the appearance of acceptance or unfairness;

- Assume everyone wants to advance within the organization. Supervisors may overlook some candidates because they assume certain employees have no interest in advancement or better salaries because of attitudes they appear to display or assumptions about family obligations. All employees should be considered for advancement;

- Avoid making decisions based on subjective "feelings" about people — rely on objective facts;

- Explain decisions to affected employees. Someone who knows he/she was considered for a promotion deserves an explanation of why he/she was passed over;

- Make sure to maintain open communication channels;

- Give clear instructions and warnings. Don't ever think that employees "should have known" what you expected;

- Always hear an employee's side of the story before taking action against him/her. Conduct a full investigation;

- Keep complete and accurate records and documentation of all incidents. This includes testimony of witnesses, employer response, charges filed and related information. Date and sign all documents;

- Reasonably accommodate disabilities, religious differences, etc.; and

- Consider putting someone in charge of measuring how well you're doing. Self-analysis now can head off litigation later.

Provide Training

Training can save you time, money and stress. If training can prevent one angry employee from filing a lawsuit, it's worth it. Diversity training, harassment-prevention training and discrimination-prevention training should occur at least once per year.

Take all steps necessary: raise the subject, express strong disapproval, develop appropriate sanctions, inform employees of their right to raise complaints and the methods of raising complaints and develop methods to sensitize all concerned.

Training is the best way for you to communicate your expectations to your employees. You should probably train supervisors and subordinates separately. They need to know about different issues, and you may not be able to conduct a productive discussion with one group when the other is present.

You can hire a professional trainer or lead the training sessions yourself. You can take advantage of videos, worksheets and many other teaching materials.

California Employer Training Regulations

California law creates specific training requirements for some employers. This section provides an in-depth overview of the regulations and answers to frequently asked questions.

Do the regulations apply to my company?

You must provide sexual harassment to all supervisors if your company employs 50 or more staff anywhere, not just in California. The state of California and its political subdivisions (local agencies, counties, public school districts and others) also count as employers under these regulations.

What is a supervisor or supervisory employee?

A supervisory employee who works in California means any individual with the authority, in the employer's interest, to hire, transfer, suspend, lay off, recall, promote, discharge, assign, reward or discipline other employees; or the responsibility to direct other employees, adjust their grievances or to recommend such actions to the employer. The exercise of that authority is not of a merely routine or clerical nature, but requires the use of independent judgment.

How do I determine if I employ "50 or more" staff?

Employees include full-time, part-time and temporary workers or contractors for each working day in any 20 consecutive weeks in the current calendar year or preceding calendar year. The 50 individuals don't need to work at the same location or in California.

I hire independent contractors as well as employees. Should I count independent contractors as part of the 50 employee minimum?

Yes; a contractor who performed services for your company for each working day in 20 consecutive weeks in the current or preceding calendar year counts as part of the 50 employee minimum.

How long must the supervisor training last?

The training must take the supervisor no less than two hours to complete. The training need not last for two consecutive hours, and the minimum duration of a training segment is no less than one half hour for classroom training or webinars. E-learning courses may include features allowing the supervisor to pause the training if the e-learning program can't be completed in less than two hours.

What constitutes classroom training?

Also referred to as "in-person" training, classroom training is instruction whose content is created by a trainer and provided to supervisors by a trainer in a setting removed from the supervisor's daily duties.

What is webinar training?

An Internet based seminar whose content is created and taught by a trainer and transmitted over the Internet or an intranet in real time. Employers using a webinar for training must document that each supervisor not physically present in the same room as the trainer actually attended the training and actively participated in it.

What is e-learning training?

E-learning is individualized, interactive and computer-based training created by a trainer and an instructional designer. Supervisors must have the opportunity to ask a trainer questions and get a response within two business days after the question is asked.

Can we provide training other than classroom, webinar or e-learning?

The regulations authorize other effective interactive training including audio, video or other computer technology only in conjunction with classroom, webinar or e-learning training.

Who can be a qualified trainer?

A qualified trainer must be:

- Attorneys admitted to the bar of any state for two or more years whose practice includes employment law under the California Fair Employment and Housing Act (FEHA) and/or Title VII of the federal Civil Rights Act of 1964; or

- Human resources professionals or harassment prevention consultants with a minimum of two years with practical experience in one or more of the following:

  - Designing or conducting discrimination, retaliation and sexual harassment prevention training; or

  - Responding to sexual harassment complaints or other discrimination complaints; or

  - Conducting investigations of sexual harassment complaints; or

  - Advising employers or employees regarding discrimination, retaliation and sexual harassment prevention.

- Professors or instructors in law schools, colleges or universities with a post-graduate degree or California teaching credential and either 20 instruction hours or two or more years experience teaching employment law under FEHA or Title VII at a law school, college or university.

What is a trainer?

To be qualified to provide sexual harassment training for supervisors, a trainer or educator must possess training and experience about:

- How California and federal law define unlawful harassment, discrimination and retaliation;

- What steps to take when harassing behavior occurs in the workplace;

- How to report harassment complaints;

- How to respond to a harassment complaint;

- The employer's obligation to conduct a workplace investigation of a harassment complaint;

- What constitutes retaliation and how to prevent it;

- Essential components of an anti-harassment policy; and

- The effect of harassment on harassed employees, co-workers, harassers and employers.

What is an instructional designer?

Instructional designers have expertise in current instructional practices and develops the training content based upon material provided by a trainer.

How often do my supervisors need to be trained?

You must provide a minimum of two hours of training once every two years. You can track compliance in either of the following methods, or a combination of the two:

- **Individual Tracking** — each supervisory employee must be trained no later than the two-year anniversary date of his or her prior training. For example, a supervisor who took sexual harassment training on July 1, 2009, must complete the next round of training in 2011 and no later than June 30, 2011.

- **Training Year Tracking** — employers may designate a "training year" when all sexual harassment training is completed. All supervisors must complete training by the end of the designated training year. If supervisors were initially trained in 2009, you may designate 2011 as your training year and those supervisors trained in 2009 must complete their training by the end of 2011.

When do my new supervisors need to be trained?

A newly hired supervisor or an individual promoted to a supervisor role must be trained within six months of hire/promotion and every two years after that using either the individual or training year tracking method.

If using the training year tracking method, newly hired or promoted supervisors who receive training within six months of hire/promotion and that training falls in a different training year, the employer may include them in the next group training year, even if that occurs sooner than two years.

> **Example:** If all supervisors were trained in 2009 and 2011 is the "training year," a new supervisor trained in 2010 would need to be trained in 2011 with the employer's other supervisors to keep them on track, or the new supervisor would have to be trained no later than the two-year anniversary date of her original training.

I hired a new supervisor who received training from a previous employer. Do I still need to train this supervisor within six months of hire?

The current employer bears the burden of proving that any training received by an employee is compliant. You must be able to demonstrate that the training the new employee received was sufficient under these regulations.

If you are able to do so, you can wait until the employee's two-year training anniversary, based on the training date with the prior employer. But you must still give the employee a copy of your anti-harassment policy and ask the employee to acknowledge receiving the policy thereof within six months of hire/promotion to the supervisory position.

TIP CalChamber recommends providing your own sexual harassment training to new supervisors. You should also make sure new supervisors fall under the same tracking method as the rest of your supervisors.

What sort of documentation must I keep relating to this training?

You must maintain documentation of the name of the supervisory employee trained, the date of the training and the name of the training provider. Keep this documentation for a minimum of two years.

What if I don't provide this training to my supervisory employees?

The Fair Employment and Housing Commission may issue an order to force you to comply with the training regulations within 60 days of the order.

What does the training have to include?

For any training method, the instruction must include:

- Questions that assess learning;

- Skill-building activities that assess the supervisor's application and understanding of content learned; and

- Numerous hypothetical scenarios about harassment; each with one or more discussion questions so supervisors remain in the training.

At a minimum, the content must include:

- A definition of unlawful sexual harassment under FEHA and Title VII;

- FEHA and Title VII statutory provisions and case law principles concerning the prohibition against and the prevention of unlawful harassment, discrimination and retaliation in employment;

- The types of conduct that constitute sexual harassment;

- Remedies available for sexual harassment;

- Strategies to prevent sexual harassment in the workplace;

- Practical examples and hypotheticals based on workplace situations and other situations that illustrate sexual harassment, discrimination and retaliation using training tools such as role playing, case studies and group discussions;

- The limited confidentiality of the complaint process;

- Resources for victims of sexual harassment, such as to whom they should report alleged harassment;

- The employer's obligation to conduct an effective workplace investigation of a harassment complaint;

- Training on what to do if the supervisor is personally accused of harassment;

- The essential elements of an anti-harassment policy and how to use it if a harassment complaint is filed;

- Either the employer's policy or a sample policy must be provided to supervisors as part of the training; and

- Regardless of whether the employer's policy gets used as part of the training, the employer must give each supervisor a copy of its anti-harassment policy and require each supervisor to read and acknowledge receiving the policy.

The Hitches, Glitches and Pitfalls of Preventing Discrimination/Harassment

Because of the serious nature of discrimination and harassment claims, you need to know what to do ahead of time. If a complaint arises, properly handling it could prevent the situation from turning into a lawsuit.

How Should I Handle a Discrimination/Harassment Complaint?

You should take all complaints of discrimination or harassment very seriously. When an employee makes a complaint, you must be prepared to conduct an investigation. A proper investigation:

- Reassures employees that complaints will be heard and resolved within the company;

- Minimizes the chance of disciplining or terminating an employee for something he/she did not do; and

- Makes it less likely that an outside agency and/or attorney will become involved.

When an employee complains, use the *Harassment Investigation Checklist*, described in Table 69 on page 275, and follow this basic process:

1. Interview the complainant and document the complaint (see page 266).

2. Determine if a formal investigation is necessary (see page 267).

3. Decide on interim actions (see page 267).

4. Conduct a formal investigation (see page 268).

5. Take quick corrective action (see page 272).

1 — Interview the Complainant and Document the Complaint

After finding out the general nature of the complaint, make sure the employee feels comfortable that you can objectively address it or that you will identify an investigator who can. Then:

- Arrange for a private, comfortable setting;

- Provide ample time and opportunity to gather the facts. Make sure the employee knows he/she can take as much time as needed, and can come back if he/she recalls other facts later;

- Encourage him/her to speak freely and make all complaints known;

- Re-state your policies against both harassment and retaliation for having filed a complaint, and ask him/her to report any retaliation to you immediately;

- Tell him/her your procedure for resolving complaints;

- Instruct him/her to keep information about the complaint as confidential as possible;

- Tell him/her that you will only disclose information on a need-to-know basis;

- Ask for any suggestions for a resolution to the problem. Stress that you may not be able to follow these suggestions, but you will take them into consideration;

- Ask if he/she would like to recommend anyone else you could speak with to back up the allegations; and

- Review the interview notes and prepare a formal statement. Although the complainant is not required to, request that he or she sign the statement.

A Note About Notes

Accurate, consistent note-taking plays a critical role in your investigation.

When you take notes on the complaint:

- Document the date, beginning and ending time of the interview;

- Record only the facts and descriptions of what occurred during the interview, not your interpretations of the interview, the employee or the situation;

- Keep these notes in a separate place from notes regarding other business issues, and don't record them in a bound notebook or format that might contain information outside of the particular complaint; and

- Keep notes about different employees on separate pieces of paper.

2 — Determine If a Formal Investigation Is Necessary

Certain situations automatically trigger your duty to investigate:

- A formal complaint, written or oral, of harassment;
- A subtle complaint that a co-worker makes the concerned employee feel uncomfortable;
- A charge from the EEOC or DFEH, or a civil lawsuit;
- An observation of harassment; and
- An anonymous note stating that harassment is occurring.

In other situations, you may need to determine if you need additional information to resolve an employee's concerns. Consider whether:

- The problem has a simple, straightforward solution or if the problem is more complex;
- It involves more people than just this complainant;
- It stems from a single incident or a pattern of conduct;
- You need more facts than the employee can provide; and
- You need the help of other experts (legal counsel, security personnel or risk management professionals).

If you need more information, conduct a formal investigation.

3 — Decide on Interim Actions

You may need to take some action during the investigation to protect:

- The health and safety of employees; and
- The integrity of the company's policies or guidelines.

Leave of Absence

If you suspect an employee of ongoing harmful behavior, you may place the individual on leave pending the completion of an investigation. Give the employee a leave of absence notice that states:

- His/her name;
- The estimated time required for the investigation;

- Who to contact if he/she has any questions or concerns;
- Any expectations of yours, such as:
  - Full cooperation and complete honesty during the investigation;
  - All information and documentation relevant to the investigation; and
  - Confidentiality.
- How you will handle his/her return to work.

4 — Conduct a Formal Investigation

Carefully plan how to conduct the investigation. A poorly planned investigation may expose both the company and the investigator to liability.

Select the Investigator

Select someone who employees view as:

- Fair;
- Objective;
- Reasonable; and
- Able to make difficult decisions.

If the complaint progresses to legal action, the investigator may be called as a witness. If you want your attorney to defend you during litigation, find someone else to conduct the investigation.

Make sure that the complainant feels comfortable with the investigator. If you choose a third-party investigator, he/she must be a private investigator or attorney licensed to practice in California.

California law prevents outside third parties from performing harassment investigations unless they are licensed attorneys or licensed private investigators. If you intend to hire an outside third party to perform investigations, make sure that person holds the proper license. An HR consultant who is not a licensed attorney or private investigator can't legally perform these investigations. Using an outside HR consultant, as opposed to in-house HR staff, could negatively impact the validity of any investigation results if a lawsuit should occur.

Gather Supporting Documents

Identify all documents relevant to an investigation. They may:

- Provide background information to help verify facts;

- Identify people to interview; and

- Identify which questions to ask.

Throughout the investigation, ask repeatedly for any documentation that might be helpful.

Interview Appropriate People

Interview the following people in this order:

1. The complainant — for guidance on conducting this interview, see "1 — Interview the Complainant and Document the Complaint" on page 266.

2. The alleged harasser — keep in mind that everyone is innocent until proven guilty.

   - State that you're investigating a complaint of workplace misconduct;

   - Review the allegations in their entirety, and give him/her the opportunity to respond generally. This allows you to get his/her emotional response to the allegations;

   - Give him/her an opportunity to tell his/her side of the story;

   - Ask questions that provide chronological answers. You can use the *Harassment Investigation Interview Guidelines*, described in Table 69 on page 275, to help you form questions;

   - Remind him/her of the company policy against retaliation, and make sure he/she understands that this applies to retaliation against him/her as well as retaliation against the complainant;

   - Tell him/her that he/she must not discuss the investigation with other employees; and

   - Prepare a written statement for the alleged harasser to sign.

3. Any witnesses — since being interviewed as part of an investigation can be quite stressful for an interviewee, make an effort to put him/her at ease.

   - Emphasize that you haven't reached a conclusion;

- Tell him/her to keep the information discussed confidential and that you will only share the information he/she provides with people who have a need to know;

- Reiterate the company policy against retaliation against him/her as well as the alleged harasser or the complainant; and

- Use the *Harassment Investigation Interview Guidelines*, described in Table 69 on page 275, to structure your interview. Go through events chronologically, and ask for any information he/she has to confirm or refute what you were told;

- Ask if he/she is aware of any other workplace misconduct; and

- Ask if he/she knows whether the complainant harbors any bias against the alleged harasser, and vice versa.

 Divulge only enough information necessary to learn what information this witness has to offer.

Examine Facts and Assess Credibility

You must determine whether the information you gathered is credible before relying on it for a conclusion. You need to make credibility assessments while conducting interviews. Ask yourself:

- Did the person raise the complaint in a timely manner? If not, why? Why did he/she raise the complaint now?

- Did similar things happen in the past that did not result in a complaint? If so, why?

- Did any person you interviewed say something that you found later to be untrue?

- Did anyone change his/her story or withdraw an allegation?

- Is the complainant's story consistent and plausible? Does it make sense? Does it correspond with the information learned from other witnesses?

- Does any evidence exist to corroborate the complaint?

- What would motivate the complainant to fabricate facts?

- Did you observe any indications of bias, hostility or self-interest? Part of this involves observing:

  - Body language;

  - Tone of voice;

  - Eye contact;

    – Reactions to questions; and

    – Word selection — for example, "girl" vs. "woman."

Don't fear making credibility decisions, but make sure you can back them up with a reasonable explanation. For additional questions to consider, see the *Credibility Assessment Guidelines for Harassment Investigations*, described in Table 69 on page 275.

Come to a Conclusion

After analyzing the facts and assessing credibility, you will conclude one of the following:

- Company policy was violated; or

- Company policy was not violated.

 You should not state that the law was violated. Only competent legal counsel should make legal conclusions. You only determine whether company policy was violated.

Document Findings and Conclusions

Write an investigation summary that includes:

- The sequence and process followed for the investigation;

- The key facts relied on to make the final decision, such as interviews and any relevant support documentation;

- The criteria used to assess credibility;

- The bottom-line factual conclusions, for example, "the alleged harasser did touch [name of complainant], and this touch was unwanted and offensive; and

- Any complaints that were not resolved in the investigation, and why.

Keep this summary and other relevant documentation, interview notes, etc. in a file labeled as "Need-to-Know, Confidential." Limit access to this file to only those with a legitimate, business need-to-know. Even the complainant and the alleged harasser do not need access to this file in the normal course of business.

Communicate Results

Notify the alleged harasser of the results. Discuss:

- The complaint(s) raised;
- The steps you took to investigate;
- How you reached the conclusion;
- Any complaints that weren't resolved and why;
- The actions you will take as a result of the investigation; and
- Whom to contact if he/she wants to ask questions or wants information in the future.

Notify the complainant of the results. Discuss:

- The conclusion you reached;
- How you reached the conclusion;
- What actions you will take that affect him/her;
- What he/she should do if he/she experiences any retaliation; and
- That you expect him/her to keep all aspects of the investigation confidential.

 While you shouldn't divulge the nature of the disciplinary action against the alleged harasser, you may want to indicate that you will take action consistent with your company policy.

5 — Take Quick, Corrective Action

You need to move quickly in determining what action to take. Consider the following:

- Do any federal, state or local laws require you to take certain actions?
- What did the company do in the past for similar violations of policy?
- How serious was the discrimination/harassment?
- Did the employee violate any other policies in the past?
- How long has the employee been employed with your company? What is his/her performance history?

After weighing these factors, determine the amount of discipline this situation warrants. Some of your options include:

- No action;
- Verbal discussion/counseling;
- Written warning;
- Training;
- Transfer;
- Suspension; or
- Termination.

You can use the *Harassment Discipline Checklist*, described in Table 69 on page 275, to help make sure you cover all the issues. Terminating a harasser is acceptable when, after an investigation, you have reasonable grounds for believing that the employee engaged in sexual harassment.

 Be careful not to give information about allegations, investigations or resulting discipline to anyone but those with a legitimate, business need to know.

What do I Need to Know About the Penalties for Discrimination/ Harassment?

The amount of liability you may face varies on the type and severity of the claim, repeat offenses and whether you can provide a relevant defense. The penalties include posting notices, reinstatement, payment of back wages and payment of damages and attorneys' fees.

Damages can total enormous sums of money. Courts have levied damages large enough to destroy small businesses. Typically, courts base fines on a business's assets.

Liability

Under California law, liability for a claim of discrimination belongs solely to you, the employer. Liability for a claim of harassment can sometimes be shared with the harasser.

TIP **Liability** is legal responsibility. In most court situations, the liable party is the one who has to pay.

Table 68. Liability

For	Employer liable?	Supervisor liable?	Employee liable?
Discrimination	Yes	No	N/A
Harassment of an employee by a supervisor	Yes, whether you knew about the harassment or not.	Yes	N/A
Harassment between co-workers	Yes, if you knew and failed to take action.	No	Yes

What Can I Do to Defend Myself Against a Claim?

The best defense is to avoid claims altogether. For more information, see "How Can I Avoid a Discrimination/Harassment Claim?" on page 256.

Discrimination Claims

You can defend yourself against a claim of discrimination by demonstrating that you have a proper defense, such as:

- **Bona fide occupational qualification (BFOQ)** — pertains to cases where you can prove that a position's requirement of religion, sex, national origin, etc., is an essential function of the job and is reasonably necessary for your normal business operations. An example of this qualification is a position for a male dancer, or a "Big and Tall" model;

- **Business necessity** — pertains to cases where apparently neutral practices create an adverse impact on a protected class, such as a vigorous physical fitness exam for a firefighter, and the adverse impact on women. You must be able to prove an overriding, legitimate business purpose necessary to the safe and effective operation of the business, and that no alternative practice could equally accomplish the task;

- **Job-relatedness** — pertains to cases where successfully performing the job in question depends on a particular criterion or qualification. For example, a secretary could be required to pass typing and spelling tests to earn a job or promotion;

- **Security regulations** — pertains to cases where your employment practice complies with applicable federal or state security regulations; and

- **Non-discrimination or affirmative action plans** — pertains to cases where your employment practice complies with a bona fide affirmative action or non-discrimination plan, or with a state or federal court's or administrative agency's order.

Harassment Claims

Defending yourself against a claim of harassment is a huge challenge. Avoiding harassment claims is your best hope. For more information, see "How Can I Avoid a Discrimination/Harassment Claim?" on page 256.

What Forms and Checklists Do I Use to Help Prevent Discrimination and Harassment?

The following table describes forms and checklists associated with discrimination and harassment.

Table 69. Forms and Checklists

Form Name	What do I use it for?	When do I use it?	Who fills it out?	Where does it go?
Credibility Assessment Guidelines for Harassment Investigations	Not required. This form will help you evaluate the people involved in your investigation.	Before and after an investigation interview.	N/A	N/A
Harassment Complaint Procedure - English	To explain your company's harassment complaint procedure.	Distribute the procedure along with your non-harassment policy to new employees and perhaps annually to all employees.	N/A	Give a copy to all employees or incorporate in your employee handbook that's distributed to all employees.

Table 69. Forms and Checklists *(continued)*

Form Name	What do I use it for?	When do I use it?	Who fills it out?	Where does it go?
Harassment Complaint Procedure - Spanish	To explain your company's harassment complaint procedure.	Distribute the procedure along with your non-harassment policy to new employees and perhaps annually to all employees.	N/A	Give a copy to all employees or incorporate in your employee handbook that's distributed to all employees.
Harassment Discipline Checklist	Not required. This form will help you decide how to discipline a harasser.	Before and after an investigation.	N/A	N/A
Harassment Investigation Interview Guidelines	Not required. This form will help you conduct a legal, useful investigation interview.	When preparing for an investigation interview.	N/A	N/A
Manager's Checklist to Avoid Discrimination	Not required. This form will help your managers and supervisors avoid discriminatory behavior.	In any situation where a discrimination complaint could be filed.	N/A	Just read it as a guideline and give it to your managers.
Sexual Harassment pamphlets	Required. This pamphlet describes the problem and the penalties of sexual harassment, and what an employee with a complaint should do.	Whenever you hire a new employee, or engage an independent contractor, etc.	N/A	Give it to your workers and make sure they understand its contents.

Table 69. Forms and Checklists *(continued)*

Form Name	What do I use it for?	When do I use it?	Who fills it out?	Where does it go?
Harassment Investigation Checklist	Not required. This form will help you run your investigation smoothly and legally.	When considering an investigation interview.	N/A	N/A

 You can find these forms in your online formspack, described in detail in "Online Forms" on page 4.

Where Do I Go for More Information?

CalBizCentral and federal and state government agencies offer a variety of resources to help you prevent discrimination and harassment.

Table 70. Additional Resources

For information on	Check out these resources
General	From CalBizCentral: • The *2010 California Labor Law Digest*, the most comprehensive, California-specific resource to help employers comply with complex federal and state labor laws and regulations; • *Sexual Harassment* pamphlets, sold separately or as part of CalBizCentral's *Required Notices Kit*; • *www.calbizcentral.com*; and • *www.hrcalifornia.com*.
EEOC	• Equal Employment Opportunity Commission 350 Embarcadero, Suite 500 San Francisco, CA 94105 (415) 625-5600 or (800) 669-4000; • Compliance Manual "Threshold Issues" section at *www.eeoc.gov/policy/docs/threshold.html*; and • The EEOC's enforcement guidance on employer liability for unlawful harassment by supervisors at *www.eeoc.gov/policy/docs/harassment.html*.

Table 70. Additional Resources *(continued)*

For information on	Check out these resources
DFEH	Department of Fair Employment and Housing Sacramento District Office 2000 O Street, Suite 120 Sacramento, CA 95814-5212 (916) 445-5523 or (800) 884-1684 ***www.dfeh.ca.gov***
FEHC	Fair Employment and Housing Commission 455 Golden Gate Avenue, Suite 10600 San Francisco, CA 94102 (415) 557-2325 or (800) 669-4000 ***www.fehc.ca.gov***

TIP CalBizCentral also provides many ongoing and comprehensive educational opportunities for small business owners, HR beginners and experienced HR professionals alike. These include online sexual harassment training, DVDs and special HR seminars. For more information, please visit our Web site at ***www.calbizcentral.com***.

Preventing Discrimination and Harassment Frequently Asked Questions

Can I fire someone who takes leave related to workers' compensation? It's illegal to discharge, threaten or discriminate in any way against an employee because he/she received an award from, filed or even intends to file a workers' compensation claim.

If found to be in violation of the law, an employer faces financial penalties of up to $10,000. The employer also may be required to reinstate the employee and reimburse him/her for lost wages and benefits. An employee who is on workers' compensation may be terminated only if the termination is clearly unrelated to the workers' compensation claim.

Do any circumstances exist where I can refuse to hire an individual because of his/her disability? An employer is not required to reasonably accommodate a qualified individual with a disability if the employer can show such accommodation would cause an undue hardship or if the accommodation poses a direct threat to other employees' health and safety. The concept of "undue hardship" includes any accommodation that is unduly costly, extensive or substantial to a particular employer, or which would fundamentally alter the nature of the operation of the business.

In general, a larger employer would be expected to undertake greater efforts and expense to make an accommodation than a smaller employer. Even if a particular accommodation would result in undue hardship, the employer would be required to provide an alternative accommodation if that accommodation was available and did not cause an undue hardship.

Under California law, an employer is not required to hire or retain a candidate or employee posing a "direct threat" to the health and safety of co-workers or themselves. Though the U.S. Supreme Court reached a similar interpretation of federal law, the Ninth Circuit Court of Appeals placed a heavy burden of proof on the employer that rejects an employee because of an alleged direct threat to his or her own health or safety.

Must I post a required poster and/or distribute a pamphlet about sexual harassment to employees? Employers must post a state Department of Fair Employment and Housing (DFEH) poster, which includes information about the illegality of sexual harassment, in a prominent and accessible location in the workplace.

In addition, employers must give employees a pamphlet on sexual harassment, and must assure distribution of this information to all employees. It's advisable to provide the sexual harassment pamphlets to independent contractors as well.

Am I required to investigate every claim of harassment? Sexual harassment claims are difficult to handle, and it's wise to be sensitive to any allegations.

An investigation is imperative, even when the allegations appear to be frivolous or when the relationship appears to be consensual. The employer must conduct a prompt, thorough investigation. Consensual relationships can change, and the parties often express reluctance to work together afterward.

In a situation where a consensual relationship ends, one employee might refuse to work with the other employee because of the changed relationship; or one employee may claim harassment by the other. In smaller companies, the employer may not be able to reassign one of the employees, and this will present a bigger challenge.

It's important that the employer acknowledge any concerns brought by one or both of the parties, and investigate promptly any claims of harassment.

If the investigation reveals no harassment, or reveals conduct that was consensual and did not reach the level of harassment, then the employer will have to address this with the complaining employee. The employer should review all allegations with the complainant and any action that will be taken that impacts the employee in the future.

When the employees involved must still work together, regardless of the findings of the investigation, the employer must clarify that the employees must still work together and abide by the work rules in force.

What protected classes do state and federal anti-discrimination laws create? Laws enforced by the California Department of Fair Employment and Housing protect applicants and employees from illegal discrimination and harassment in employment based on race, color, religion, sex (pregnancy and gender), sexual orientation, marital status, national origin (including language use restrictions) ancestry, disability (mental and physical, including HIV and AIDS), medical conditions (cancer or genetic characteristics), age (40 and above), denial of pregnancy disability leave or reasonable accommodation.

Federal discrimination laws protect against discrimination on the basis of race, color, religion, sex (including payment of wages), national origin, individuals with disabilities and veterans.

Chapter 8

Ending the Employment Relationship

Ending an employment relationship, often called "termination" or "separation," involves more than just your employee leaving your working environment. It's a very complex situation: You need to manage your potential for liability, fill out paperwork and properly calculate and deliver the employee's final paycheck.

You can protect yourself from an overly complicated separation or even lawsuits with good preparation and by using a consistent approach in the separation process.

In this chapter, you can find answers to questions about:

- Legal termination procedures;
- Layoffs;
- "Just cause"; and
- Much more.

Minimum Compliance Elements

1. Hang your **Employment Notices Poster** (available from **www.calbizcentral.com**), which includes mandatory postings that all employees and applicants must be able to see, in a prominent place (such as a breakroom).

2. Use the *Termination Decision Checklist* to make sure you fill out all the required paperwork for every employee who leaves your company (see Table 74 on page 296 for a description of this form).

3. Use the *Termination Checklist* to alert you to possible negative repercussions that could follow a termination decision (see Table 74 on page 296 for a description of this form).

4. Provide the employee's final paycheck in the correct amount and within the required time period (see "What Do I Need to Know About the Basic Process for Ending the Employment Relationship?" on page 285).

The Basics of Ending the Employment Relationship

Use the following guidelines to help you through the separation process:

1. Determine the type of separation:

   - Voluntary quit;

   - Discharge (involuntary termination);

   - Layoff;

   - Change in status;

   - Job abandonment; or

   - Refusal to accept work.

   For detailed definitions and examples of each type, see "What Do I Need to Know About the Different Types of Separation?" on page 283.

2. Assemble all of the relevant documentation.

   This includes the employee's personnel file, disciplinary notices and forms required at separation. See "What Forms and Checklists Do I Use to End the Employment Relationship?" on page 296.

3. Assess the risk of your situation.

   Different rules about unemployment insurance benefits and wrongful termination lawsuits apply to different situations and different types of separations. See "The Hitches, Glitches and Pitfalls of Ending the Employment Relationship" on page 290.

4. Maintain an established procedure and follow it consistently.

   For specific information on what steps to take in each type of separation, see "What Other Steps Do I Need to Take to Cover Specific Situations?" on page 287.

What Do I Need to Know About the Different Types of Separation?

Several distinct types of separation exist, and different laws and guidelines apply to each. This section provides required processes and best practices to guide you through each of these separation events. The following table provides definitions for each of the separation types.

Table 71. Separation Types

Separation Type	Definition
Voluntary quit	When an employee quits, either with or without notice, the separation is called a "voluntary quit."
	When someone quits, see "The Basics of Ending the Employment Relationship" on page 282 and "Voluntary Quit" on page 287.
Discharge (involuntary termination)	California is an at-will employment state so you can discharge employees at any time if they're not under contract and if the discharge isn't based on a discriminatory reason. To avoid possible wrongful termination lawsuits, you should follow the parameters of your company policy or union agreement.
	Before you fire someone, see "The Basics of Ending the Employment Relationship" on page 282 and "Discharge (Involuntary Termination)" on page 288.
Layoff	A "layoff" occurs when available work ends either temporarily or permanently and through no fault of the employee.
	Before you lay off employees, see "What Do I Need to Know About the Basic Process for Ending the Employment Relationship?" on page 285 and "Layoff" on page 288.
	❗ Specific notice requirements exist for employers laying off a large number of employees. These requirements vary, depending on state or federal law. Read them carefully.

Table 71. Separation Types *(continued)*

Separation Type	Definition
Change in status	You and your employee may decide to alter the employee-employer relationship, known as a "change in status," in a number of significant ways: from an employee to an independent contractor, a demotion, an employee on leave is fired or resigns or the employee will work fewer hours. ❗ Use caution when changing an employee's status to independent contractor. If the employee performs the same or similar job duties, he or she will not be properly classified as an independent contractor. Always consult with legal counsel before classifying someone as an independent contractor. Before you change an employee's status, see "What Do I Need to Know About the Basic Process for Ending the Employment Relationship?" on page 285 and "Change in Employment Status" on page 289.
Job abandonment	"Job abandonment" means that the employee is missing in action and doesn't show up to work. You can set a policy that limits the number of days an employee can fail to show up for work without contacting you before you consider the job abandoned. The law doesn't require you to terminate an employee who doesn't show up for the number of days defined in your policy. But if you maintain an established and objective policy and you deviate from it, you could be challenged in cases where you apply it. ❗ Specify in your policy that job abandonment amounts to a "voluntary quit" under company policy. This gives you 72 hours to prepare the final paycheck. If you do terminate the employee and he/she later presents a reasonable excuse for the disappearance, you can choose to hire the person again. See "How Do I Hire an Employee?" in Chapter 2, page 8, for more details. When someone abandons his/her job, see "What Do I Need to Know About the Basic Process for Ending the Employment Relationship?" on page 285 and "Job Abandonment" on page 289.

Table 71. Separation Types *(continued)*

Separation Type	Definition
Refusal to accept available work	"Refusal to accept available work" means that the employee refused to perform work that's: • Appropriate to the individual's health, safety, morals and physical condition; • Consistent with the individual's prior experience and earnings; and • A reasonable distance from the individual's residence. When the employee refuses appropriate, available work, you can exercise your option to terminate the employee, though the law doesn't require you to terminate an employee who refuses to accept work. You can choose to offer other work or to put the employee on a temporary leave of absence. If you maintain an established and objective policy and you deviate from it, you could be challenged in cases where you apply it. This type of separation is likely to occur when something about the work changes; for example, your management changes, you reassign an employee to a new work unit or you begin a new project. When an employee refuses available work, see "What Do I Need to Know About the Basic Process for Ending the Employment Relationship?" on page 285 and "Refusal to Accept Available Work" on page 290.

What Do I Need to Know About the Basic Process for Ending the Employment Relationship?

There are many different ways to end an employee-employer relationship, but all types require you to perform essentially the same group of tasks. Table 72 on page 286 describes the guidelines to follow for all types of separation. For information about what else you need to do for a particular type of separation, see "What Other Steps Do I Need to Take to Cover Specific Situations?" on page 287.

See "How Do I Protect Myself Against Wrongful Termination Lawsuits?" on page 290 for information on how to protect your company against potential lawsuits.

Table 72. Basics of Ending Employment Relationship

Before	• Using the information in Table 71 on page 283, determine what type of separation applies to the situation. • For a list of the important legal issues to consider when terminating an employee, review the *Termination Decision Checklist*, described in Table 74 on page 296. • Depending on the type of separation, either the employee or the employer provides written notice. Use the *Notice to Employee as to Change in Relationship*, described in Table 74 on page 296, to document the separation event. • For a list of the forms you must fill out or provide to the departing employee, review the *Termination Checklist*, described in Table 74 on page 296.
During	**1.** Gather the employee's personnel records and relevant documentation. **2.** Provide the EDD's ***For Your Benefit, California's Program for the Unemployed*** pamphlet, described in Table 74 on page 296 and located in CalBizCentral's ***Required Notices Kit*** available from ***www.calbizcentral.com***. **3.** If the employee receives health benefits, fill out and provide the appropriate health insurance and COBRA forms, described in Table 74 on page 296. See COBRA and Cal-COBRA in the "Glossary of Terms, Laws and Agencies" on page 305, for more details. **4.** Prepare the employee's final paycheck, including all wages and accrued, unpaid vacation. You can use the *Final Paycheck Worksheet*, described in Table 74 on page 296 to help you prepare the paycheck. **5.** Provide the final paycheck to the employee in the appropriate manner within the required time period, based on the type of separation. In most circumstances, you must provide the final paycheck on the employee's last day of work. See "How Do I Calculate a Final Paycheck?" in Chapter 5, page 187, for more details. **6. Optional:** ask the employee to sign the *Final Paycheck Acknowledgment*, described in Table 54 in Chapter 5, page 203, to document that you met the last paycheck deadline, as required. It also gives you an opportunity to clarify with the employee that proper payment was received. **7. Optional:** conduct an exit interview on the employee's final day of employment or allow him/her to take the *Exit Interview* form (described in Table 74 on page 296) home and return it by mail. The exit interview gives you a chance to learn the employee's thoughts about employment with your company, and to document any employee claims.

Table 72. Basics of Ending Employment Relationship *(continued)*

After	The employee may be eligible for unemployment insurance (UI) benefits.
	1. The employee schedules an interview with the EDD to apply for benefits.
	2. The EDD mails a notice to you, advising you whether the claimant is eligible and whether your account will be charged for benefits paid to the former employee. Respond to correspondence from the EDD promptly; the agency is serious about its deadlines.
	3. You can use the *Responding to a Claim for Unemployment Insurance* form, described in Table 74 on page 296, to determine how to respond to the EDD notice that a claim was filed.
	4. To appeal a claim, see "What Do I Need to Know About Unemployment Insurance?" in Chapter 4, page 131.
	Follow your company's policy on references for former employees.
	Be careful what you tell remaining employees about the termination. A privacy and/or defamation lawsuit could result from sharing too much information with other employees. If you need to communicate the reason for the termination to other employees, consult your legal counsel first.

What Other Steps Do I Need to Take to Cover Specific Situations?

For specific types of employment separation, you may need to complete additional tasks to ensure that you protect yourself from potential lawsuits.

Voluntary Quit

Follow the basic process described in Table 72 on page 286.

You may wish to confirm the voluntary quit by asking for a letter of resignation. Or you may use the *Notice to Employee as to Change in Relationship*, described in Table 74 on page 296, because it contains all the important information.

Be sure to provide the final paycheck:

- Within 72 hours of the employee's final employment date (if you received less than 72 hours' notice); or

- On the employee's last day of work (if you received more than 72 hours' notice).

For a definition of voluntary quit, see Table 71 on page 283.

Discharge (Involuntary Termination)

Follow the basic process described in Table 72 on page 286.

Review the questions in the *Termination Decision Checklist*, described in Table 74 on page 296.

You must provide written notice for involuntary termination. Use the *Notice to Employee as to Change in Relationship*, described in Table 74 on page 296.

Layoff

Follow the basic process described in Table 72 on page 286.

Document the layoff with a *Notice to Employee as to Change in Relationship*, described in Table 74 on page 296. Provide the employee with any information about severance packages that you offer.

 Under California law, if you employ 75 or more staff and the layoff will affect 50 or more of them, you must provide advance notice of the layoff.

Under federal law, a mass layoff is

- For a period of 30 days;

- Of 50 or more full-time employees (provided it affects at least 33 percent of the workforce); and

- If 500 or more employees will be affected, then the 33 percent requirement does not apply.

You must provide advance notice of the layoff. Consult legal counsel before taking any action.

If you need to lay off an employee on a certain statutory leave (PDL, family and medical leave, workers' compensation leave or disability leave), the employee has no greater rights than if he/she had been at work.

You may want to consider alternatives to layoffs, including job sharing. See "Where Do I Go for More Information?" on page 302 for helpful agencies and Web sites.

For a definition of layoff, see Table 71 on page 283.

Change in Employment Status

Follow the basic process described in Table 72 on page 286.

Review the *Employee Orientation* checklist, described in Table 8 in Chapter 2, page 40, if the employee changes status.

Fill out the necessary forms:

- A *Notice to Employee as to Change in Relationship*, described in Table 74 on page 296;

- Any required reporting forms associated with the new status [for example, *New Employee(s) Report (Form DE 34)* and *Independent Contractor(s) Report (Form DE 542)*, described in Table 8 in Chapter 2, page 40];

- Any financial paperwork affected by the new status (for example, the *W-4 Form – Employee's Withholding Allowance Certificate*, described in Table 8 in Chapter 2, page 40); and

- Any benefits paperwork associated with the new status (health care, retirement or time off).

Provide an orientation session explaining the details (timesheets or paycheck deductions) that result from the change in relationship.

For a definition of change in employment status, see Table 71 on page 283.

Job Abandonment

Follow the basic process described in Table 72 on page 286.

Prepare the final paycheck immediately upon determining that the job was abandoned, unless your policy specifies that job abandonment is a voluntary quit (see "Voluntary Quit" on page 287).

The law doesn't require you to mail or otherwise deliver the final wages. You should make the check available to that employee at the place wages normally get paid. You should notify the employee that he/she has been terminated, and that he/she should pick up the paycheck. The employee can request his/her final check to be mailed. For more information, see Table 52 on page 193.

For a definition of job abandonment, see Table 71 on page 283.

Refusal to Accept Available Work

Follow the basic process described in Table 72 on page 286.

Consider the questions in the *Termination Decision Checklist*, described in Table 74 on page 296. It will alert you to possible negative repercussions that could follow a termination.

If the former employee makes a UI claim, use the *Responding to a Claim for Unemployment Insurance* form, described in Table 74 on page 296.

For a definition of refusal to accept available work, see Table 71 on page 283.

The Hitches, Glitches and Pitfalls of Ending the Employment Relationship

The increase of wrongful termination lawsuits in the past few decades makes the idea of terminating an employee a frightening one. When faced with an unexpected lawsuit, there's not much you can do. If you prepared for the possibility of a wrongful termination lawsuit, you'll have much less to worry about. This section provides helpful information about:

- "How Do I Protect Myself Against Wrongful Termination Lawsuits?" on page 290;

- "What Should I Know About the Most Common Kinds of Wrongful Termination Lawsuits?" on page 293; and

- "How Should I Handle Employee References?" on page 295.

How Do I Protect Myself Against Wrongful Termination Lawsuits?

Avoiding a wrongful termination lawsuit begins long before you actually terminate an employee. An error or miscommunication in any part of the employment process, from job applications to interviews to employee handbooks to performance reviews, can open you up to a wrongful termination lawsuit. You must take early action to protect yourself against legal action.

Document! Document! Document!

Nothing creates a strong defense against an angry ex-employee like a personnel file documenting that you consistently followed your established disciplinary process, gave the employee honest performance evaluations, tracked any behavior/work problems, attempted to accommodate the employee's needs/complaints and precisely followed your termination policy and process. It is a good idea to keep copies of:

- A signed *Acknowledgment of Receipt of Notification of COBRA Rights*, described in Table 74 on page 296;

- A signed *Confirmation of Receipt*, described in Table 13 in Chapter 3, page 92;

- A signed *Notice to Employee as to Change in Relationship*, described in Table 74 on page 296;

- Job description(s);

- Performance reviews;

- Records of pay changes and promotions/demotions;

- Records of disciplinary actions/warnings; and

- Written complaints, both by and about the employee (for example, harassment or discrimination charges) and records of each complaint's investigation and resolution.

Establish Company Policies Ahead of Time

An employee handbook sets forth your rules and expectations and creates a fair and simple way to resolve disputes. Once you set forth policy, you need to follow that policy until you discontinue or change it. If you need to discontinue a policy or implement a new or updated policy, make sure you communicate the new information to employees and document the distribution of the updated handbook.

 For more information on creating employee policies, see "The Basics of Developing Policies" in Chapter 3, page 58.

Be careful when you write your policies that you don't paint yourself into a corner.

Example: You may follow a disciplinary process that allows for a verbal warning, written warning and suspension before terminating an employee. If you terminate an employee without following your own policy, you may face a claim for a breach of contract.

To avoid this situation, you should describe the disciplinary process, but reserve the right to follow whatever course of discipline is warranted in a particular situation. See "Progressive Discipline" in Table 12 in Chapter 3, page 69, for specific guidelines, and see "The Basics of Developing Policies" in Chapter 3, page 58, for tips on writing sound and sensible policies.

Watch Your Language

In all communication with employees, be careful to avoid language that could limit your right to terminate an individual employee.

California is an at-will state, but certain language or conduct may create an employment contract, written, oral or implied, that may override the legal presumption that employment is at-will. See "Don't Create a Contract" in Chapter 2, page 37, for details.

Train Supervisors and Managers

No matter how much you know about avoiding a wrongful termination lawsuit, if your managers don't follow your guidelines, you will be the one to pay the price. Take the time and resources to ensure that your managers and supervisors follow the policies set forth in the employee handbook and know how to:

- Avoid creating oral or implied employment contracts;
- Prevent and deal with harassment or discrimination in the workplace;
- Handle problem employees; and
- Implement the company's discipline policy.

Be Aware of Public Policies

State and federal laws include many exceptions to the doctrine of at-will employment, primarily to create protections from discrimination against people who belong to protected classes. For more information, see "What Is Discrimination?" in Chapter 7, page 244. When faced with the prospect of terminating an employee in a protected class, be sure you gather all the documentation you will need to show that the termination happened for legitimate, not discriminatory, reasons.

Be Aware of Protected Activities

In addition to protecting certain characteristics, state law also protects certain activities. You can't terminate someone for:

- Performing service — serving jury duty, performing military service or acting as a volunteer firefighter;

- Asserting legal rights — refusing to commit an illegal act, "whistle-blowing" if he/she believes the company is violating the law, exercising a statutory obligation to report apparent victims of abuse or neglect, and refusing to participate in abortions;

- Maintaining privacy — keeping private any arrest records that don't lead to convictions, refusing to authorize disclosure of medical information and disclosing or refusing to disclose wages; and

- Engaging in lawful behavior — participating in political activity, enrolling in an adult literacy program, taking time off for a child's school or day care activities and refusing to patronize the employer.

Follow a Standardized Method of Separation

To make sure that all employees get treated the same way upon separation, create a standard separation process and don't deviate from the established method. No specific law requires you to terminate an employee in person, so if you terminate someone by phone or letter, create a standard "script" or form letter that the terminating manager can use.

The sample *Termination Decision Checklist*, described in Table 74 on page 296, can help you decide whether to go forward with the termination and how to proceed. The sample *Termination Checklist*, described in Table 74 on page 296, can help you make sure you've done everything you need to during the separation event. For specific guidelines for different types of separation, see Table 71 on page 283.

What Should I Know About the Most Common Kinds of Wrongful Termination Lawsuits?

In every employment relationship, an implied covenant of good faith and fair dealing exists. If an ex-employee feels he/she received unfair treatment, he/she may file a wrongful termination suit against you.

> **TIP**   **Good faith and fair dealing** means that you should make decisions on a fair basis, and you should treat similarly situated employees in the same manner.

Ex-employees may file several types of wrongful-termination lawsuits against you. Some of the most common are listed in "Types of Lawsuits" in Chapter 8, page 294.

Table 73. Types of Lawsuits

Discrimination	The employee claims the separation was based on his/her possession of certain characteristics rather than for legitimate reasons. For examples of these characteristics, see "What Is Discrimination?" in Chapter 7, page 244.
Wrongful termination in violation of public policy	The employee must show that the public policy involved is derived from an administrative regulation or state or federal statute and is fundamental and of benefit to the general public, rather than just to the employee or employer. You, in turn, must show that you based your decision to terminate the employee on legitimate business reasons. A well-documented separation process can help you defend against this type of lawsuit. See "How Do I Protect Myself Against Wrongful Termination Lawsuits?" on page 290.
Breach of contract	The employee claims that you did not fulfill an understood employment contract. This includes written, oral and implied contracts. The employee must prove that the contract exists and that he/she was terminated in violation of that contract. Your best defense against this type of suit is to not create a contract in the first place. A copy of the *Confirmation of Receipt* signed by the employee can defeat his/her claim that an implied/oral contract existed. A clause in a written contract that allows for termination at-will can protect you from wrongful termination claims.

Table 73. Types of Lawsuits *(continued)*

Fraud based on misrepresentation at hiring	If you make promises at the time of hiring that you fail to keep, you may be liable for fraud when the employee is later terminated. *Example:* If at the time of hiring you promised regular pay raises that you never delivered, you committed fraud. Be careful of the promises you make when recruiting for a position. See "3 — Advertise and/or Recruit for the Position" in Chapter 2, page 12, for more details.
Constructive discharge	In this type of suit, the employee claims that you made working conditions so intolerable that a reasonable person would be compelled to resign, effectively terminating him/her and breaching your implied covenant of good faith and fair dealing. This most often happens when the employee claims that he or she was harassed at work, and that you did nothing to stop it. An open door policy may present your best protection against constructive discharge claims. Make sure you document and address employee concerns in an appropriate manner.

An **open door policy** encourages employees to bring employment issues to the attention of the employer, rather than going outside the company.

How Should I Handle Employee References?

You do face some risks in providing references for former employees. You need to protect yourself from liability that stems from:

- Failing to provide enough information to protect future employers and co-workers — for example, not revealing an employee's record of sexual assault in the workplace;

- Invading the former employee's privacy — for example, disclosing an employee's sexual orientation;

- Defaming the former employee — for example, alleging that the former employee is a "womanizer"; and

- Exposing discriminatory motives for termination — for example, talking about how your former female employee just "didn't fit in" in your male-dominated work environment.

You should develop a company policy for handling employee references and follow it consistently. See "Employee References" in Chapter 3, page 91, for more details.

What Forms and Checklists Do I Use to End the Employment Relationship?

The following tables describe required and recommended forms and checklists associated with the termination process.

You can find these forms in your online formspack, described in detail in "Online Forms" on page 4.

Table 74. Forms and Checklists

Notification/ Form	What do I use it for?	When do I use it?	Who fills it out?	Where does it go?
Acknowledgment of Receipt of Notification of COBRA Rights	Required for **all** types of separation if your insurance plan covers 20 or more participants.	Within 14 days of the time you receive notification of a qualifying event.	Employee signs the notice.	Send via certified mail to the employee and the employee's spouse.
Affidavit to Collect Compensation of Deceased	Provide this form to the surviving spouse, registered domestic partner, guardian or a conservator of an estate (affiant) to allow collection of the decedent's salary or other compensation. The maximum amount may not exceed $5,000.00 net.	After the death of an employee.	The surviving spouse, registered domestic partner, guardian or conservator an an estate.	Maintain in deceased employee's personnel file.
Authorization to Release Personnel Records	To authorize your company to release various information regarding an employee or former employee's employment.	Upon termination.	An employee or former employee should sign this form.	Maintain in employee's personnel file.

Table 74. Forms and Checklists *(continued)*

Notification/ Form	What do I use it for?	When do I use it?	Who fills it out?	Where does it go?
Cal-COBRA – Notice to Carrier	Required for **all** types of separation if your insurance plan covers between two and 19 participants.	Within 31 days of the time of the qualifying events of either separation or reduction in hours.	The employer.	Send the original form to your insurance carrier within 31 days of the qualifying event. Keep a copy of the form in your personnel records.
Cal-COBRA – Notice to Employee	Required if you change health plans and Cal-COBRA protects former employees.	At least 30 days before a change in group plans.	The employer.	Send the original form to each individual who chose Cal-COBRA coverage. Also, send information about the new group benefit plan(s), premiums, enrollment forms, instructions and anything else necessary to allow the individuals to continue coverage. Keep a copy of the form in your personnel records.

Table 74. Forms and Checklists *(continued)*

Notification/ Form	What do I use it for?	When do I use it?	Who fills it out?	Where does it go?
Certificate of Group Health Plan Coverage **TIP** This form is also known as the "HIPAA Certificate."	Required for **all** types of separation if you carry a health insurance plan.	Within 14 days if the employee is eligible for COBRA, or otherwise within "reasonable" time.	The employer.	Send the original certificate to the employee by first class or registered mail. Dependents may need their own certificates. Keep a copy of the certificate in your personnel records.
COBRA Continuation Coverage Election Notice (California Employees)	Required for **all** types of separation for employers with 20 or more employees, provide an employee health plan and self-administer COBRA.	Within 44 days of a qualifying event.	Employee fills it out.	Send via certified mail to the California employee and the employee's spouse.
COBRA Continuation Coverage Election Notice (Outside California)	Required for **all** types of separation for employers with 20 or more employees and some of whom are outside California, provide an employee health plan and self-administer COBRA.	Within 44 days of a qualifying event.	Employee fills it out.	Send via certified mail to the employee and the employee's spouse.

Table 74. Forms and Checklists *(continued)*

Notification/ Form	What do I use it for?	When do I use it?	Who fills it out?	Where does it go?
COBRA – Notice to Plan Adminis-trator	Required for **all** California employers with 20 or more employees and that outsource COBRA adminis-tration.	Within 30 days of a qualifying event.	The employer.	Send to the plan administrator.
Employer Proof of Identity and Disbursement of Final Pay	Complete this form upon receipt of the "Affidavit to Collect Compen-sation of Deceased – Not To Exceed $5,000 Net."	After the death of an employee when their survivor(s) request the employee's final pay.	The employer fills it out; the affiant signs it.	Place a copy of this completed form in the dece-dent's file and provide a copy to the affiant.
Final Paycheck Acknowledgment - English	To ask an employee to certify receiving his/her final paycheck.	Upon termina-tion.	The employer fills it out and the employee signs it.	In the employee's personnel file.
Final Paycheck Acknowledgment - Spanish	To ask an employee to certify receiving his/her final paycheck.	Upon termina-tion.	The employer fills it out and the employee signs it.	In the employee's personnel file.
For Your Benefit, California's Program for the Unemployed	Required for **all** types of separa-tion.	Upon termina-tion.	N/A	Give a copy to the employee. Use the *Termina-tion Checklist* to document his/her receipt.
HIPP Notice (English)	Required for **all** types of separa-tion.	Upon termina-tion.	N/A	Give a copy to the employee. Use the *Termina-tion Checklist* to document his/her receipt.

Table 74. Forms and Checklists *(continued)*

Notification/ Form	What do I use it for?	When do I use it?	Who fills it out?	Where does it go?
HIPP Notice (Spanish)	Required for **all** types of separation.	Upon termination.	N/A	Give a copy to the employee. Use the *Termination Checklist* to document his/her receipt.
Notice to Employee as to Change in Relationship	Required for: • Discharge; • Layoff; and • Leave of absence. Recommended for **all** types of separation. Written notice must be provided by: • Letter; • Employer's own form; or • The form in your online formspack.	In your preparations to terminate an employee.	The employer. You should request the employee's signature, but the law doesn't require you to do so. The notice must include: • Employer name; • Employee name; • Employee Social Security number; • Indication that the action was a discharge, layoff, leave of absence or a change in status; and • The date of the action.	Give a copy to the employee. Keep a copy in the employee's personnel records.

Table 75. Recommended Forms and Checklists

Notification/Form	What do I use it for?	When do I use it?	Who fills it out?	Where does it go?
Appealing a UI Claim to an Administrative Law Judge (ALJ)	To help you prepare an appeal to an ALJ for a UI claim you want to protest.	During the appeal process.	The employer.	Keep a copy in the employee's personnel file.
Appealing a UI Claim to the UI Appeals Board	To help you present your final case to the UI Appeals Board.	At the final stage of the appeal process, after an ALJ rejected your appeal.	The employer.	Keep a copy in the employee's personnel file.
Exit Interview	Recommended for **all** types of separation.	On the final day of the employment, or ask the employee to return a paper form by mail.	Employee fills it out unless the interview is conducted orally; in that case, you may fill in the employee's answers.	Keep the exit interview in your personnel records.
Responding to a Claim for Unemployment Insurance	Recommended for **all** types of separation.	After the separation process.	The employer.	Keep the checklist in your personnel records.
Termination Checklist	Recommended for **all** types of separation.	During the separation.	The employer.	Keep the checklist in your personnel records.
Termination Decision Checklist	Recommended for **all** types of separation.	Before deciding to terminate an employee.	N/A	N/A

Where Do I Go for More Information?

CalBizCentral and federal and state government agencies offer a variety of resources to help prepare you for the separation process.

Table 76. Additional Resources

For information on	Check out these resources
General	From CalBizCentral: • The *2010 California Labor Law Digest*, the most comprehensive, California-specific resource to help employers comply with complex federal and state labor laws and regulations; • *2010 California Labor Law Administration*; • *www.calbizcentral.com*; and • *www.hrcalifornia.com*.
State government	California's Employment Development Department at *www.edd.ca.gov*

Ending the Employment Relationship Frequently Asked Questions

Do I have to provide terminating employees with a HIPP Notice? Yes, if you provide health insurance benefits to your employees. California's Health Insurance Premium Payment (HIPP) Program requires all California employers to provide terminating employees with notice of special state programs under which the state pays the COBRA premium under certain circumstances.

May I fire someone for complaining about working conditions? No. Employees can discuss working conditions with other employees, and Labor Code Section 232.5 protects employees from discipline or termination for discussing working conditions.

Employers may not require, as a condition of employment, that employees refrain from discussing working conditions. Employers may not require an employee to sign a waiver of that right, nor discharge, formally discipline or otherwise discriminate against an employee for discussing working conditions.

How can I get my equipment or uniforms back from an employee who decides to terminate his or her employment? Employers can't make deductions from an employee's final paycheck for unreturned employer property, such as tools and uniforms. You may need to seek recourse in small claims court if the employee refuses to return your property.

Must I give severance pay when I fire someone? California law doesn't require severance pay. The employer may follow its own policy, past practice or union contract, if applicable.

Must I provide a written termination notice for the Unemployment Insurance program? Unemployment Insurance (UI) Code Section 1089 requires that employers give immediate written notice to an employee of a change in the employment relationship, including discharge, layoff, leave of absence and change in status from employee to independent contractor. No particular form is required for the notice, but it must include the name of the employer, the employee's name, Social Security number, the date of the action and the action taken. The reason for the action is not required.

The employer may create its own notice or use the sample form created by the Employment Development Department (EDD). The notice must be given to the employee and a copy should be retained for the personnel file.

Can I fire an employee on workers' compensation? It's illegal to discharge, threaten or discriminate in any way against an employee because he/she received an award from, filed or even intends to file a workers' compensation claim.

If found to be in violation of the law, the employer faces financial penalties of up to $10,000. Further, the employer may be required to reinstate the employee and reimburse him/her for lost wages and benefits. An employee on workers' compensation may be terminated only if the termination is clearly unrelated to the workers' compensation claim.

Am I required to follow the Worker Adjustment and Retraining Notification (WARN) Act if someone buys my business? The WARN act does not apply where employees get transferred from the payroll of one company to the payroll of another as a result of a sale of assets.

What rules must I follow in paying unused sick and/or vacation time to an employee when that employee terminates employment? All accrued but unused vacation must be paid out at the termination of the employment relationship at the final rate of pay, even if the employee was not yet eligible to take the vacation time.

Sick leave does not need to be paid out upon termination of employment when the employer maintains a separate sick leave policy.

Glossary of Terms, Laws and Agencies

4/10 workweek

A weekly schedule that allows the employee to work four 10-hour days each week; for exemption from overtime requirements, the schedule must be under an approved alternative workweek.

9/80 workweek

A two-week schedule that allows an employee to work nine days and 80 hours — five days in one calendar week and four days the following week; for exemption from overtime requirements, the schedule must be under an approved alternative workweek.

accrue

To accumulate or have due after a period of time.

ADA

Americans with Disabilities Act of 1990. Administered by the federal EEOC, prohibits employers of 15 or more employees in the private sector, and state and local governments from discriminating against qualified individuals with disabilities. It requires employers to provide reasonable accommodation for individuals with disabilities, unless the accommodating measures would cause undue hardship. *See also* reasonable accommodation.

ADEA

Age Discrimination in Employment Act of 1967. Prohibits employers with 20 or more employees from discriminating against individuals 40 years of age and older.

administrative control

Procedural improvements intended to reduce the duration, frequency, and severity of work-related injuries and illnesses. Examples include job rotation, work pacing, and work breaks.

adverse action

An employment decision that has a negative impact on hiring, promotion, termination, benefits, or compensation.

affirmative action

An active effort to improve the employment or educational opportunities of members of protected classes.

ALJ

Administrative Law Judge. A judge appointed by an administrative agency for the purpose of conducting hearings and rendering decisions under the agency's unique jurisdiction. Typically, an ALJ's decisions are reviewed by the agency and by the courts.

alternative workweek

An alternative scheduling method that allows employees to work a standard workweek over less than a five-day period in one week or a 10-day period in two weeks without incurring overtime.

arbitration

A non-court procedure for resolving disputes using one or more neutral third parties as decision makers.

at-will employment

A legal concept, mandated by California law, assuring both employer and employee that either party can terminate the relationship at any time and for any reason or no reason.

back pay

A type of damages awarded in an employment lawsuit that represents the amount of money the employee would have earned if the employee was not fired or denied a promotion illegally.

bereavement leave

Time off for a funeral or for mourning when and employee's family member dies.

BFOQ

Bona fide occupational qualification. Qualifications and characteristics reasonably necessary to perform duties, tasks, or processes required to conduct normal business operations.

cafeteria plan

A type of employment benefit plan in which the employee selects benefits from a "menu," up to a specified dollar amount.

California Labor Commissioner

Sets and enforces regulations for employee wages, paycheck deductions, breaks, vacation, jury/witness duty, or temporary military leave, the workweek, minors, employee access to personnel files, "lawful conduct" discrimination, exempt status, and independent contractor status. The Commissioner also assesses fines and files charges with the District Attorney on behalf of underpaid employees, and investigates, holds hearings, takes action to recover wages, assesses penalties, and makes demands for compensation.

Cal-COBRA

California Continuation of Benefits Replacement Act. Requires insurance carriers and HMOs to provide COBRA-like coverage for employees of smaller employers (2–19 employees) not subject to COBRA.

Cal/OSHA

California Occupational Safety and Health Administration. Enforces California laws and regulations pertaining to workplace safety and health and provides assistance to employers and workers about workplace safety and health issues.

CFRA

California Family Rights Act. Provides employees 12 weeks of leave for bonding with a newborn or adopted child, caring for a family member with a serious health condition, and/or caring for the employee's own serious health condition. This law applies to companies with 50 or more employees.

Civil Rights Act of 1991

Amended Title VII, creating, among other things, the right to jury trials, and allowing those claiming intentional discrimination or harassment based on sex, race, religion, national origin, or color under Title VII, or disability under the ADA or Rehabilitation Act, to obtain compensatory and punitive damages measured by the size of the employer's workforce, up to a maximum of $300,000.

claimant

Individual making a claim for unemployment insurance, workers' compensation or other benefit.

COBRA

Consolidated Omnibus Budget Reconciliation Act of 1985. Requires employers with 20 or more employees to offer all employees covered by health care the option of continuing to be covered by the company's group health insurance plan at the worker's own expense for a specific period (often 18 months) after employment ends.

collective bargaining agreement

An agreement resulting from "collective bargaining," or the negotiations between representatives of a union and employers. A collective bargaining agreement establishes employees' terms and conditions of employment, such as wages, hours of work, working conditions and grievance procedures.

commission

Compensation paid to an employee based on a proportional amount of sales of the employer's property or services.

compensation

Any monetary payment related to work, including wages, commissions and bonuses.

compensatory time off (CTO)

Gives a nonexempt employee time off for extra hours worked instead of paying overtime; commonly referred to as "comp time" and almost always illegal for private sector employers.

concurrent leave

Two different types of leave (for example PDL and FMLA) that are used up simultaneously. Table 19 in Chapter 4, page 114 provides an overview of the ways PDL, FMLA/CFRA, workers' compensation, and disability leaves interact concurrently.

conflict of interest

A conflict between the private interests and the official responsibilities of a person in a position of trust.

constructive discharge

A wrongful termination claim that the working conditions were so intolerable that a reasonable person would be forced to resign.

CTD

Cumulative trauma disorder. *See also* RMI.

CTO

Compensatory time off. Gives a nonexempt employee time off for extra hours worked instead of paying overtime. It is also commonly referred to as "comp time" and is almost always illegal for private employers

deduction

An amount of money withheld from an employee's gross earnings for legally required or permitted purposes, such as taxes, garnishments, contributions to retirement plans or health plan premiums.

DFEH

California Department of Fair Employment and Housing. Enforces California's non-discrimination laws. DFEH has jurisdiction over private and public employment, housing, public accommodations, and public services. DFEH receives and investigates discrimination complaints, and provides technical assistance to employers regarding their responsibilities under the law.

DIR

California Department of Industrial Relations. Seeks to improve working conditions for California's wage earners and to advance opportunities for profitable employment in California. DIR has these major areas of responsibility: labor law, workplace safety and health, apprenticeship training, workers' compensation, statistics and research, mediation, and conciliation.

disability

In California, a physical or mental impairment that limits one or more of the major life activities.

disability insurance

A voluntary plan, for employers who do not want to participate in SDI, that provides short-term benefits for employees who are disabled by a non-work-related illness or injury.

disparate (unequal) impact

An employment practice that appears neutral but discriminates against a protected class in practice.

disparate (unequal) treatment

Disperate treatment refers to an applicant or employee that belongs to a protected class receiving different treatment because of his or her membership in a protected class.

DLSE

California Division of Labor Standards Enforcement. Investigates wage claims and discrimination complaints and enforces California's labor laws and IWC Wage Orders.

DOL

U.S. Department of Labor. Administers a variety of federal labor laws including those that guarantee workers' rights to safe and healthful working conditions, a minimum hourly wage and overtime pay, freedom from employment discrimination, unemployment insurance, and other income support.

domestic partner

Either one of an unmarried heterosexual or homosexual cohabiting couple, especially when considered as to eligibility for spousal benefits.

DOSH

Division of Occupational Safety and Health. Enforces California's occupational and public safety laws, and provides information and consultative assistance to employers, workers, and the public about workplace and public safety matters.

double-time

Two times an employee's regular rate of pay. *See also* overtime.

EAP

Employee assistance program. A workplace program provided by the employer to assist employees in recovering from or dealing with personal issues or problems.

EDD

California Employment Development Department. Part of the California Health and Human Services Agency, helps California employers meet their labor needs, job seekers obtain employment, and the disadvantaged and welfare-to-work recipients to become self-sufficient. It supports state activities and benefit programs by collecting and administering employment-related taxes (UI, SDI, Employment Training Tax, and Personal Income Tax).

EEOC

Equal Employment Opportunity Commission. A federal agency that interprets discrimination law, collects employment data, and handles employee complaints.

employee

Any person rendering actual service in any business for an employer for wages, or a person who offers to work for no pay to gain experience.

employee benefit plans

Welfare and pension plans voluntarily established and maintained by an employer, an employee organization, or jointly by one or more such employers and an employee organization. Governed by ERISA.

employer

Any person engaged in any business or enterprise in California with one or more persons in service. An employer can be an individual, association, organization, partnership, business trust, limited liability corporation or corporation.

employment at-will

See at-will employment.

engineered controls

Protective devices designed to reduce or eliminate the risk of workplace injury. Examples include machine guards, adjustable fixtures, and tool redesign.

English-only policy

Prohibits the use of other languages in the workplace. It is illegal in California unless certain conditions are met, including business necessity and employee notice.

Equal Pay Act

Part of the federal Fair Labor Standards Act and the California Labor Code, both of which require "equal pay for equal work." Employers are required to pay employees of the opposite sex in the same establishment equal wages for equal work without regard to an employee's gender.

ergonomics

The scientific study of the relationship between people and their work environments. The goal of the field is to minimize workplace injuries and illnesses through improved workplace design.

ERISA

Employee Retirement Income Security Act. Regulates employee benefit plans and the numerous persons (for example, employers and unions) involved in establishing and maintaining these plans. ERISA sets uniform minimum standards to assure that employee benefit plans are established and maintained in a fair and financially sound manner. In addition, employers have an obligation to provide promised benefits and satisfy ERISA's requirements for managing and administering private pension and welfare plans.

essential functions

Fundamental job requirements of the position, or the reason the job exists.

exempt

An employee who is not subject to any of the laws pertaining to overtime, meal periods, and rest periods.

family leave

Family and medical leave, typically called "family leave," is time off available to employees for specific reasons, as defined in federal and state statutes. Family leave covers time off for bonding with a newborn or adopted child; caring for a family member with a serious health condition; caring for the employee's own serious health condition; caring for an ill or injured servicemember; and qualifying exigency related to a close family member's military service.

FCRA

Fair Credit Reporting Act. Requires specific disclosures in a specific format, in addition to any waiver that might be on an application, before checking the applicant's credit, and restricts an employer's ability to use credit reports for employment purposes.

FEHA

California Fair Employment and Housing Act. Prohibits discrimination/harassment on the basis of race/color, religious creed, national origin/ancestry, physical disability, mental disability, medical condition (including no genetic testing), marital status, sex, age, and sexual orientation. This law provides more protection than the ADA.

FEHC

California Fair Employment and Housing Commission. Hears complaints brought before it by the DFEH, and has the power to levy fines and assessments for damages.

fitness for duty

A medical practitioner's certification releasing an individual under his/her care to assume or resume full or modified duties before hire or following a leave of absence due to illness or injury.

flat rate

Pay based on a job completed, not the number of hours spent completing it.

flexible schedule

An eight-hour work schedule where some employees begin the shift early in the day and others begin their work later in the day.

FLSA

Fair Labor Standards Act. Regulates minimum wages, overtime, and working conditions for all employees of businesses that engage in interstate commerce and have an annual gross volume of sales of not less than $500,000, or an individual employee who is involved in interstate commerce, contracts to do work for a firm engaged in interstate commerce, or travels across state lines in the course of employment.

FMLA

Family and Medical Leave Act. Provides up to 12 weeks of job-protected, unpaid leave during a pre-defined 12-month period for employees who work for a public agency, a local education agency, or an employer in the private sector who has 50 or more employees each working day during at least 20 calendar weeks in the current or preceding calendar year.

front pay

A type of damages awarded in an employment lawsuit that represents the amount of money the employee would have earned if he or she was reinstated or hired into the higher-paying position from which he or she was illegally rejected.

full time

An employee who works the number of hours designated by the employer as "full time."

garnishments

Money withheld by court order from an employee's check to pay for debt, back taxes, or child support.

good faith and fair dealing

Employment decisions that are made fairly, treating similarly situated employees in the same manner.

harassment

Behavior toward a person that a reasonable person would find unwelcome or hostile.

HAZCOM

Hazard Communication Program. Requires all employers to communicate workplace hazards to employees, particularly when employees handle or may be exposed to hazardous substances during normal work or foreseeable emergencies.

HIPAA

Health Insurance Portability and Accountability Act. Limits the extent to which a new employer's health plan can establish barriers, such as pre-existing conditions, that will delay or prevent new employees from becoming fully covered under a new plan. The law was designed to limit or eliminate what Congress called "job lock," which occurs when employees are unable to change jobs because of inability to financially withstand the typical pre-existing condition limitations in a new employer's medical plan.

HIPP

Health Insurance Premium Payment program. A California program that requires all employers to provide departing employees with notice of a state program that pays COBRA payments under certain circumstances.

HMO

Health maintenance organization. An organization that provides comprehensive health care to voluntarily enrolled individuals and families in a particular geographic area by member physicians with limited referral to outside specialists, and that is financed by fixed periodic payments determined in advance.

hostile work environment

An unproductive work environment caused by unwelcome sexual comments, touches, or visual displays.

IIPP

Injury and Illness Prevention Program. A company's general plan for keeping its workforce free from work-related injuries and illness, mandated by California law.

independent contractor

A person or company that supplies goods or services to an individual or business. The independent contractor should not have any of the characteristics of an employee.

INS

U.S. Immigration and Naturalization Service. The INS has been renamed to the U.S. Citizenship and Immigration Services (USCIS). The USCIS is an agency of the Department of Homeland Security (DHS), which enforces the laws regulating the admission of foreign-born persons to the U.S., and administers various immigration benefits, including work visas and the naturalization of qualified applicants for U.S. citizenship. The USCIS investigates violations of IRCA.

intern

Students who perform work in the course of their studies, as part of the curriculum, receiving no payment for their work and no financial credit toward their school fees.

IRCA

Immigration Reform and Control Act. A federal law requiring employers to verify all employees' legal eligibility to live and work in the U.S.

IRS

Internal Revenue Service. The nation's tax collection agency, which administers the Internal Revenue Code enacted by Congress.

IWC

Industrial Welfare Commission. A California agency that monitors the hours and conditions of employment; investigates employee health, safety, and welfare; and determines the Wage Orders.

just cause

A fair and honest cause or reason, acted on in good faith by the employer.

kin care

Care of a sick child, parent, spouse, registered domestic partner, or child of a registered domestic partner.

Labor Commissioner

See California Labor Commissioner.

lay off

To cease to employ a worker, often temporarily, because of economic reasons.

living wage

A wage sufficient to provide the necessities and comforts essential to an acceptable standard of living. Generally mandated by local ordinances.

Log 300

A series of record keeping forms for recording workplace injuries and illnesses. Part of a Cal/OSHA record-keeping requirement.

major life activities

Caring for oneself, sleeping, learning, walking, interacting with others, working, and other physical, mental, and social activities. Used to determine whether a worker is disabled.

makeup time

Allows nonexempt employees to request time off for a personal obligation and make up the time within the same workweek without receiving overtime pay.

mass layoff

The laying off of 50 or more employees, under WARN.

meal period

An upaid, 30-minute block of time for nonexempt employees for every period of work that lasts for more than five hours; must begin no later than four hours and 59 minutes into the employee's work period.

medical certification

A statement from an employee's health care provider as to the necessity of time off from work. Usually required by an employer when an employee is off for a reason protected by law.

minimum salary

The smallest amount a salaried exempt employee can make, in order to be considered exempt. On January 1, 2008 the amount increased to $2,774 per month.

minimum wage

The smallest hourly wage a nonexempt employee can make. Currently $8.00 per hour. *See also* regular rate of pay.

minor

Any person under the age of 18 who is required to attend school, or any person under the age of six.

misdemeanor

A criminal offense that is more serious than an infraction, but less serious than a felony. A misdemeanor is punishable by fine, incarceration in county jail, or a combination of both.

MSD

Musculoskeletal disorder. See RMI.

MSDS

Material Safety Data Sheet. An information sheet provided by the manufacturer of a product that describes the product's chemical properties, potential hazards, and instruction in safe handling.

NLRA

Federal National Labor Relations Act. Prohibits employers from basing any employment action on employee participation in labor organization (union) activities. Such activities include attending union meetings, speaking with union representatives, and discussing union activities with other employees.

negligence

A lack of prudent care (neglect).

noncompete agreements

An agreement between an employer and an employee, which says that, when an employee leaves the company, the employee will not work for a competitor for a certain amount of time. With few exceptions, non-compete agreements are illegal in California under most circumstances.

nonexempt

An employee who is subject to the laws pertaining to overtime, minimum wage, meal periods and rest periods.

occupational wage order

Same as Wage Order. Contains the instructions for payment of wages to nonexempt employees as well as specific rights and responsibilities of the employee and the employer. There are currently 17 Wage Orders, organized according to industry and occupation, plus a Minimum Wage Order. The purpose of your business determines which Wage Order applies to you. *See Wage Orders.*

open-door policy

A policy encouraging employees to bring employment issues to the attention of the employer, rather than going outside the company.

open enrollment

A period of time during which employees can sign up for an employer's group health plan or benefit plan, such as a retirement fund.

OSHA

Occupational Safety and Health Administration. The federal agency that ensures safe and healthful workplaces by issuing standards, performing inspections, and levying penalties for violations.

overtime

Hours worked beyond a "normal" amount of hours for a day or week. For nonexempt employees with a regular workweek, normal is eight hours per day. For employees with an alternative workweek, normal could be nine or 10 hours. For more information on alternative workweeks, see Chapter 5, "Paying Employees." *See also* pyramiding of overtime.

part time

An employee who works less than the number of hours that qualify him/her as a full-time employee, according to your policy.

PDA

Pregnancy Discrimination Act of 1978. An amendment to Title VII, requires that employers treat a pregnant employee the same as any other employee, and that when a female employee becomes unable to work due to pregnancy, childbirth, or related medical conditions, the employer treat her disability the same as any other disability.

PDL

Pregnancy Disability Leave. California employers with five or more employees must provide as much as four months of leave for employees disabled by pregnancy and pregnancy-related conditions.

pension plan

Provides retirement income or defers income until termination of covered employment or beyond. Governed by ERISA.

personal days

Time off associated with a particular event, such as an employee's birthday.

PFL

Paid Family Leave. A wage replacement program funded through employee contributions and administered by the Employment Development Department for employees unable to work when they are needed to care for a family member.

piece rate

An amount paid for completing a particular task or making a particular piece of goods.

plant closing

The shutting down of a facility or laying off 50 or more employees. *See also* WARN, *mass layoff.*

PPE

Personal protective equipment. Items such as gloves, masks, and special clothing used to protect against hazardous, toxic, or infectious material.

Proposition 65

Requires that employers with 10 or more employees warn any person (employees and others who may enter a laboratory) prior to their exposure to a chemical known to the state of California to cause cancer, birth defects, or other reproductive harm.

Proposition 209 (1996)

Bars California's state and local governments from granting preferential treatment to any individual or group on the basis of race, sex, ethnicity, or national origin in the operation of government hiring contracting, and education. This state measure does not affect the affirmative action programs required by the federal government.

protected class

Different classes of individuals who receive specific legal protection against discrimination and harassment based on the individuals belonging to a protected class, including individuals over the age of 40.

PTO

Paid time off. An informal term referring to an employer-defined combination of sick pay, holiday pay, and/or vacation.

pyramiding of overtime

Not required by California law, exists when an employee earns overtime on top of overtime already paid.

qualifying event

For benefits purposes, one of several defined events that permits a change of benefits enrollment status outside of open enrollment periods or that entitles an eligible beneficiary to COBRA or Cal-COBRA benefits.

qualified beneficiary

An employee covered under an employer's group health plan.

quid pro quo

Latin, meaning "this for that." A type of sexual harassment that conditions job continuance, promotions, benefits, etc. in exchange for sexual favors.

rate of pay

A fixed amount of payment based on a unit of time or a piece of work performed.

reasonable accommodation

Any change in the work environment or in the way a job is performed that enables a person with a disability to enjoy equal employment opportunities. *See also* disability.

regular rate of pay

The calculated amount of an employee's actual earnings, which may include an hourly rate, commission, bonuses, piece work, and the value of meals and lodging.

religious holidays

A day specified for religious observance. Employers must make reasonable accommodations for employee requests for time off for religious holidays.

reporting time pay

Payment to a nonexempt employee who reports to work at his/her normal time and is not put to work, or is given less than half the hours for which he/she was scheduled.

rest period

A 10-minute, paid block of time for nonexempt employees for each four hours worked; should be scheduled near the middle of the work period.

retaliation

California regards retaliation as any adverse employment action that results because an individual has opposed practices prohibited by the Fair Employment and Housing Act, or has filed a complaint, testified, assisted or participated in any manner in an investigation, proceeding or hearing conducted by the Fair Employment and Housing Commission or Department of Fair Employment and Housing or their staffs.

retirement plan

A fund that provides individuals with income after retirement. Employees and employers contribute money to a fund during an employee's term of employment, and employees receive a defined income from the fund upon retirement.

RMI

Repetitive motion injury. A problematic injury that builds over time, caused by overuse or overexertion of some part of the musculoskeletal system. RMIs are characterized by inflammation, pain, or dysfunction of the involved joints, bones, ligaments, and nerves. Often referred to as cumulative trauma disorders (CMDs) or musculoskeletal disorders (MSDs).

salary

A fixed amount of money for each payroll period, whether weekly, bi-weekly, semi-monthly, or monthly.

SDI

California State Disability Insurance. Provides temporary disability benefits for employees who are disabled by a non-work-related illness or injury. Benefits are paid by the Employment Development Department from employee contributions in the form of a tax.

seventh day rule

Nonexempt employees who work on each day of your established seven-day workweek are entitled to overtime at the rate of time and one-half for the first eight hours worked and double time for any hours worked beyond that on that seventh day.

severance pay

Money paid to an employee at the time of termination or layoff, to compensate in part for the sudden job loss. Not required by law.

sexual harassment

Unwelcome verbal, visual or physical conduct of a sexual nature that is severe or pervasive and affects working conditions or creates a hostile work environment.

SIC

Standard Industry Code. System that classifies businesses by their primary activity. The SIC is used for a variety of statistical purposes.

split shift

Any two distinct work periods separated by more than a one-hour meal period.

standby

Time the employee spends on call that cannot be used for his/her benefit. Depending on the limitations on the employee during this time, the standby time may be paid or unpaid.

statute

A law enacted by the legislative branch of a government.

telecommute

To work at home by the use of an electronic linkup with a central office.

Employees may use an electronic linkup with a central office or other technology to work from a location away from their office.

TICP

Targeted Inspection and Consultation Program. A Cal/OSHA program that identifies certain high-hazard employers, and requires a fee paid to fund a special inspection unit.

time-and-one-half

The regular hourly rate for the job an employee is doing, plus one-half the regular rate of pay. *See also* double-time, *overtime*.

Title VII, Civil Rights Act of 1964

Prohibits employers of 15 or more employees from discriminating on the basis of race, color, religion, sex, or national origin.

UI

Unemployment Insurance. An employer-paid tax, which is held in reserve for employees in case they become unemployed.

USERRA

Uniformed Services Employment and Reemployment Rights Act. This act prohibits discrimination or reprisals against past and present members of the uniformed service. No employer may deny a person initial employment, retention in employment, promotion or any benefit of employment based on a person's membership, application for membership, performance of service, application to perform service or obligation for service in the uniformed services.

VETS

Veterans' Employment and Training Service. Federal agency that enforces the Uniformed Services Employment and Reemployment Rights Act.

volunteer

If a person intends to give his/her time for public service, religious or humanitarian objectives without wanting pay, classify the individual as a volunteer for the organization receiving the services.

Wage Orders

Contain the instructions for paying nonexempt employees their wages. There are currently 17 Wage Orders, organized according to industry, plus a Minimum Wage Order. The purpose of your business determines which Wage Order applies to you.

wages

Money received by an employee for labor performed of every description, whether the amount is fixed or determined by the standard of time, task, piece, commission or other methods of calculation.

WARN

Worker Adjustment and Retraining Notification Act. A federal law requiring employers to give employees advance notice of a plant closing or a mass layoff if the action involves a requisite number of employees. California has a similar law that provides more protection than that

of federal law, therefore more employees are covered by state law.

welfare plan

Provides health benefits, disability benefits, death benefits, prepaid legal services, vacation benefits, day care centers, scholarship funds, apprenticeship and training benefits, or other similar benefits. Governed by ERISA.

whistle-blowing

Any report made by an employee of suspected illegal activity on the part of an employer.

work permit

A document establishing the maximum number of days and hours a minor may legally work during the workweek. The permit may also impose other limitations on the scope of the minor's work.

workday

Any consecutive 24-hour period starting at the same time each calendar day. If an employer doesn't define the workday, the California Labor Commission will presume a workday of 12:01 a.m. to midnight.

workweek

Any seven consecutive 24-hour periods, starting on the same calendar day and at the same time each week. If an employer doesn't define the workweek, the California Labor Commissioner will presume a workweek of Sunday through Saturday.

workers' compensation

A mandatory "no-fault" insurance program, paid for by employers, to cover medical treatment and wage replacement for an employee who suffers a work-related illness or injury.

Index

A

Absence Request, 203–204

Absenteeism policy, 81

Access Standard, 222

Accident, Injury and Illness Investigation Form, 214, 234

Acknowledgement of Receipt of Notification of COBRA Rights, 291, 296

Acupuncturist, workers' compensation and choice of, 140–141

ADA. *See* Americans with Disabilities Act (ADA)

Advances on wages policy, 85

Adverse Action Notice, 40

Advertising for job opening, 12–13

Affidavit to Collect Compensation of Deceased, 296

Affirmative action rules
employers subject to, 2
Proposition 209 and 256

Age discrimination, 246

Age Discrimination in Employment Act (ADEA), 246

Agencies, glossary of, 305-319

Agriculture workers, when to pay, 195

AIDS/HIV+ status and discrimination, 246

Alcohol/drug rehabilitation. *See* Drug and alcohol abuse policy

Alimony, wage garnishments, 189

Alternative workweek, 173
regulations about, 201

Americans with Disabilities Act (ADA), 247
employers subject to, 2

Appealing a UI Claim to an Administrative Law Judge, 133, 301

Appealing a UI Claim to the UI Appeals Board, 133, 301

Appeals, Cal/OSHA inspection results, 231-233

Arbitration
defined, 97
employee handbook statement, 69

At-will employment, 12–13, 37
discharge of employee, 283
employee handbook statement, 65
termination policies and, 90

Authorization to Obtain Consumer Credit Report, 20, 40

Authorization to Release Personnel Records, 296

Authorization to work, verifying, 26–30

Automatic payroll deposit policy, 84

B

Back taxes, wage garnishments, 189

Background checks, 18–22

Benefits
See also Specific types of benefits
FAQs about, 163–168
forms and checklists, 156–161
information resources, 161–163
minimum compliance elements, 100
optional benefits (table), 101

Personnel files
    employee's right to inspect, 55
    policies about in employee handbook, 75

PFL. *See* Paid Family Leave (PFL)

Phone interviews, job applicants, 14–15

Physical fitness, paid non-working time, 178

Physical harassment, 254

Physician
    overtime exemption, 181
    workers' compensation and choice of, 140–141

Plant closing laws, employers subject to, 3

Policies
    See also Employee handbooks
    benefits of written policies, 59–60
    communication methods, 61
    compliance, mandatory elements, 58–59
    compliance, minimum elements, 58
    legal documents, 60

Poster and notice requirements, employers subject to, 3

PPE. *See* Personal Protective Equipment

Pre-Adverse Action Disclosure, 48

Pre-Hire Checklist, 44

Pregnancy and discrimination, 249

Pregnancy disability leave (PDL), 101–104
    employee handbook policy, 70
    employers required to provide, 3
    PDL Timeline, 159

Pregnancy Discrimination Act, 249

Privacy laws, employers subject to, 3

Privacy rights of employees, personnel files, 55

Process Safety Management of Acutely Hazardous Materials standard, 222

Professionals, 43

Progressive discipline policy, 90

Prohibited conduct policy, 80

Property. *See* Company property; Employee property

Property Return Agreement, 44

Proposition 65, warning requirements, 218

Proposition 209 and affirmative action, 256

Protected activities leave. *See* Leave

Protected classes and activities, 246–251

PTO. *See* Paid Time Off (PTO)

Public policy violation, wrongful termination lawsuits and, 294

Punctuality and attendance policy, 81

Q

Qualified trainer defined, 261

"Quid pro quo," sexual harassment, 255

R

Race/color and discrimination, 249

Reasonable accommodation, 252–253

"Reasonable suspicion" and drug testing, 242

Record keeping
    See also Form I-90
    HAZCOM, 218
    injuries and illnesses, 214, 226–227
    Log 300 regulation, 226–227
    payroll information, 196–198
    Repetitive Motion Injuries Standard, 220
    training of supervisor/supervisory employee, 263
    work surfaces, control devices and emergency equipment inspections, 217

Records Retention Requirements, 94

Recreational activities policy, 89

Recruiting Checklist, 48

References for employees
    avoiding problems with, 295
    hiring process and, 22
    policy about in employee handbook, 91

Refusal to accept available work, 285, 290

Registered domestic partners. *See* Domestic partners